PENGUIN BOOKS
RETHINK THE COUCH

Allison Heiliczer is an American psychotherapist who has been living in Asia for over a decade. She is the founder of Rethink the Couch and works with adult individuals and couples in Singapore and around the world. Heiliczer was the former Head of Corporate Psychology at OT&P's clinics in Hong Kong.

While the hundreds of individuals and couples she has supported in clinical and private practice settings face various challenges, the common thread is they are navigating relationship and work issues.

She graduated *summa cum laude* from New York University (NYU) with a Bachelor of Science, a master's also from NYU, and a second Master's in Counselling from Monash University (Australia). Heiliczer is the first therapist in Asia to be certified in Relational Life Therapy (RLT), a transformative form of couple's therapy, pioneered by *New York Times* bestselling author Terry Real. In addition, she is an ICF-certified coach and has offered extensive coach trainings with executives and at leading multinational corporations.

T0150638

ADVANCE PRAISE FOR *Rethink the Couch: Into the Bedrooms and Boardrooms of Asia with an Expat Therapist*

'A highly engaging, insightful read from the first certified Relationship Life Therapist (RLT) in Asia. Allison provides a rare window into the unique challenges couples grapple with in Asia, highlighting intricate cultural layers, while also exploring the universal themes present in so many relationships.'

—Terrence (Terry) Real, *New York Times* Bestselling author of *Us: Getting Past You and Me to Build a More Loving Relationship*

'In this page-turning debut, Allison Heiliczer invites us into her psychotherapy office, where her clients' stories provide the scaffolding for a riveting exploration of modern Asian marriage, sex, work, parenting, and everything in between. Not shying away from difficult realities, like the couples who end up divorcing when their marriage can't heal, Heiliczer teaches us there's always hope, especially when we care about and believe in each other. She is the master weaver, threading her intimate knowledge of East and West into a stunning exploration of life in the modern world.'

—Anna Lembke, MD, *New York Times* Bestselling author of *Dopamine Nation: Finding Balance in the Age of Indulgence*

'A ground-breaking book that transports you immediately to Asia. This book offers remarkable perspective on culture, relationships, and work including neurodiversity issues. You won't be able to put this book down, and it'll inspire you to transform.'

—Peter Shankman, Bestselling author of *Faster Than Normal: Turbocharge Your Focus, Productivity, and Success with the Secrets of the ADHD Brain*

'Allison's book is a real page-turner and powerfully explores all the complexities of Asian cultural influences in relationships and at work in Asia. This is an important resource for people looking for insights into and help for universal issues like toxic offices, workaholism, neurodiversity and more along with those wanting to learn about the unshakable connection that work in Asia has with relationships. It's also a profound call to end the stigma of mental health challenges in Asia.'

> —Celina Lee, Executive and Career Coach and
> award-winning author of *Live Your Dream*,
> 꿈을 이뤄드립니다"

'This book is a profound call to action to change the mental health landscape in Asia. Allison has been a champion in the region for wellbeing, supporting AXA in our efforts to democratize and make mind health accessible to all.'

> —Gordon Watson, Chairman of AXA Asia

'Allison's work with our teams has been invaluable. When the pandemic hit, we realized immediately the toll it would take on our employees' mental health and jumped into action. Our employees' well-being is our number one priority and Allison has been a vital partner in supporting that aim.'

> —Ken Cooper, Global Head of
> Human Resources of Bloomberg

'In this groundbreaking book, Allison Heiliczer illuminates the hidden lives of people living in Asia . . . written with a candid honesty and an endearing sense of humour. . .'

> —Danielle Lim, award-winning
> author of *And Softly Go the Crossings*

Rethink the Couch

Into the Bedrooms and Boardrooms of Asia with an Expat Therapist

Allison Heiliczer
edited by Sylvia Yu Friedman

PENGUIN BOOKS

An imprint of Penguin Random House

PENGUIN BOOKS

USA | Canada | UK | Ireland | Australia
New Zealand | India | South Africa | China | Southeast Asia

Penguin Books is part of the Penguin Random House group of companies
whose addresses can be found at global.penguinrandomhouse.com

Published by Penguin Random House SEA Pte Ltd
9, Changi South Street 3, Level 08-01,
Singapore 486361

Penguin
Random House
SEA

First published in Penguin Books by Penguin Random House SEA 2023

Copyright © Allison Heiliczer 2023

ISBN   9789815144062

Typeset in Garamond by MAP Systems, Bengaluru, India

www.penguin.sg

To my husband, who is much more than my 'make-it-go-away man'. Thank you for saying yes to Asia and all that unfolds.
To my sons, who are forever in the Uncontrollable Laughter Club. May you be there for each other and others.
To Sylvia Yu Friedman, thank you for believing in me and this book. Let's live in the gratitude bubble.
To past, present, and future clients, thank you for the incredible privilege of journeying together.

Contents

Part V: Work and Relationships

Foreword

'The wound is the place where the light enters you.' These words by the poet Rumi ring as true now as they did in the 13th century.

In this ground-breaking book, Allison Heiliczer illuminates the hidden lives of people living in Asia, a region where the relentless pursuit of success is thrust into the spotlight from a young age, and where long hours of work are pervasive. We are offered a rare glimpse into the unseen loneliness of high-powered executives, the unspoken fears and heartaches of outwardly successful couples facing relationship breakdowns, the inner anguish of ordinary people when things fall apart, and at times the quiet courage they show in working towards healing and transformation. Many of us will be able to connect with these experiences, for often we, too, share a similar bewilderment at how easily things can go wrong, and how easily relationships can break down.

In these pages, written with a candid honesty and an endearing sense of humour, we become awakened to the truth that beneath all the wealth and glitz of cities like Singapore and Hong Kong, there is a tremendous amount of psychological and emotional pain, and many broken relationships. As Allison points out, there is a great underlying pressure to be defined by one's business card and bank account. This pressure often leads to personal and relationship problems.

Depression among adults increased three-fold during the Covid pandemic. This has led to mental health being discussed more openly in Asia. The crossing into emotional distress and/or mental health difficulty is a silent one. The crossing of relationships into stormy waters often begins insidiously. Humans have, since time immemorial, been at the mercy of whatever derives its power from being unheard, unseen. Be it mental illness or Covid-19, we often seem helpless against that which we cannot see. The battle becomes one of unseen wills against an unseen enemy.

Our personal and relationship struggles often involve deep emotional wounds, childhood traumas, mistaken assumptions, and destructive thought patterns. The past and its wounds are often buried in the present, leading to behaviours that can destroy our relationships. To heal, we have to dig deeper into ourselves and our relationships to understand the real problem in order to find a way forward. The willingness to change is necessary for improved relationships; marriages and relationships have to be worked on. The stories and insights which Allison shares, together with the human courage and determination to heal and transform, point us towards finding a way out. The path out of our distress has to go through the wound causing that distress.

Allison and I share a desire to bring more awareness to the need for emotional and psychological healing in our individual lives, our relationships, and our society. My books strive to convey that what lies at the heart of life is not only pain, but also great beauty, possibility, healing, and hope. To push towards hope, we must be more attuned to the unseen changes which sometimes besiege us; we must pay heed to the silent crossings of the human heart and mind which inevitably change the threads of our lives, impacting not just ourselves but our relationships as well. Collectively, we must become more aware of how societal structures and systemic pressures can lead to broken relationships and families.

The personal and relationship issues we face are often complex with no simple solution. We have to avoid simplistic responses such as pointing a finger at 'chemical imbalances' or assuming that having a few more counsellors in schools or workplaces will solve the problem. Although healing and transforming ourselves and our relationships is not easy—it takes courage, action, and hard work—we can change ourselves and our relationships for the better. The stories in this book show us that we are not alone in striving to rise above our predicaments. The insights Allison shares from her years of experience as a professional therapist can guide us towards a more wholesome life and more fulfilling relationships.

I am privileged to have met Allison in our work towards a common vision. You, too, are invited to join us in this journey of possibility, hope, and courage. Together we can push boundaries— from what is to what can be.

Danielle Lim
Author of award-winning
And Softly Go the Crossings and The Sound of SCH

Introduction

Many therapists half-joke that their training began as toddlers. Although my own family of origin was overflowing with chaos and trauma, my real voyage to being a psychotherapist unfolded when I was a teenager working at an exquisite farm stand in San Diego, California.

When I moved from New York City to San Diego at the age of 16, I read a *New Yorker* article by Mark Singer profiling the Chinos, the Japanese owners of a family farm. I felt deep in my gut I needed to work with them. And, like so many times when my gut takes over, I had no idea why.

I landed a job at the Chinos farmstand in a customer-facing role and found them to be the most remarkable family I had ever met. Their lives are worthy of an epic, their story taking them from imprisonment in America's World War II era Japanese internment camps to becoming the farmers behind California's most coveted produce.

Most of all, the Chinos gave me the tremendous gift of a value system that heavily informs my worldview and how I practise therapy to this day. Curiosity, humility, creativity, and hard work were the core values the Chinos seeded in me. Ultimately, they were the springboard to *rethinking the couch* and doing therapy differently in Asia.

I moved to Hong Kong and pursued my dream of being a therapist in Asia well over a decade ago. Walking down the streets in my adopted city was an adventure for my senses—the bright neon street signs, elegant Chinese writing on billboards, and an endless row of storefronts of dried fish and goods, Chinese medicine, fresh meat, and produce. Around many corners were gleaming glass office towers, extending to the sky, some of which housed the headquarters of some of the largest corporations in the world. The juxtaposition of tradition and modernity was reflective of what I would see in many of my clients in Asia, who longed to hold onto tradition, such as rituals and values, while also yearning to evolve.

During a festive holiday like Lunar New Year, many Asian cities reveal their vibrancy, showcasing values of family, hard work, and tradition. Red lanterns line the streets and incense burns at temples as families dressed in traditional clothing carry fragrant foods to share and give out red packets—*lai see* in Cantonese and *hong bao* in Mandarin—that include money as a gift for special occasions.

Discussions swirl around the anticipated joys and challenges of the year ahead—many informed by the Chinese Zodiac. It reminds me of the Japanese New Year celebration *mochitsuki* I used to celebrate with the Chinos and of how important it is to pause and reflect on the year that has passed and be intentional about the one to come.

Every New Year, I reflect on the precious lessons they taught me and am reminded of the power of asking someone *O-genki-desuka* in Japanese, which, very roughly, translates into 'How are you?'

I would often hear the Chinos ask people this question with a focus and deliberateness that seemed foreign to me as an American. I was culturally conditioned to understand 'How are you?' as a kind of casual, throwaway question as in, 'Hey, how are you? Did anyone order pizza?' *O-genki-desuka* has a different vibe; it is a deeply personal question to ask in Japanese culture. Years later,

I'm reminded just how deep and intimate this is to ask my clients
and what an incredible privilege it is to witness their deepest truths,
secrets, dreams, shames, desires, and needs. I'm sometimes the only
person with whom my clients share these innermost thoughts, and
that is a powerful and precious gift to behold.

This cultural imprint became a guide to living and working in
the collectivistic cultures of Asia, where I have spent most of my
adult life.

Whenever we move somewhere, there are push and pull
factors. While there were things 'pushing' me to leave the United
States, it was the 'pull' of Asia that was—and is—far more
compelling and powerful. I am reminded of this every time I hear
the perennial question expats around the world like to ask one
another: 'When are you going home?' In all my years living in
Hong Kong and Singapore, whenever I have been asked this, I
have responded, 'Asia is my forever home.' This is where I feel
my feet grounded and my soul connected, and I have a deep
reverential connection to my work out here.

I have worked with more than a thousand people from
various cultures, including couples, corporate clients, and
individuals, both in clinical settings and private practice. I have
started and led various support groups, including ones for male
refugees and asylum seekers, men becoming fathers, domestic
workers and women with postnatal depression and anxiety.
I specialize in supporting people with relationship and work
challenges, and what I've come to learn is how intimately these
two are linked in much of Asia. The health of our relationships
and our experiences at work determine so much of our physical
and mental wellbeing.

Part of what I've learned working in Asia is how deeply
culture informs our experience of the world. There are universal
experiences and feelings, for sure, yet there are also unique ways
we walk through the world and unique ways we seek support.

This book tells the true stories from my therapy room. I have gone out of my way to disguise the details of my clients to ensure confidentiality. If you see yourself in this book, then that's purely coincidental. Any resemblance to actual persons—living or dead—or actual events is sheer chance.

You'll meet the Singaporean maneater who measures the manhoods and salaries of hundreds of expat lovers in a physical portfolio, the Indonesian tycoon who struggles with unlimited power, the Chinese workaholic litigator devoted to a feng shui master, a high-powered professional Taiwanese woman debating whether to freeze her eggs, and more.

If you've struggled with the challenges that life sometimes throws at us—heartache, affairs, toxic offices, control issues, divorce—then you might find this book to be a useful self-help guide.

For so long in Asia, mental health has been a taboo subject, for both individuals and couples alike. Encouragingly, the pandemic has shifted this somewhat out here. This is the right time to talk about this important topic and I'm incredibly grateful that Penguin Random House Southeast Asia is at the forefront of this.

In light of the rise of Asian hate crimes globally during the pandemic, this book also illuminates the humanity and common ties that bind us all in the East and the West. Culture may inform how we experience the world, yet we are all still people seeking deep relational connection and meaning. We all want to feel that we matter to someone, to something. There are many walls but not enough bridges in this world. I hope this book will help to build some bridges between cultures and nations.

It's my highest privilege to work with clients from such diverse backgrounds. I wake up every morning with a deep curiosity and commitment to supporting them on their journey through this world.

With that, welcome to my therapy room.

Part I

Power, Control, and Sex for Sale

Chapter 1

Who's in Control? (She's a Maneater)

Lin swaggered into my therapy room, oozing sex appeal and dripping with power. She first came to see me on her own to talk about her Canadian fiancé, Paul, and whether she would marry him. 'I have many choices, just so you know,' she told me in a seductive tone. I had been practicing in Hong Kong for less than a year and was immediately intrigued by her confidence. She was unlike any of my female clients—they ranged in personalities and job roles and included powerful expat executives, stay-at-home mothers, and local Chinese professionals.

Lin was Singaporean Chinese and had worked in Hong Kong and London for the past twenty-five years as a portfolio manager of sprawling, mixed real estate investments across the world. At forty-nine, she looked fifteen years younger. Her lean muscular legs were accentuated by sky-high white stilettos and hugged by a powder pink micro miniskirt and matching tailored Chanel blazer. She carried a beige Birkin 35 handbag with a silver lock hanging off the tassel. Her long black hair had caramel highlights and was tamed into a perfectly coiffed Brazilian blowout. She had cat-like eyes, made up with a dark-grey smoky shadow; these had a laser focus and could penetrate a man, making him do her bidding.

Everything about her facial demeanour was controlled and seductive all at once.

As she spoke of her demanding job, she knew exactly what she needed to do and how to go about it. She applied the same vim and vigour with her lovers. She shared in a composed way that she had a portfolio of men in descending rank. It detailed their wealth and annual salary measured against her earnings, estimated bonus, ethnicity (she preferred 'non-Asian men, easier to control'), a photo, penis size, sexual performance, and an extra column for best sexual positions. She said there were dozens on this list of expat men she would sleep with on a rotational basis and hundreds in total. Because she had climbed so high in finance, she had raised the bar with the men she seduced. They were conquests to her, like mountains to a climber.

My first thought was to wonder whether Lin really did have such a portfolio. Before I could ask, though, she pulled out a beige folder, labelled 'Investments', and started flipping through the pages. I thought to myself, *wow, she's serious—and seriously acting like many entitled men I've met.*

She reminded me of a Korean client, Albert, who once came into a session with two printed copies of an Excel spreadsheet that compared his past lovers to his fiancée in terms of height, weight, education, employment, salary, net worth, and bra size. Financially, Albert coded his fiancée as 'X'. He was '12X'.

Lin admitted freely that she had been 'inspired' to make her own spreadsheet after dating a British man who ranked his lovers.

'When I date, I'm always thinking of what a man can offer me financially. I've expanded the spreadsheet into a portfolio as it's easier to keep all this information organized. Penis size, sexual positions, all great. But what I'm really focused on is whether a guy is able to offer me something financially satisfying.'

Expanding her portfolio was one thing. Expanding her empire was another. My guess was that Lin was more after control and power than money. I even sensed she was trying to mould me into the therapist she wanted me to be, to serve her agenda.

I've had many male clients divulge that they freely exchanged this kind of sexual information with other men on spreadsheets, websites, social media, you name it. How many women can they sleep with? How big were her breasts? How to make them scream? How good was the sex? Lin was the first woman I had met who not only asked these same questions of the men she slept with, but also had it all organized in a neat portfolio. She was one in a billion and certainly shattered any stereotypes of Asian women being compliant and obedient. She was anything but.

I asked her what her end goal with the portfolio was and how it related to the question of whether she wanted to marry Paul, who had stayed with Lin even after learning about the portfolio and being told he didn't measure up.

I had to be careful not to get distracted with her detailed and ruthless stories of seduction. The risk: the hour would pass, she would feel she had controlled me enough, that I was under her spell, and if Paul joined us, I would collude with her.

'My end goal? My end goal is to be with a man who is even more powerful than me. Not an easy hunt,' she said.

'Is that what you really want? Let's play this forward for a second. Let's pretend you do hunt down a really powerful man. Then what? There will always be more powerful men. So, is this a forever hunt as in capture and then release when the next man presents himself?' I asked, leaning towards her ever so slightly.

'I will never be controlled by another man. I will control my destiny,' she replied.

'When you said, "another man", who controlled you in your past? Who is the other man?' I asked.

'Let me make this easy for you. My father is who I'm talking about. For him, money meant control, and he had the most influence in the family. My mother had no power and no independence, always needing to save money because my father only gave her enough to buy groceries. My family in Singapore was a typical Chinese family where my father made all the decisions. I felt powerless, and we had to listen to him. I'm the oldest of two girls, and he made it very clear he always wanted boys. It was his go to: "I wish I had boys,"' she said with rising anger.

'You've certainly experienced a lot. How were you able to survive?' I asked.

'I did what I needed to do to make sure no man ever controlled me,' she responded, still with a touch of anger in her voice.

Lin, like many who were controlled early on, went in one of two extreme directions. She would either give up her sense of agency or try to control others fiercely. We sat together for a few moments in silence, and I could sense that Lin wanted to regain control.

'Look, I think the lamest of therapists could piece this one together. At a young age, I was never the smartest or prettiest, yet I remember my mother putting my sister and me in a local beauty pageant. I won. And I remember the time my father finally looked at me like I was something. I can't recall another time he told me he was proud.

'But I'm not stupid. I knew early on that beauty fades, and I can't compete with a twenty-year-old perky-breasted woman with perfect skin and a sex drive like an animal. So, I went to business school, did what I needed to play in the arena with the big boys, and knew that my intellect would save me when beauty fades or in the unlikely event that I wouldn't meet a man who made more money.'

I was impressed with her level of self-awareness. It was said in quite a robotic way, as if she had prepared beforehand: 'Speech 32—What to Say if a Therapist Asks'. And yet, I could sense Lin's humanity and understood how she responded to the challenges in her childhood. The question was whether she could understand how those adaptations negatively impacted her current relationships while honouring that at one point they had made sense given her upbringing. I wondered how she would be in the room with Paul.

She leaned in towards me, crossed her legs, and said, 'Let's cut to the chase. There's nothing wrong with me. I get all this stuff we're discussing. Yes, my father's had an impact. But Paul is the one with the problems, and he sent me here to meet you. I'm really just here to see if you're good enough to help.'

With that, she picked up her Birkin 35 handbag, put her hand on the doorknob, looked me straight in the eye, winked, and said, 'Paul and I will see you next week.'

Chai lattes and disco balls

'Why don't we speak about the fucking engagement, Lin?' Paul asked.

Paul was a Canadian investment banker at a top global institution and had been living in Hong Kong for the past fifteen years. He was divorced with two sons who were living with his ex-wife in Canada. With his broad shoulders, 'bad boy' vibes, dark brown hair, and olive skin tone, he looked more like a retired professional boxer than a banker and liberally dropped F-bombs as if on autopilot. When he spoke directly to me, he was quite kind and gentle, with only the occasional F-bomb escaping. Yet, with Lin, it was as if a different Paul had shown up—a spiky, frustrated man, with F-bombs falling like rain in a downpour.

Instead of speaking about the engagement, Lin pulled the ring out of her bag to show it to me. 'Do you like this ring?' she asked as if, woman-to-woman, she wanted my solidarity that it was just an average ring. In reality, it looked like a humongous disco ball, a blinding diamond that was likely worth more than a mortgage for a multi-million-dollar house.

I didn't respond and had to pull back from her invitation to play ball. Instead, I redirected the conversation and asked about the actual engagement.

'Is there a story you wanted to share about the engagement?' I asked, looking at both of them and squinting my eyes slightly to signal interest.

Paul took up the mantle.

'Yeah, I'll just tell the story. I flew her to Bali last Christmas and arranged a private villa for the weekend. I went all out. We were having dinner outside the villa, watching the sun set, drinking champagne, and I got down on bended knee to propose and opened the ring box to Lin to ask if she would marry me. A fucking US$250,000 ring. You know what she did? She merely glanced at the diamond, looked down at her fucking nails, and asked petulantly, "Where's my chai latte? If you're going to propose outside of a restaurant, you gotta get me my favourite drink!"'

Paul had a mocking tone as he shared this story, but he looked enraged, and his lower lip started to quiver.

'What's wrong with that?' asked Lin. 'It's a decent ring. But come on, I know men who can do better,' she sniffed, as she inspected her ring, looking at it as if it came from a Cracker Jack box.

As if on cue, Paul exploded. 'You're such a maneating bitch.'

I was lost in a sea of chai lattes. Sometimes couples will speak in code or converse in their own secret language, reflective of experiences and years together. I am usually able to follow just enough to make progress, yet with the chai latte, I was genuinely perplexed. Was it code for something, or were we actually speaking tea?

I thought clarifying would help by redirecting them away from their ping-pong game of insults.

'Please pause for a second. I want to be sure I'm following. What does a chai latte have to do with an engagement? Is the chai latte code for something?' I asked.

'Code? No. No code. The diamond ring is one thing. So, check, the guy got me a US$250,000 ring. Many could have bought me that ring, as I said. But the chai latte is the true litmus test,' Lin said unapologetically.

She was both serious and sadistic. No chai latte, no deal. I sensed this was really a pretext, her way of signalling that she wanted to return to her portfolio, that she had other mountains to climb.

The two of them bickered and glowered at each other continuously. You would never have guessed they were a couple. They sat several feet apart with no sign of compatibility. In fact, they seemed like each other's worst enemy.

'Don't you know there are hundreds of men in my portfolio? I imagine many would have ordered me a chai latte,' she said coldly, crossing her slim, defined legs and folding her arms smugly over her short red dress.

'You narcissist!' he snarled.

She replied super calmly that she had a date lined up and could swat Paul away.

'His penis was bigger,' she said, looking straight into Paul's eyes. A master manipulator, she got off on his rage and jealousy.

Each time I would pause or try to redirect the session, I was going nowhere. I finally put my foot down. 'What do you want from me and this process? What are we doing?' I asked. I needed to make sure they were clear I wasn't there to pull out popcorn.

'Look, I just want Lin to stop it with this portfolio stuff. And by that, I mean stop sleeping with other men, when I'm clearly not OK with that, and stop torturing me by comparing me with other men and make up her damn mind if she wants to get married. And, marriage definitely means no cheating,' Paul said.

'Marriage? You think I want to marry you still?' she said coldly, her eyebrows raised.

At this point, I was riding the currents of resistance. Maybe they did just want to torture each other, I thought. I put this to them, as I needed to check that I had understood their goals and was not being more ambitious than they were.

'Maybe you two enjoy playing with each other's life and want to continue like this indefinitely. At that point, you don't need to come to waste your time and money seeing me. Maybe there is another type of therapy out there to consider if you want to do this, yet it's not the kind of therapy I do,' I said and paused deliberately.

Lin stood up and looked at me in a very controlled manner. 'Thank you, Allison, for your time and candour. I'm not willing to change anything and don't need to. I have many options, as I've already told you.'

Then she looked at Paul, pointing her perfectly manicured, long red fingernail in his eye and said, 'You're done.'

With that, she stormed out of the room.

Bye-bye, Maneater

'He's all yours.'

An email with this subject line appeared from Lin in my inbox a week later. Paul was copied in. She let me know she would no longer come to therapy yet encouraged, *in her own way*, Paul to continue with individual sessions. I sensed that the subtext of her email, paradoxically, was, you better fix him, and you better not fix him. This wasn't the first time in my career I had received this kind of paradoxical request.

In our first individual session, Paul focused on Lin and how he could not get over how she treated him. I could sense Paul building a victim narrative, and at the same time I could sense he needed some space to share his feelings about her. I wondered if he had anyone else with whom he could share this. I imagined he was quite proud to have Lin hanging off his arm yet utterly ashamed to tell other men or family what happened outside the bedroom.

'I don't know what I'm doing with Lin. She's wicked. She plays with my life just constantly. And, you know what's crazy, she shits all over me, and I just take it. And, if I'm totally honest, I'm obsessed with her,' Paul exhaled.

'Why are you obsessed with her?' I asked.

'I don't know. Sex with her is amazing. Just the opposite of what I had with my ex-wife, which was sexless, there was no love, just boring, except we have good kids. I am wildly attracted to Lin when she's not such a bitch. Yet, even when she's a bitch, there's something about winning her over. I was one of those men, you know, in her portfolio. I remember the first time meeting her, staring at her incredible legs, just wondering what it would take to be with her and be inside those legs. The first time I found the portfolio, I was incredibly angry and wanted to break up with her. And you know what? She just said, "Fine with me, bye!" And like a fucking loser, that made me want her more,' Paul said.

Sex was one thing. Yet, when Paul was talking, it occurred to me that he may never have experienced a relationship in which he loved someone and felt loved. Even when he very briefly spoke about his ex-wife and kids, it all seemed very matter of fact.

I tested my hypothesis. 'Have you ever felt loved?' I asked gently.

I watched him swallow deeply and could see his Adam's apple going up and then descend back into his throat. 'No. Never,' he said.

'Do you want that?' I asked.

'Yes,' he said in a resigned tone, as if he wanted it yet didn't believe it was possible.

Paul had grown up in a rough part of Hamilton, Ontario in Canada and learned how to defend himself on the streets. As a child, he was always fighting. He fought the bullies who made fun of his crooked teeth, the teachers who told him he was a 'failure at math', and the absent father who would dodge paying child support. He also fought for his mother's attention. Paul's parents had divorced when he was five, and although his father was rich— he led a publicly listed business whose transactions have totalled more than US$1 billion—Paul had never received a cent.

His mother had worked a job as a receptionist during the weekdays and as a waitress on the weekends to make ends meet. She was a 'difficult person', and they hardly communicated as he grew up. She often abused him verbally, and he cried under his blanket just about every night as a child. He was practically raised by surrogate fathers and mothers—aunts, family friends, a priest.

Even now, it seemed like there was always a storm brewing over his head; his eyes looked clouded every time I saw him, reflecting the lack of clarity in his thoughts and decisions.

Paul spoke eloquently about his choice to become an investment banker. 'It was fuelled by my desire to win, to outdo my father, as a fuck you to the teacher who told me I suck at math, and as a fuck you to the bullies who I imagine are flipping burgers now. I always wanted to outdo the son of a bitch I had as a father. I hate my work, if I'm being honest. I work with a bunch of assholes who are also just looking to make money. But anyway, I have two kids to support and an ex-wife, so it is what it is. I guess I won, but I'm fucking lost. I wake up miserable going to work and have nobody to keep me warm at night,' Paul said.

This idea of 'winning' became a window into a long history of trying to win. Winning at his career. Winning the heart of a maneater. Lin wanted control, he wanted to win—a toxic combination, at best.

'Have you ever tried to win your boys' hearts?' I asked, knowing that parents don't aim to win their children's hearts, yet needing to match his language.

Paul's eyes started to swell. 'No, I've let them down.'

I asked him what he meant and whether he wanted a relationship with his boys. He said that because his father had never supported him financially, he had focused all his energy on doing so for his own children. He had never considered that there was a different way to be a father. His marriage had disintegrated after years of him chaining himself to the investment banking ladder. He and his ex-wife barely spoke anymore.

We worked on what he wanted in his relationship with Lin, and as we spoke more about his past relationships and Lin, it emerged that he wanted love and respect as the cornerstones of a partnership.

Even though she had shown no sign whatsoever of wanting this in the past, he was 'obsessed' with her and wanted to stand up for himself, lovingly and firmly. Paul was clear the portfolio needed to go, along with all the manipulative games they would play with each other. He wanted a relationship in which 'Bye!' wasn't a cheap, easy exit, one where there was passion yet depth too, and a shared commitment only to each other.

The moment Paul started to assert himself and set boundaries, Lin broke up with him.

'Maybe I dodged a bullet?' he wondered.

'If I was a betting therapist, then I would say you more than dodged a bullet,' I said, my eyes wide open and my head nodding yes.

Paul was nodding too; we were sharing a reality.

Paul continued therapy for the next couple of months, and we redirected some of the obsessive energy he experienced towards Lin to training for a marathon instead.

What he really wanted, though, was to repair his relationship with his sons. The summer after the break-up, he flew to Canada to be with them, promising himself he would get the job done before returning to the world of dating.

Instead of trying to 'win' his boys over, as he had once done with Lin, he recognized that his presence, attention, and energy were worth more than any bonus from the bank.

Breaking barriers

Lin certainly broke the mould.

For centuries in this part of the world, men have wielded all the power in relationships, with many cultures viewing them as being entitled to women and gratification.

Women, meanwhile, have been oppressed and controlled by foot binding, the concubine system and patriarchal family structures that consider them the property (literally) of their husbands; their bodies and minds not their own.

Today, this oppression, this emotional foot binding, lives on in new guises, such as the plastic surgery craze that has swept South Korea and beyond. Globally, the market for cosmetic surgery is projected to reach US$48 billion by 2030, according to Vantage Market Research[1]. In China alone, it is already worth US$25 billion.

However, I do see signs of hope in Singapore and Hong Kong.

In the past few generations, Asian women have climbed to the top of the corporate ladder. They have broken through barriers in ways unimaginable to their female ancestors, who were taught to be obedient and submissive. Arguably, there are more successful career women in Asia today than at any other time in history.

When Lin talked about her father's gender discrimination, I felt for her. I have had many women clients tell me their families impressed upon them what therapists refer to as a 'negative identity'. Negative identities are when someone is defined by what they are not—in the case of these women, they were defined by not being boys.

I had a visceral experience of this myself during my first pregnancy in Hong Kong.

When I asked the doctor the sex of the baby, she hesitated and said, 'Why do you want to know? The reason I ask is because this year we're seeing so many sex-selective abortions, and we believe it's because parents consciously time their pregnancy and want to give birth to a son in the Year of the Dragon.'

---

[1] 'Cosmetic Ingredients Market – Global Industry Assessment & Forecast', Vantage Market Research (Dec 2022) https://www.vantagemarketresearch.com/industry-report/cosmetic-ingredients-market-1918 (accessed 15 Feb, 2023).

I was shocked and saddened. I had, of course, heard about sex-selective abortions, yet hearing it from the mouth of a doctor while I was pregnant made me physically sick.

The preference for boys in China has been culturally engrained over centuries and is linked to the desire to carry on the family name. China is not unique in this regard, but the one-child policy it pursued from 1978 to 2015 greatly exacerbated the situation, as, for decades, parents turned to sex-selective abortions and infanticide to ensure that their one child was a boy. Largely as a result of this, today, in China, there are 20 million more men than women.

While I was aware of this cultural preference for boys, I had no idea that Dragon boys in particular were so auspicious. I learned that many Chinese and East Asian families believe these children will be cleverer and more successful than those born in the other eleven Chinese zodiac years. Research has shown fertility rates spike during this period in Hong Kong, Singapore, and Taiwan. And so it was in 2012, when there was both a baby boom and significantly more boys born.

In my personal experience, people were not shy in wondering aloud if my pregnant belly was carrying a Dragon boy. Soon enough, they got their answer.

When I arrived at the hospital in Hong Kong on 8 October 2012, I was screaming from my contractions and ready to push.

In the West, such an entrance would have been unremarkable, but on this ward, I must have appeared out of control. Every other baby had been born by C-section and taken out according to a feng shui master's direction at a precise minute, often the eighth minute on the eighth day of the month.

Eight is an auspicious number in Chinese culture and, to this day, people remark approvingly when they hear of my eldest son's date of birth or read his Chinese name, which contains the character for 'dragon'. My younger son, born in the Year of the Pig, doesn't get anything like the same positive energy from strangers.

That's not to say there aren't drawbacks to being a Dragon boy. The over-abundance of males means greater competition in finding a mate, a job, and even an education. We found it hard to get my eldest into school for this very reason.

Perhaps that just goes to show that even Dragons—whether by birth, like my son, or by character, like Lin—can't have everything their own way.

Chapter 2

Risky Trades

Jed shared proudly in our first session that he once 'snorted a line of cocaine off a hot stripper's breast' in a dark alley after work one evening in New York City.

He sniffed and fidgeted, his legs trembling as he nervously scanned the framed certificates, art, and photos on my wall. His eyes darted to and fro as he introduced himself: New Yorker from the Bronx, trader on Wall Street, work pressure 'made him' do lines of cocaine on conference room tables.

We were both from New York City, and yet the New York he described seemed oceans away from mine. Jed grew up in Queens; I grew up in Manhattan. It was his dream to 'make it' and come to Manhattan to work on Wall Street, whereas my dream was to make it to Asia and in Asia. His New York City was full of glitter, glamour, drama, money, sex, and power; mine was basically home, school, and exploring different neighbourhoods.

I've always felt more in tune with the people and lifestyle of Asia, a collectivistic society, and I enjoy interacting cross-culturally. It's striking when you meet someone abroad from the same city and feel like you're in a cross-cultural exchange. I have, at times, felt more connected to the distant foreigners I met than to my own countrymen. This is one of the many mysterious threads of living abroad—I feel more at home in Asia.

Back to Jed. At forty-three, Jed still worked as a trader and made clear that if we worked together, then we would need to meet ten minutes after the Hong Kong Stock Exchange closed at 12 p.m. for lunch, so that he could run from his desk to mine and end the session ten minutes early so he could run back to the trading floor for the reopening. Like clockwork, he would show up at 12.10 p.m. for each session, and at 12.50 p.m. he would jump from his chair and walk out, even at times interrupting his own sentence. He would bring a sandwich to each session, wolfing it down as quickly as he could as if he had never left Wall Street.

Jed spoke in quickfire sentences, and in between comments about 'stopping the bleed on massive losses' and his 'big trades', he would pause and stare at me for a second as if waiting for me to say, 'Wow, you stopped the bleed! Wow, big trades! You're such a big man!'

But with all the chaotic energy in the room, I made a point of keeping things laser-focused and refused to stroke his ego.

'Jed, if our work together is a super success, then what would that look like? What will you have gained?' I asked directly.

'Uh . . . my wife wants to divorce me,' he said, his left leg shaking nervously.

'And you do or do not want a divorce?'

'Oh, actually I don't really care,' he replied, as if sharing that his tenth favourite baseball team had just lost the World Series.

'You don't really care if your wife divorces you? It's striking you seem to have very little emotion or opinion on it. Is there anything else you want to share about your marriage or her desire to divorce?' I wondered.

'Lisa is Malaysian Chinese from Kuala Lumpur. Former workaholic banker. From a wealthy family. Was a real ballbreaker. Her mother still is. We have three daughters aged two, four, and seven. She wants to leave me and go back to KL,' he said, with little emotion.

I asked him about when they had got married and how they had met to see if maybe the emotion had died but was once alive.

'We've been married for twelve years. I don't love Lisa anymore. I don't want to be married. The only thing I care about is that she's threatening to take the kids to Kuala Lumpur to live with her family,' he said. 'We met at a friend's wedding and hit it off right away. She was sexy as hell and a confident banker, and I was hooked. But love? Eh, I guess at one point. Yet, when the girls came along, she became a stay-at-home mom, and our marriage just died—no time together.'

'Why do you think your marriage died?' I asked to see if he could say anything about their dynamic without laying the blame on changing endless diapers.

'I don't know. I was on the trading floor all day. My wife was pissed that I wasn't helping more. But she decided to leave work and hired helpers, so why would I help more? And besides, I'm a dude. I was planning to spend time with the kids when they were older, like hiking on the weekend or something fun. I don't know, when I look back after the girls were born, it's like Lisa didn't care about me anymore, and so I just stopped caring,' he said, shrugging his shoulders.

I held back from telling him the only things men cannot do with babies is breastfeed or give birth. Instead, I focused on where he was right now—did he want to work on his marriage? Was his wife willing? Or was I helping him to prepare for divorce?

'My wife thinks I've been cheating over the past year. She doesn't understand why our bank account has been drained and why I've been absent from home so much. Her friend told her to give me one more shot and told me to go to therapy. I have no idea if she wants to work on the marriage. I was just told to come here,' he said matter-of-factly, as if the therapy room could have been a sandwich shop or a dental clinic.

'Is that true? Have you cheated and drained your bank account?' I asked.

'Nope and nope,' he said, one hand on each leg, moving his trousers up and down.

'So, it sounds like your wife has told you she will divorce you and has put therapy on the table as a last resort. But to be clear, does she want to join you in this process and do couples therapy eventually, or is she asking that you do individual sessions?' I asked.

He laughed. 'Oh, fuck no, she doesn't want to come here.'

'Fair enough. So, your wife wants to divorce you, puts therapy on the table for you, and you are sharing that you don't love her anymore, maybe never did, and you don't really have interest in the marriage? If ultimately what you want is to prevent her from taking the kids to Malaysia, then there is perhaps an emotional component of shifting how you two are interacting. However, there's a real practical component here. Have you consulted a lawyer yet?'

I wondered if he understood what would happen if Lisa did divorce him. I also wondered why he cared so much about Lisa taking the kids to Malaysia, but I held onto this question about his relationship with the children. He raised his eyebrows as if I had just asked at once the world's stupidest and most helpful question, so I waited to feel the energy of his response. 'Nope. Haven't done it,' he said, before getting distracted by the clock. It was 12.49 p.m., so he leapt from his chair and threw down some bills on the table next to me dramatically, as if he were paying a prostitute.

I looked down at the money and then up at Jed and said, 'We're not doing this. Please hand me the money directly. I will work with you only if we both commit to a respectful relationship.' He recoiled but then picked the cash back up and handed it to me. He then ran out of the door.

I knew he would not have respected me, or the therapeutic process, had I not said something straight away.

Jed reminded me of a wound-up toddler, jacked on sugar and wanting to run in every direction, yet craving containment and boundaries at the same time.

Lifting the veil

'Can I trust you, Allison, with what I want to tell you? It might shock you,' he asked me in a subsequent session, after a full two minutes of small talk about his most recent big trade. He appeared restless, visibly hesitant to bring up this question. I met Jed after years of practicing and knew well enough to sit with him in the tension before jumping in too quickly.

'The chances of me falling off my chair are next to zero, but try me,' I responded.

'I was thinking about our conversation,' he said anxiously.

I kept my mouth shut and waited for more.

'I'm in love with a woman, May. We met at a bar in Wan Chai. OK, I said it.' His eyes stilled, and he breathed in deeply. I could tell he was ready to share his stories, seeking relief.

'Are you open to telling me more? I'm asking so that I can help you,' I said.

He had met May at a brothel, and she was literally inside a cage, with other young women, when they first met. The idea was that a man would walk into the brothel, look at the women inside the cage, and then choose the one he wanted. I had chills when he told me this and still do when I reflect back years later.

Jed said that when he looked at May in the cage, he 'knew' there was something 'special' about her and that he could somehow 'save her'. She had been occupying his thoughts for most of the past year. He had spent a lot of time and money on tracking her down and trying to win her affections. He was nearly bankrupt, his wife screaming at him day and night, wondering where their money had gone, threatening divorce and to take the girls to Malaysia if he didn't give her clear answers soon.

'May is so sexually adventurous and gives the best blow jobs. We had threesomes and chemfun,' he said in a giddy tone, his eyes wide open. 'But it's not just the amazing sex. She pays attention to me, even asks how I'm feeling, and she comes from such a tough background. She's a real tough, sexy cookie.'

'Chemfun? What is that?' I asked with trepidation.

'It's a drug party, an orgy with ice,' he said without skipping a beat.

He waxed on obsessively about falling in love with May and was convinced she loved him back. He fantasized about running off with her, getting married, and saving her from her 'shitty, horrible situation' in the Philippines. He would meet May after work and party with her on the weekends, lying to his wife that he needed to sleep at the office some Sunday evenings to 'do research' before the market opened on Monday morning. Because, you know, big trades.

The more I listened, the more I realized Jed was not only obsessed with May and all the 'fun' they had but also possessed by the idea that he could save her. He appeared to give no thought to the destruction he could cause to his wife and children. I experience this often when people are in the throes of an illicit relationship—a near addiction to the idea that one person can save another, or that the relationship will save them both, often ignoring any collateral damage.

'While I understand you feel you're saving May, you're perpetuating a system, a very dark web, that could one day trap your daughters. Do you see that?' I asked boldly.

He squirmed, then blurted out, 'I'm not perpetuating a dark web.'

There was something else that made his preoccupation with May even more troubling. Due to compliance issues, Jed and his peers were not allowed to use phones during their twelve-hour shifts on the trading floor. But Jed had taken to running out of the building several times a day to read messages from a private investigator (PI) he had hired to spy on May. The PI, a Chinese man who spoke Tagalog, would check up on May at the bar in Wan Chai and collect intel about her family in the Philippines. In particular, he kept an eye out for any potential boyfriends.

'It ain't cheap. This PI charges me USD five figures a month. Plus, my sessions with you, Allison, actually cost more than my time with May,' he said.

That made me feel nauseated. I tried not to let it show.

Jed continued that on one occasion when he had left the floor to check his messages, there had been a massive drop in a position in his book. 'I was just obsessed, and I didn't even tell anyone I was going off the desk. We took a steep loss, and I got placed on a PIP [performance improvement plan], but it still didn't stop me.'

He was totally out of control. Drugs, paid sex with an exploited young woman, private investigator, possessed by ideas of love and being a saviour, and diminishing work results? I could see his bank account draining before my eyes, not to mention the relationship with his family.

While telling me about the PIP, Jed stopped mid-sentence and said, 'You should see the difference, then you would understand.'

He showed me a photo of May on his phone, then one of his wife and three daughters. I was confused as his wife looked eerily similar to May, so much so that they could pass for sisters, but I decided against saying that out loud. I was also deeply concerned for his three girls. I couldn't help but think that while he was focused on saving May, he was ignoring the risk that his daughters could end up like her one day. Trafficking and exploitation can happen to anyone from any background.

'I understand all too well, Jed,' I said. 'I sit with people like you all the time and watch them blow up their lives. I can sense you're a good guy. We've sat together now for two sessions.

The longer you have your double life with May, though, the more collateral damage it will cause to your finances, job, work visa, and children, and this could all very likely blow up if changes aren't made. I understand also that you want to "save" May, yet you're perpetuating a dark web that one day could trap your three girls.'

This time he was silent.

I paused for a moment to let him reflect and asked, 'What would you like to do, Jed? It's your life. I care about helping you enough to see the destruction this is causing your family. At the same time, nobody can take a bath for you.'

'I don't know. I don't know how to stop. I feel possessed,' Jed cried.

'When did you start feeling possessed, Jed?' I asked. I could sense he was being genuine, and so I gave him some space for this.

'I'm not sure. It was just the first time in my life that I felt special. It's almost a *Revenge of the Nerds* kind of feeling, that finally I am special after feeling like a loser for most of my life, and I've found someone who tells me this always and desires me. And things have just been hard,' Jed mumbled.

Once the tap turned on with Jed, he started pouring out stories. He told me about his unhappiness with Lisa's unwillingness to work, which was causing his 'head to spin with stress', and about his terrible relationship with his father. Jed's father had been a workaholic with a hugely successful career as an attorney for a sports league but had been absent for most of Jed's childhood and teenage years. When he was around, his caustic tongue lashed at Jed for not excelling at school and in athletics. Jed was terrified of his father, so much so that his physical presence could cause him to break out in hives. 'I was allergic to my own dad,' he joked.

'Your girls may become allergic to you if you continue with this behaviour,' I told him. 'Jed, my suggestion, take it or leave it, is you need to take action right now, or you're going to have a huge fall. The bad news is the fall will be very big. The good news is we may have enough time now to prevent that, but again, only if that's what you want.' I said these words with a deliberate calm to signal that I knew I could not control his actions.

There was quite possibly a connection between his past and his wife's unwillingness to work and his current obsession with May. But at this point in time, I saw this as a red herring. For now, we didn't have the luxury to wonder how much of his childhood wounds contributed to his behaviour. I couldn't understand what was driving his wife's decision to not work. I couldn't tell whether it was a sense of entitlement on her part or the result of a deal that she and Jed had made long ago—with him making money, her staying home—and that she had come to resent this now that he was draining their account. But I tucked away my questions in a mental 'To Discuss Later' file, as right now we had a crisis on our hands. He was clearly addicted to May, quite possibly to substances too, and there were a lot of lives at risk.

'What would be the first step?' he asked as the nervous shaking in his legs returned.

'My recommendation is that you go see a lawyer to understand the consequences of a divorce,' I said confidently.

'A lawyer?' He tilted his head to the side and looked perplexed.

'Yes, see a family lawyer, and let them know your situation— that you have an American passport, your wife a Malaysian one, that you work in Hong Kong on a visa, and you have three young kids. Tell them about the financial situation with your work, all of it. Then we can speak about the step after that. Are you willing to do that?' I asked.

'Right. OK,' he said, as if I had just sent him to prison.

I advised Jed, as I have many clients in similar situations, to see a lawyer as a first step because this usually sobers them up. The more I listened to Jed's stories and language, the more

I felt he needed to understand what he could lose as opposed to what he might gain. I sensed he had no awareness of how massive a bleed he could cause to his family and his own life.

Lawyers make for expensive therapists. Their primary focus is not on helping people emotionally. Jed needed one because he needed to start thinking practically.

Practicality is important because it is often the first step in stopping, or at least slowing, what I call the '2 a.m. Anxiety Train'—a particular anxiety that hunts us down in the middle of the night when we are facing high levels of uncertainty with challenges in our relationships, finances, jobs, or health. It's the anxiety that wakes us up at an unthinkable hour, knocks so hard that we can't sleep, and causes the wheels to come off, spinning our minds and bodies into torment. With this kind of anxiety, I will often separate the intervention into two buckets: practical and emotional. I find that if we can get certain answers, that reduces the grip the anxiety has on us.

Sending Jed to the lawyer was meant to wake him up. The 2 a.m. Anxiety Train hadn't yet pulled into the station, but if he didn't act now, it would be arriving soon.

2 a.m. Anxiety Trains

Jed came in for the next session ashen faced. No time for fluff or big trades. He was clearly nervous as he spoke.

'The lawyer told me there is a good chance, given my risk-taking behaviour, that if Lisa applies for relocation and wants to take the kids to Malaysia, she will win, and I may not see them much. The lawyer also told me that if she divorces me, all our financial information will be on the table, in some kind of Form E, and I will owe Lisa child support and alimony. What's worse is he said that my visa could be taken away if I violate compliance issues on the desk. He ended by telling me to "be very, very careful".'

'Jed, you ultimately need to decide what you want in your life. Being with May and draining your bank account are mutually exclusive of being married, providing for your family, and having a relationship with your kids and wife. How was it hearing that warning from the mouth of a lawyer?' I asked, genuinely curious.

'I don't want that. I won't lose my girls. I will be shipped back to New York City and what? I'm that loser guy who couldn't make it in Hong Kong, and worse, who has three kids who now live in Malaysia? No, thanks,' he said.

'I can help you get out of this if you're willing to do the work. No guarantee, though; I don't know if Lisa has already made up her mind,' I said.

'I'm willing to do the work. I adore my girls. I wish I had more time to be with them, yet I work such crazy hours,' he said.

'The good news is that you made plenty of time to be with May. If you're telling me that you genuinely value your children, which I can feel you do, then you've already shown yourself able to make time. That's the least of our concerns,' I said.

I needed him to avoid falling into this 'finding time' myth. Over the years, I have worked with people who have incredibly demanding jobs and other commitments, and yet if people want to make time for something, then they will. I wanted to suggest to Jed the potential treasure here: a better relationship with his kids. 'What do you adore about those girls?' I asked.

'My eldest and I have always been the closest. She's feisty like her mom, but she's incredibly sweet. We can talk for hours,' he said.

The next step for Jed was to work with a psychiatrist to discuss his substance usage as that greatly reduced the chances of him changing his behaviour.

The psychiatrist helped him withdraw from the drugs, and we both spoke with him about regulating his lifestyle choices so that he could be home right after the market closed, eat dinner with the girls, and go to bed early enough that when he awoke for another day of gruelling trading hours, he felt well rested and focused.

We also eventually spoke more about his parents and his resentment about Lisa not working. I asked him why she wasn't working and how he felt about that. He said they had agreed when Lisa was pregnant with their first daughter that she would not work outside of the home. He also said his resentment had dissipated now that he had more control over his decisions and finances.

Eventually, Jed stopped seeing May, but he never did tell his wife about his cheating. Over the years, I have often wondered whether he should have. Some therapists feel this is necessary for relationships to grow, especially if truth is a core value for those involved. Yet, I do not believe there is a clear-cut answer.

But whether Jed had truly wanted this never really became clear. The priority in his case was to stop the bleed, work on his relationship with his children, and get his work and finances in order.

Yet even when that started to happen, he showed no interest in repairing his marriage. He managed to kick the substance abuse and get off the performance improvement plan but remained at most 'just civil' with his wife, though they did stay married. His relationship with his daughters, on the other hand, improved immeasurably. He began cultivating a better relationship day by day, coming home each night after work for dinner and bedtime and committing his weekends to the family.

During his last session, he shared that he still loved May and wondered some days how she was doing. But he realized, too, that as intoxicating as his double life was, he couldn't afford financially or emotionally to remain tangled in this web.

Indeed, perhaps the biggest trade of his life came from this realization. He traded in a life of gratification for one of connection with his daughters.

'My girls now ask me every Friday evening what the plans are for the weekend. As soon as I'm home, they come running in their pajamas to grab my legs,' he shared with a big smile, his left leg shaking ever so slightly.

Trafficking in Asia

Something about Jed's struggle and obsession with May hit me on a very deep level. At the time of seeing Jed, I had already been working with domestic workers, male and female asylum seekers, and refugees, and started the first therapy group for male refugees and asylum seekers in Hong Kong—many of whom were trafficked. However, working with Jed lifted the veil on a very dark world—that of sex trafficking in Asia.

Over the years I would come to learn that Jed was not particularly unusual as a high-powered expat male pursuing a relationship with a trafficked woman (even if his use of a PI was). Many locals also pursue relationships with trafficked women.

A surprising number of expats in Asia engage in this kind of activity. Thousands of miles from home, they feel safe, far from prying eyes and untethered by family or community—distanced from their homes and distanced from their actions.

Like Jed, many fool themselves into believing they are somehow 'saving' these women, perhaps as a way to ease their conscience. But what they are really doing is perpetuating the business cycle that causes the suffering of women like May.

According to the International Labour Organization, as of last year, an estimated 50 million people in the world were living in conditions of modern slavery, about half of them in Asia.

Many are trapped in forced marriages (about 22 million) or otherwise sexually exploited (a further 6.3 million). In the commercial sex industry, seven in ten victims live in the Asia Pacific region and nearly all (99 per cent) are women or girls. And it's not only sexual exploitation. About 60 per cent of modern slaves are associated with manufacturing supply chains, often used in the growing of crops or making of clothes. The number of modern slaves is growing ever faster, propelled by an industry that makes US$150 billion annually, with the United Nations estimating there are more in the world today than at any other time in history.

If all that sounds bleak, there are reasons for hope, among them the work of non-profit organizations like the Mekong Club, a leading Hong Kong-based international charity that helps companies of all sizes understand how human trafficking works and ensure they are not unwittingly supporting it.

The chances of a woman like May being saved—by anyone—are exceedingly small. So, there was a heavy counterweight to any hope I felt when Jed told me of his improving relationship with his daughters. To this day, I do not know what happened to May or Jed. This is one of the challenges of being a therapist—stories don't always get tied up with a clean, bright bow. I am sometimes left guessing and hoping.

Chapter 3

Billion-Dollar Baby Daddy

A referral letter from a midwife arrived with 'urgent' in the subject line early on a Monday morning. It read, 'Allison, please see Toni ASAP. She is 28 weeks pregnant, not eating well, very anxious, on Class X medication for anxiety (highest risk medication for the baby) and is terrified the baby's father will leave her.'

When we first met, Toni sashayed into the room in a gorgeous floral green dress that camouflaged her considerable bump. At seven months pregnant, she looked immaculately put together. The only giveaways to her discomfort were her flat sandals and swollen feet. Toni had an entitled attitude that was unmistakable and knew how to wield her power. Her presence exclaimed, 'Hello! I'm here! I want you to help me immediately!'

At thirty-two, she was a platinum blonde with a voluminous wavy hairstyle, a Barbie-like aesthetic with the requisite perky nose, smoky blue eyeshadow, gorgeously long eyelash extensions, and an hourglass figure. I later learned that her perfect proportions and frozen Botox-ed forehead and lips were made possible by the best plastic surgeons and dermatologists that money could buy.

Although I had the referral from the midwife, I wanted to hear from Toni directly why she was here and what she wanted us to work on together. There is often a mismatch between what a professional might feel a client needs and what a client feels he or she needs. Part of my work is understanding why there may be a mismatch. Yet, I've learned that listening to the client's point of emotional urgency first is often the only gateway to making progress. And, when clients come in, they often come in with others in their psychic space—people who are haunting or hooking them in some way—and want to share what they are often painfully carrying, what is often invisible to the outside world.

Before I could finish asking Toni, she interrupted to tell me about how her billionaire benefactor and father of her baby, Mr Wong, was both 'generous' and 'demanding'. 'I've been *chosen* by Mr Wong. He wanted me to give him a son. He's in his fifties now and has a wife and two daughters in Shanghai. We met at a bar. I was doing some modelling in China and Japan. I didn't know that he was a billionaire when we hooked up. We've stayed at the best hotels and travelled by private jet to Paris, London, New York, and Tokyo,' Toni said coldly.

I could feel her unbearable sadness in my body. I wondered if she could feel me feeling her sadness; her eyes appeared full of frozen tears. She had come a long way from a poor village in the Czech Republic and was alone in Hong Kong with no close friends or family nearby. Mr Wong wanted her to stay in Hong Kong and essentially set up a sham job for her at his company so that he could visit, when he wanted, all the while keeping her at a distance from his family in Shanghai. He was leading a double life and liked to keep his two realities neat and separate.

She lived in the most expensive neighbourhood in Hong Kong, The Peak, in a palace of an apartment owned by Mr Wong. In addition to the personal trainers, plastic surgeons, and dietitians he paid for, Mr Wong provided for Toni a small army of staff to wait on her every need: a cook, midwives, nurses, domestic workers, assistants, and a driver, all chosen by him. Once the baby was born, there were nannies and night nurses already on deck. They served her hand and foot, 24/7, and she wouldn't go out of the door without at least four of them in tow. Her staff were collectively making US$100,000 a month while Toni received an allowance of US$22,000 a month, paid through her 'job'.

Days would pass in this gilded cage, and Toni's loneliness grew in lockstep with her baby bump. Instead of connecting with the son growing inside her, she spent her days obsessively consumed by anxiety that Mr Wong would leave her. There was no legal basis to their arrangement, so she worried constantly about whether he would continue to provide for her after she gave birth. She didn't have much of a relationship with her family in the Czech Republic and no friends in Hong Kong.

'I wake up after a night of broken sleep with nonstop anxiety throughout the day. I can't stop thinking that he will leave me. Why wouldn't he? He's so powerful. He has *chosen* me for now, but I'm not stupid—he will leave me once he gets his son. I am so worried that this pregnancy will break my body. I've tried to control my eating as much as I can and I am still exercising, but I've heard that women's boobs sag and their bodies get destroyed from a pregnancy. I already notice cellulite, and this could not be an attractive thing,' she said convincingly.

I spent years working at a midwives' clinic in Hong Kong, owned by two Icelandic sisters-in-law, so I know that doing therapy with an individual or couple expecting a baby has a particular shape. People in this situation can be very motivated to change, and quickly. That's because there's a deadline involved—even if it's an imprecise one—and many people feel motivated to improve themselves for the baby, even if they're unwilling to do so for their partner. I've lost track of how many clients will make changes for an unborn baby but not for their significant other.

I couldn't sense Toni's connection with her own feelings or the baby, though, and I wondered if she would stay focused on Mr Wong. I knew if I didn't first hear more about him and try to support her anxiety, she was unlikely to hear my ideas relating to pregnancy or her son. I also held in my mind the letter from the midwife and was aware we would eventually need to address her food and medication intake.

So, I asked more about her arrangement. I got the impression I was the only one with whom she could openly share. Toni's army of staff made her feel powerful and in control, at least momentarily, but in truth, she had much in common with those she lorded over. Toni and the army were terrified of the same thing—being fired by Mr Wong. She and they knew that with one stop of a payment, they could be erased.

It didn't take long for Mr Wong to energetically enter the room with us. I knew reducing her anxiety about him leaving her would be a tall order. She wasn't sharing much that made either of us feel hopeful. My stomach turned as she shared details of their *arrangement*.

Before the pregnancy, he would fly in once a month and compliment her lingerie or the way she looked, yet even over several nights together, they would not speak much. After she became pregnant, the trips grew less frequent and the compliments non-existent. He refused to have sex with her, telling her that pregnant women were 'useful only for the baby that's inside'. That line tortured Toni most nights. What happens once the son is born? What if the son isn't who Mr Wong wants him to be? Excitement, get the son, turn off, review arrangement.

Perhaps even harder for Toni was that there was no emotional connection. They barely spoke when he was out of Hong Kong, and when he was in Shanghai with his wife, he would turn off the phone he used to communicate with her. He didn't ask her questions, and he responded with silence when she asked about his work and personal life. She was somehow good enough as a baby vessel yet not good enough to be a human. While they were together, he was always working on his iPad or phone. He cared nothing about her culture when she would share about life in the

Czech Republic and told her that his only interest in her home country was '*some* of the beautiful women it produces'.

He could shut it all off. Put it in a lingerie box on the shelf and forget about both her and their son. Go back to Shanghai, or possibly to another city with another family. What made Toni interesting, though, was that she didn't delude herself with an idea of specialness. I sometimes wondered if she would have been better off if she had.

Toni asked me if I'd heard of similar arrangements before and if so, then, 'What are the chances he would leave me after the baby is born?' She swiftly followed up with, 'Actually, don't answer that,' and then fell silent.

I honoured her request and did not tell her just how common these sorts of mistress stories are in Asia. In what seems to me like an echo of the ancient concubine system, it is not so unusual for a travelling businessman to have a wife and children in one country and an affair partner and another set of children in another.

I've had several clients come to me to process their shock and grief over finding out that their father had a second wife and set of children elsewhere, even in another country. For instance, I had a client a few years before Toni, called Bernice. After years of suspicion, Bernice hired a private investigator to follow her father in China where he was spending an inordinate amount of time supposedly managing his business. The investigator discovered her father had a ten-year-old son and a wife in her thirties— around the same age as Bernice. Another client found out about the second family in her father's will and said hello to a brother and a sister in Argentina she never knew she had. Another woman was sent a photo of her husband with his second wife pushing a stroller together along the streets of Beijing.

Toni broke the silence. 'I'm so afraid he's going to cut the money off. How do I maintain it?' She then told me they had flown to Thailand three times to choose the sex of the baby by using in vitro fertilization (IVF) and preimplantation gender testing (PGT).

He was bent on having a son. In Hong Kong, one cannot choose the sex of a baby unless there's a medical reason, and it's also largely discouraged to find out the sex of a baby before birth to discourage sex-selective abortions.

To nail down the date for giving birth, she was also forced to consult Mr Wong's feng shui master who chose a date for her C-section.

'I'm sorry you feel so anxious. Your concerns are real, and I can understand why you would be feeling that way. It's very helpful you've shared all these details. I've noticed when you're sharing these stories, Mr Wong seems to be at the centre, yet I don't hear a lot about your feelings about this arrangement or your pregnancy. I care about you,' I said gently.

I knew she would either blow past my attempt to connect or would reach for it, yet my words were genuine. I have learned over the years to say these words only when I mean them. If I don't, then clients can smell the disingenuousness. Once Toni's mask of entitlement fell, she was warm and wanted to connect, yet I sensed her mind was utterly tortured, likely by design.

When speaking to Toni, I very deliberately used the word 'arrangement' and not 'relationship' as I was attempting to mirror her language. There's an ocean of difference between an arrangement and a relationship; on some level, she realized this. We agreed to meet for another session later in the week, and as I turned my chair to the computer to check the schedule, she asked, 'Allison, I want to meet again, but I need some kind of reassurance he won't leave. Can you please give me something?'

Whenever clients ask for reassurance, it's challenging. There's always a part of me that wants to take the client's pain away and say *the thing* that temporarily will. The client is often explicit with what that thing would be, and even if they're not, it's usually clear. All of us, at some point, are overwhelmed by uncertainty, and anything reassuring is like a steroid shot to the soul, temporarily reducing pain.

Yet, there is a reason why I do not give that 100 per cent reassurance to Toni or any client. I am not Mr Wong. He may or may not leave her.

There is also a power imbalance in the therapist–client relationship, and I feel it's an abuse of power to offer reassurance to a client on a matter I have no clue about. Instead, I can speak about pattern recognition—here are potential outcomes I've seen—and about building enough belief in not only in one's self but also one's community to feel more resilient riding the currents of life.

With this, I encouraged her to consider a different frame: that he was not her supply of oxygen and self-worth in this world. I said, 'Toni, I want to be able to tell you that he won't ever leave you. I am not able to because I do not know what Mr Wong will or won't do. I do know that you have inherent worth as a human, and that is something nobody can take from you. I am also confident we can work on ways to build your confidence so that regardless of the outcome, you will be able to handle it. Even after just knowing you for an hour, I can already sense your resilience. What comes to you when I say all of this?'

I'll never forget hearing her saying repeatedly under her breath, holding her belly, 'My self-worth isn't based on him. My self-worth isn't based on him.'

Those words were chilling and true all at once.

An army of one's own

Toni and I met later the same week, and she sashayed once again into the room.

I knew for this session we would need to focus on her pregnancy to ensure her mental and physical wellbeing. It was inevitable that Mr Wong would make his way back into the room, yet I was aware of containing this as we were working on a tight deadline to make some considerable change.

'How would you feel if today we discuss your pregnancy and feelings about becoming a mother? I am aware that your midwife has some questions about your nutritional intake and medication usage that I am wondering if you're open to discussing?' I asked.

'I am terrified of gaining weight. I keep asking the dietitian how I can lose weight after I give birth. She won't answer my questions, look me in the eye, or anything. I feel like a number to her. She keeps speaking about needing this and that nutrient for a healthy pregnancy and tells me to stop thinking about weight loss. Easy for her to say. I know I need to eat so the baby grows, but why won't she acknowledge my anxiety or tell me how to lose weight?' she wondered.

I understood from having worked with many pregnant women and having been one myself a couple of times, most of us worry about losing the weight, to some extent. With Toni, though, there was more to it—weight loss was a hedge against Mr Wong leaving her for a younger body, and she was utterly consumed by the anxiety that her body would change forever.

I knew she was not really after the quasi-reassurance that plenty of other pregnant women worried about their weight. Even so, I thought telling her so might still diffuse some of her loneliness by pointing out her connection to other women, however imaginary that community may be. I was even starting to wonder if she might eventually want to connect with other mothers, but I put that idea on hold.

'You're not alone, Toni. I have worked here for a few years, and the vast majority, let's say more than 90 per cent, of pregnant women bring up concerns about gaining weight and how they will be able to lose it. The midwife mentioned, though, that you're not eating well, and this is something we need to take very seriously for your son's health and yours to sustain pregnancy and labour. May I ask, what is your eating like these days?'

I needed to probe, on a basic level, to see what the midwife meant by not eating 'well', so I could know what kind of support she would need.

'I didn't know other women worried about this also. I look at them with their husbands, and I just imagine maybe those kinds of men don't care about weight, or maybe other women don't care. I *need* to care. My care is about my survival. Anyway, the food, umm . . . well, most days I get up and I take two of those anxiety pills with a big glass of water with lemon. I've heard lemon boosts metabolism so even though I hate the taste of the sour water, I drink it. Then I wait until lunch to eat a salad and then I sometimes snack on a few chocolate-covered almonds, which is naughty, I know. And then at dinner I am so hungry, I will eat fish or meat plus veggies and some brown rice. I hate my body when it feels so hungry. Sometimes the anxiety is high before I go to bed, so I take another anxiety pill. It's better than any dessert.'

'Toni, speaking of the anxiety medication, are you comfortable sharing which medication and how often you're taking it?' I asked.

'I'm on medication for anxiety, yes. I got it over the counter while in Thailand with Mr Wong,' she admitted openly.

She showed me the bottle of pills, and the midwife was correct—these were considered 'Class X' medications for pregnancy in the United States.

My role as a therapist, rather than a medical doctor, meant I could not comment on her use of these pills, so I tried to steer her towards help instead.

I asked Toni directly, 'I understand why you would be hesitant to speak with the dietitian if she is not hearing your concerns. How would it be if I handpick another dietitian to work with you closely and ensure she is hearing your concerns? I would also like you to see a psychiatrist to discuss the medication and can recommend someone as well. That way, Toni, if you give me permission to collaborate with them, we can build *your own* army of support, people you can hopefully trust.'

Eventually, she agreed, and the dietitian, the psychiatrist, and I all worked together. Toni and I met for a few more sessions during the pregnancy and worked on building a healthier mindset with her body and weight. The dietitian and I worked with her on setting healthier expectations, and she began to accept that she could likely lose weight at a healthy pace after pregnancy, even though her body would change in significant ways out of her control.

She scheduled regular physical training sessions and a tummy tuck for after giving birth. I suspect this ultimately may have been what moved the needle with her healthier mindset. Regardless, she was eating better and not obsessing over weight loss. She was also seeing a psychiatrist regularly.

We explored whether she could reconnect with her mother and sister in the Czech Republic. I asked gently whether any family would visit after her son was born. She shared that she had cut ties with her family during her modelling career as they tried to 'steal' her earnings. She said she would 'consider' reconnecting with them but would first need to ensure they had changed.

I did not see Toni again until one year after the birth.

She sashayed right back into the room. She was still with Mr Wong and still worried he would leave her. The difference now: she had alternative plans and the confidence to execute them. She was speaking regularly with her family in the Czech Republic, connecting with other mothers, feeling 'some' connection with her son, and had launched an online bikini business.

He may or may not try to erase her.

On a good day, her newly forged connections with her friends, family, and son meant she could swat away this niggling doubt. On a bad day, Mr Wong's power felt as debilitating as before.

And thus she beat on against the current, army and baby in tow.

Chapter 4

Bitter Truths

The truth was simmering in a pandemic pressure cooker.

At the end of 2021, the second year of the coronavirus pandemic, Chiori and Donald, a young couple in their mid-thirties, came to see me in Hong Kong. They had been together for eight years, engaged for one, and wanted to consult on whether to get married or split up. At this point, I had seen countless couples reckoning with the same question. Chiori and Donald, though, wore this question heavily in their facial expressions, body language, tone, and word choice. Either option, marrying or splitting up, felt like a burden.

With her fluffy pink shoes, jogging pants and sweater, her baby face features, round eyes and button nose, Chiori looked like a fifteen-year-old schoolgirl. And when she opened her mouth, her high-pitched sweet voice only added to her girlish aura. Chiori was from Kobe, Japan; Donald was from Hong Kong. They had met while attending graduate school in London. During our first session together, Donald sat down and pulled Chiori's chair close to his in a protective manner. He looked at me, then prodded her, 'Tell her.'

'I was a compensated dating girl. A sugar baby,' she said flatly, with no emotion. Her eyes were glazed over like she was not all there. She certainly wasn't in the room with us—she was somewhere else.

I was perplexed but kept a neutral look on my face, so Chiori explained.

Years ago, when Chiori was a high-school student in Kobe, she had registered on a website frequented by wealthy men, in their forties to seventies. These men would *choose* her and fly her first class from Japan to Hong Kong, Singapore, Australia— wherever their wildest fantasies would take them.

Men in their sixties and seventies in Hong Kong took a particular shine to her. They would place her at the Four Seasons Hotel and give her luxury handbags and money in exchange for sex and companionship at dinners.

This arrangement was a form of 'compensated dating', a phenomenon that has spread from Japan to all over Asia and is sometimes known in Hong Kong as 'part-time girlfriend or boyfriend'. The idea is similar to the Western concept of a 'sugar baby', with a modern slant: most of these hook-ups are facilitated online on websites or apps.

'Thank you for sharing all of this, Chiori. How long have you been involved in compensated dating?' I asked gently. I had not encountered anything like this in my therapy room before, and I needed to start with the basics before attempting to go deeper. I also needed to do all I could to make her feel safe and reassure her that I could connect with her humanity.

'I've been doing this since I was fourteen. I've been with thirty different men. No, thirty-three. Or is it thirty-two? I only saw one of them recently, though,' she said. I breathed in deeply as the reality of this woman selling her body at fourteen years old weighed heavily on my heart.

Once again, the veil had lifted, revealing a darkness so intense I would need to move slowly, with a deliberate focus, and make sure to respect both words spoken and those left unsaid.

'How did you get involved with this?' I asked calmly. She told me of her traumatic past and family life in Kobe as an only child.

Her father beat her and her mother with regularity. Her mother told her she was a nobody and threw steel utensils and glass objects at her. Both parents told her often she should never have been born, that she was a burden. Unwanted. The worst kind of unwanted in Asia: born a girl.

'My parents told me so often that I never should have been born. I was always sensitive to my parents' words and stress. I couldn't relax any time they were around. They were always stressed out about money. My dad's business was failing. When his stress was high, he would come after me with a stick and beat me. It's the stress that caused them to hit me or scream at me, and I probably deserved it as I did place a lot of burden on my parents. I sometimes used to cry loudly, and I think this caused my dad too much stress. I knew, though, that I needed to find a way to make money and never cause my parents to worry. That was my only chance of them loving me. I remember one time, when I was around ten years old, my mother chased me around the apartment with a sharpened knife, yelling, "Baka! Baka! Baka!"'

She looked down at her neon pink nails, shuffling her Chanel bag to the right of her chair. She took a few deep breaths, and before I could ask what *baka* meant, she looked up and told me that it was a Japanese slang word for 'idiot'.

Her response commanded a couple of minutes of silence.

This is something I had learned over many years in Asia— deep respect and reverence for silence and the power of using it judiciously in the therapy room.

As we sat in silence, I heard Donald breathing deeply, aggravated and uncomfortable by all that was filling the room. Chiori was holding back twenty years of tears. I was trying to hold them both in this pain.

I placed one hand on my chest, took a deep breath and said, 'I'm very sorry to hear about this stress and that you couldn't feel safe around your parents. No child ever deserves to be a punching bag for their parents' stress. No child ever deserves to be told they are a burden or unwanted. I can see how you adapted to this by turning to compensated dating.'

I was taking a risk saying this to Chiori. Many adults I work with in Asia whose parents hit them as children feel they deserved it, that they weren't compliant enough, or that it was culturally appropriate to be hit. Yet, what Chiori described went too far to fit these narratives, these excuses. Her parents had wanted to erase their child's existence and burdened her psyche with the knowledge her existence was unwanted.

I was keen to help her make sense of why she chose compensated dating. It was her way of adapting to her pain. Men looked at her lovingly and helped ease her very real stress of needing to make money. Too many women could tell similar stories.

Chiori stayed silent for another minute, fighting hard to contain those tears. I handed her a box of tissues. 'Take your time. If those tears could speak, then what would they say?' I asked.

Her tears were for so many. There are no words.

A painful discovery

I found Donald fidgeting in the chair, looking as if he were about to cry and, at the same time, seething with anger, like he wanted to punch someone. His face was turning red, almost like he was fighting back a visceral sadness buried beneath his obvious anger.

'How did you find out, Donald?' I asked.

'I found out when one of the sugar daddies tried to contact her on her phone,' he said, staring angrily at Chiori.

'We were both at home during the pandemic and had a lot of time on our hands. We were originally separated for a few months at the beginning when I was stuck in the UK because flights were cut off to Hong Kong. I kept dreaming about being back with Chiori, and although I knew the pandemic would continue to be stressful, I thought we would get through it together. Clearly, I was living a delusion, thinking I had a partner who was honest and trustworthy,' he said.

He was working for a British airline, and she was a marketing executive at a spa in Hong Kong. His income was cut when flights were grounded, and she went on months of unpaid leave when the spa closed, so it was tough for them to make ends meet. It was during the heaviest restrictions, when people were opting to stay indoors, that Donald happened to see the random text on her phone that was on the dining room table. It said, 'Can you meet at the Four Seasons for breakfast? Don't forget to shave, my darling.' Donald wanted to throw the phone out of the window and hunt this man down. Instead, he followed Chiori to the hotel.

He found her sitting across from a seventy-five-year-old man and watched them for five minutes before his skyrocketing blood pressure and pounding pulse overcame him. He confronted them and grabbed her by the arm. She tried to calm him down, saying, 'Donald, this is my old friend, a lovely man named Tom. He's offering to help me with money.'

Donald went ballistic. 'Who the hell is he? Why the hell is he offering to help you with money?' he screamed.

Back at home, Donald yelled at Chiori and accused her of cheating on him. He refused to return her phone. She went mute, curled into a ball, and stared past her feet into oblivion. As I listened to Donald's retelling of the situation, I couldn't help but wonder what Chiori must have thought during the confrontation. Was she reliving the trauma of her childhood? The longer Chiori's silence continued, Donald would undoubtedly have grown angrier too. Would she, once again, have felt unwanted, like a burden? Feeling like a burden psychologically can be one of the most torturous experiences.

Donald had always felt there were 'ghosts' in her past. He found it suspicious that she had ten Chanel bags and an endless array of lingerie, all the way from vanilla to red hot chilli pepper. Each one of these bags cost more than her monthly salary, while the underwear appeared designed to meet an array of appetites. He had wondered who had funded her luxurious lifestyle before they began dating, yet, like so many in relationships, he chose to ignore his suspicions, those inconvenient gut feelings, and went on with daily life.

Wake up, eat breakfast, have a sneaking suspicion, wonder if your gut is on to something, try to forget it, get back to work, sleep. Rinse and repeat.

Whenever Donald asked about Chiori's childhood, she would stay silent. So, he told himself stories about what it must have been like instead. One of those stories was that her silence reflected her culture, as he knew it was valued highly by many Japanese people. He had considered suggesting going to therapy with Chiori, yet he was against the idea of 'airing their dirty laundry' to a stranger. His British boarding school days had taught him the value of a 'stiff upper lip'—the need to carry on no matter what else was going on—while his family echoed the narrative: on, and on, and on.

Once in a while, Chiori would punctuate the silence with *just enough* details to make Donald think that she had a fine childhood, fine parents, fine experiences. Nothing to look at here. She minimized the reality as many traumatized people do. She would even share a story here and there of how 'generous' her parents were to her to signal that maybe, just maybe, those Chanel bags came from them. Donald knew not to inquire further.

All of this was simmering in a pandemic pressure cooker that was about to bubble over. There is nothing like a crisis to clarify a bottom line in a relationship. Donald wanted Chiori never again to be involved in 'compensated dating', a term he hadn't even heard of until that meltdown at the Four Seasons. He said he would never marry her if this were part of the deal. When she spoke of how much money these men had, it ravaged him psychologically;

he could not even sit still in his seat. He was keenly aware that his bank account balance was puny in comparison; that was the only part of his pain he could quantify.

Donald's psyche was ravaged by the thought of his fiancé not only *seducing* other men, but of doing so *in the first-class section of an airplane* or *in one of the world's most expensive hotels.* Then he imagined the Chanel bag Chiori would carry while with him, then the potential STDs, the unwanted pregnancies, and the potential loss of face in being married to a woman engaging in this. It was all too much for him.

As the session continued, Chiori explained that her experiences with these men were all scripted. She could spend a week at the Four Seasons, and every hour would be planned out.

The 'John' would choose when and where they would have sex, whether he *wanted* to use protection, when to take her to dinner at a classy restaurant, and which dress and heels she would wear. She belonged to him. He owned her time, her body, the way she would respond to his every touch, the dainty salad she would eat and how much, and if a blow job was desired, there she was, down on her knees, dead inside. Then he would transfer US$20,000 to her account. This was about fantasy, power, gratification, and objectification. She knew deep down she neither loved these men nor was loved—something Donald needed to hear her say aloud—but for fleeting moments she would pretend to feel loved and that was worth more than any fancy handbag.

From her teens, she drank heavily to numb the pain and would sometimes make herself vomit. 'It was my purge. It was my revenge against my parents,' Chiori shared chillingly.

There was an added complexity to this story. Donald was a committed Christian and against any form of prostitution on moral grounds. He saw these men as sinners; Chiori as one as well and couldn't connect with her story of desperation. As she shared her stories and any ounce of emotion, Donald's rage eclipsed his compassion. He would shake his head in disbelief while insisting he wanted to hear about her past traumas and how they shaped her choices. Yet, he couldn't bear to hear it. He was lost in a thick fog of judgement, disappointment, and utter betrayal.

It was all too much. 'I will kill these men if I see them,' he said.

Still cheating

When they came to see me for the third time, Donald knew she was still selling her body. He was following her and checking her phone texts on their laptop and taking photos of the men.

'I promise you it's over,' she would plead.

'You're doing it again. You're cheating on me and lying, even with cold, hard evidence in hand,' he would say through clenched teeth, shaking. He was no longer prepared to ignore the Chanel bags and gut hunches. He now knew what that blind eye had cost him. He was overwhelmed by what the pandemic had brought to his life—the initial pain of being separated from Chiori, being stuck in the UK, and catching a bad case of Covid, worrying about his elderly parents and returning to a job that had slashed his salary. He was able to endure all of this except for the devastating truth of Chiori's deception. He couldn't bear her narrative being integrated into their narrative one day.

I suggested we pause couples counselling and that Donald hold off on deciding about the marriage until he and Chiori each had individual support. He agreed but added, 'No guarantees.'

I suggested to Donald that he see an individual therapist and possibly speak with one of his spiritual leaders if he found comfort or support there, and I suggested Chiori see a trauma specialist as I felt she needed a different type of therapy.

While Chiori and I had a strong rapport, I was (and still am) very aware of my limitations, not only as a human but also as a therapist. I regularly refer out to specialists or other kinds of professionals when clients need it.

Chiori asked to meet for one individual session to understand how a trauma specialist would support her differently. She started the session by asking if the trauma specialist would tell her to stop seeing these older men, make her relive the past, or increase her chances that Donald would marry her. These three questions swirled with an intensity as she asked me them one by one. There was a sense of arrested development, like she was frozen in time, a little girl overwhelmed by abuse, determined enough to rise from that pain, and never to become a 'burden' to anyone again.

I tried to hear more about the woman sitting across from me, yet Chiori kept responding with stories about the men. She said many were 'turned on' because she was engaged, and she would need now to think of how to make herself more attractive. The men loved being with a committed woman—she wouldn't ask them for more. *Be grateful for what I give you, little girl, and don't ask for a penny more.* They never asked directly about Donald yet were happy to outsource any emotional labour to him. They didn't want any of that. A flow of cash from their bank accounts to hers was reasonable, yet nothing flowed from the heart.

She knew each man's favourite sexual position, what eyeliner to wear, the tone to use in response to a joke or a story told, and how to make each man feel he was king of the world. She recalled a sixty-year-old man who had handed her a list of criteria for 'being hired again' and on that twisted list was 'Wanting to feel like the most powerful man in Hong Kong'. When I asked how she felt sharing this with me, she didn't respond.

Chiori was seduced by the idea of making a lot of money in a short amount of time; she had to emerge from the hellish conditions of her childhood. She knew that taking this on would be more efficient than babysitting or working as a barista at

Starbucks. In her mind, she could make enough money to support her studies while also feeling desired and loveable as a person for the first time. The plan, for so many years, had been to one day leave these repulsive arrangements behind. Yet here she still was. The years had passed, she had finished two degrees and started her career, but she remained utterly entangled in a dark ball of wax. She ended the session by asking whether the trauma specialist was needed because she was broken.

I told her no, she wasn't broken. Her life had been stolen.

Pandemic reckoning

To varying degrees, we were all brought to our knees during the pandemic. Donald and Chiori certainly were. Historically, mental healthcare, including couples counselling, in Asia has been stigmatized and neglected at a great cost to society due to 'saving face' and false beliefs that the mentally ill are dangerous or morally deficient.

In Asia, many people seeking help are still considered 'crazy' and become a liability to the good name of their parents. Seeking help for mental health issues simply isn't acceptable, and it has been that way for decades or centuries even. Many clients of mine kept it a secret from their friends and family that they were seeing me regularly. The concept of 'saving face' is a set of behaviours and customs operating in different cultures. and it is highly important in Singapore, Hong Kong, and across the rest of Asia. 'Face' is one of the factors behind the stigma associated with therapy because it brings dishonour or embarrassment to one's parents and family. It's a blend of respect, reputation, honour and social standing. Embarrassment, criticism, or disagreement causes one to 'lose face'.

A Singaporean study found that half of the country believed that mental illness was a 'sign of personal weakness' and that it was the fault of the patient; hence there is a sense of shame around it.

One of the first documented official facilities that offered treatment for the mentally ill in Asia was the *Bei Tian Fang*, a charity facility administered by monks, during China's Tang Dynasty (618–907 CE). One of the first foreigners in Asia to set up a Westernized psychiatric hospital was an American missionary, John Kerr, and he helped the homeless.

For many, the pandemic, though, translated into a 'Dark Night of the Soul', a reckoning that shook our cores and many who resisted therapy in the past saw it as the final option, a last attempt to connect, make sense of their relationships, their lives. Do I want to be *here*? Do I want to be in this relationship? How about this job? What really matters in my life?

For more than a decade, the steady stream of clients in my private practice, and previously at medical clinics, have given me an insight into relationships, marriages, and work issues in Asia. The pandemic, though, was a professional bootcamp. The issues and perspectives have given me a window into not only the culture of Asia and its people but also the changing landscape of mental health awareness.

While I still had a steady flow of expat clients, the number of local clients, particularly Chinese, and Asian expats visiting my therapy room had soared because of a new openness surrounding mental health. Celina Lee, a career and executive coach in the US and Korea, explained to me that Asian societies are collectivist, which means that group identity is much more important than an individual identity, so fitting in, belonging to the group, and behaving according to the group norm is extremely important. She said many people suffer in silence by suppressing their individual needs. 'Those with mental illness do not share with others or get treatment or go to therapy because they're afraid of bringing shame not only to themselves but also to their family. This stigma impacts Asians in the workplace too. Since they fear judgement, criticism, and embarrassment, and also fear losing career opportunities, they do not get the help or treatment needed which often exacerbates their mental health struggles,' she said.

Therapy also became somewhat demystified during this period with more companies talking about it (and providing resources to access it), more people accessing online therapy, people using mental health apps, and conversations happening on social media. The barriers erected by cultural stigmas around seeing a therapist were beginning to break down, little by little, in Hong Kong and other parts of Asia, such as Singapore. The wall of stigma was, and is, still there, but I was beginning to see the cracks.

The topics that clients were reckoning with included: redundancies, terminations, overwork, underwork, stress, burnout, toxic bosses, toxic co-workers, toxic policies, toxic you-name-it, separation, divorce, high conflict, fights over custody, domestic abuse, substance issues—the list goes on.

Clients were also reckoning with the other side of the psychological coin: promotions, career changes, supportive bosses, caring co-workers, compassionate teams, increased mental health resources, mental health programming, marriages blooming (yes, still stressed), deeper connection with a partner, deeper conversations, a commitment to making more efforts to date or meet others, commitments to commit.

The bedrooms and boardrooms of Asia were shaking. Yet, they were also blooming.

The pandemic also forced me to reckon with how I relate to clients. I could no longer get away with pre-cooked, reflexive responses. Clients, even before the pandemic, sometimes as a courtesy, other times out of anxiety, would often start a session by asking me, 'How are you, Allison?' My reflexive 'I'm fine thanks! Now, onto you!' just wasn't cutting it during those long, dark days. People wanted to know I was in the same boat with them. And boy, was I.

Hong Kong at the time had an ultra-strict quarantine policy that separated infected people from their immediate families, even in cases involving babies. My clients wanted to know that my fear of being separated from my children was as real as theirs, that the fear of getting ill was keeping me up at night as well, that I too had no idea when this would end. Would it ever?

I have always been conscious never to make a session about me and contain my responses, yet people wanted confidence that their therapist could genuinely connect with some of their experiences.

For better or worse, we all have our pandemic stories. Mine are replete with burnout and purpose. I truly witnessed the best and the worst of humanity and relationships throughout the pandemic. Each hour, a toss-up.

I recall a client at the end of a session saying as he got up from his chair, 'You talk to so many people, Allison. Do you believe that humanity bends towards light or darkness?'

'It depends on the hour you ask that question,' I said, reflecting on my time with Chiori and Donald.

Part II

Infidelity

Chapter 5

We Don't Bump into People Naked

Rex was silent. Serena, his wife, was seething with anger. They were sitting facing me to discuss the problems in their marriage and the gulf between them wasn't narrowing even after several sessions.

She dominated each session while he could barely get a word in, which was a great surprise considering he was a renowned litigator. He was a wordsmith, known for his eloquent probing speech, yet his mouth was frozen. With some people, I watch the words migrate into their throats only to get stuck there. With Rex, there were no words anywhere to be found. He would often look down, into his hands, signalling utter deflation. I would try to imagine a confident version of him in the courtroom and invite that Rex to join us. I am often trying to invite different versions of a client into the room. I would meet only this Rex, the one replete with words, in individual sessions, and that said a lot about his marriage. Out in the world and in the courtroom was a confident Rex; yet here in the therapy room, he was shackled in a contemptuous marriage, a shell of himself.

On my third session with them as a couple, through a typhoon of tears, Serena told me she could not proceed with Rex in the room and asked if he could wait outside for a few minutes while she shared something. After Rex obediently walked out, Serena's tone changed. It went from hurt to grandiose in the blink of an eye. Serena said she had found Rex's emails and learned he was physically intimate with his 'affair partner', a paralegal who worked at his law firm. Rex had sworn his affair was 'purely emotional'. It's a confounding description I hear most days in the therapy room.

Serena pulled out photos of the woman and said, 'I need to show you who he was with! She's so ugly! Allison, she's so ugly! Like, I just can't believe *how* ugly!' She showed me a photo on her phone and began to tear into the other woman. As she looked to me for a response, I kept a neutral facial expression and did not say anything, yet I could see there was a stark difference in appearance between these two women. I wondered about the story Serena, like so many, would tell herself about how superficial qualities keep a partner faithful. Did she believe that Botox and perky boobs would prevent a man from cheating? Did she choose Rex as a partner, at least in part, because she was the better-looking one, and therefore believed there was no way he would stray?

The woman in the photo was make-up free with straight, cropped hair. Serena was a lean fitness maven in pastel pink yoga gear and matching pink lipstick; her long tresses were accentuated by a Brazilian blowout, dark smoky eyeshadow framing her small set eyes, adorned with jet-black, fake eyelashes that looked as though they weighed more than she did. It's often assumed that men cheat with people who are better looking than their partners, but that's not always the case. I had a client cheat on his partner who was a supermodel. Over the years, I have witnessed every affair permutation under the sun, from the most superficial to the deepest emotional bonds. With some affair stories, I have to pinch myself as it all sounds so similar. Others have me almost falling off the chair.

Serena's attempt to understand Rex's unfaithfulness made sense given her worldview, yet in my professional experience, affairs can rarely be explained solely by reference to another person's looks.

I imagined Serena kept pushing on this woman's looks in part because she was in disbelief, in part out of narcissism, and in part because she wanted to believe that whatever her husband and this woman experienced could not have been anything 'real'. The word 'real' comes up often with affairs. Was my experience real? Did it mean anything? Were my feelings real? Did my partner really like/love/lust after that other person? People will often feel temporary relief from their pain if they believe that what their partners felt and did with another wasn't 'real' or meaningful.

Reeking of entitlement

Rex and Serena were both Hong Kong Chinese and met in university. They married soon after. He went on to have an illustrious career as an incredibly precise litigator who would prepare for cases overnight at his law firm, sometimes even forgetting about the camp bed by his desk. Serena became a yoga instructor and motivational speaker. They had three young children, each three years apart. Rex was serious about fencing and nearly went on to compete internationally before injuring his knee. With his athletic build and boyish features, he looked a decade younger and wouldn't have been out of place in a Gap advertisement. On the surface, this couple had it all—they were the 'perfect' family. He gave the appearance of 'My wife is the love of my life. I'll be obsessed with her for the rest of my life.' Serena gave the appearance of being chosen, of how could she not be chosen? But from the moment I met them, it was clear there was something underneath their perfect image. The image, I would come to learn, was a straitjacket for Rex.

Rex and I met separately so I could listen to his story. The tap turned on faster than I could close the counselling room door. He looked me right in the eye and said, 'I so regret marrying her. I knew, I knew deep in my gut, it was the wrong thing to do.

We shared a similar family background, and I was seduced by the idea that Serena's looks and our shared background would be enough. I buried for years this knowing that I should not have married Serena. When I met the other woman, not only did those feelings come rushing back, but I realized how much connection, deep connection, matters.'

I inquired further about this connection and asked what sort of a person he was when he was with this other woman. All of us get to be different people, or at least share different parts of ourselves, in different relationships. While I never condone cheating, understanding who the client is when they are with another person can often be illuminating. I watched his body language, I listened closely to his words and tone, and I kept my ear out for the narrative to try to understand his story.

Rex was articulate in describing the connection with the other woman. 'She was curious about me and listened to me in a way my wife never has. I wasn't sharing deep, dark secrets. We weren't having esoteric conversations. We weren't having mind blowing sex. She simply would ask me "How are you?" and took the time to listen, understand, and connect. I was also deeply curious about how she was and equally took the time to listen, understand, and connect. If you asked me to name a time when Serena and I shared that, I'd be at a loss. With my wife, it's "The Serena Show". I fight for airspace, and after fighting for so long, I gave up. What's the point?'

What is the point? That's the question we all need to answer in relationships, and one many couples answer multiple times throughout their marriages, especially after a crisis. For some couples, the point is to maintain appearances, and that's enough. For others, culture, religion, and/or family bind them. For others, they want connection. And the list goes on.

Rex was haunted by the idea of a divorce being shameful in his culture, and even more so by the thought of a life devoid of deep connection. Would he ever be able to experience that again, he asked himself. Rex said he did feel remorseful about cheating but felt uneasy about using that remorse as a starting point for a real conversation with his wife, fearing it would be weaponized.

We continued with couples counselling, and during every session, Serena's sense of entitlement filled not only the therapy room but also all twenty-seven floors of the building. She threatened to ruin Rex's career, take away the kids, poison the relationship he had with them, drain their shared bank accounts, and tell his and her parents lies about him if he didn't declare his unwavering commitment to her and her idea of the marriage. 'You're lucky to even be with me!' she said throughout the sessions. The more silent Rex became, the darker Serena's threats would become. They were caught in a very common pattern in marriages—the distancer and the pursuer—yet Rex ultimately didn't just want to distance himself; he wanted to get the hell out. And Serena ultimately wanted to endlessly pursue and torture him.

In the first phase of the stormy aftermath of an affair, there's often lots of venting of emotions from the hurt partner, in this case Serena. During this phase, I fancy myself as a pilot navigating a huge aircraft, carrying suitcases of history and resentment, all of it through wildly turbulent emotional storms. These storms are often precipitated by drip-by-drip disclosures in which the involved partner does not share the whole truth at once but rather little by little. They can also be precipitated by the hurt partner being overwhelmed with a mingling of emotions while the involved partner is trying to move on.

Usually, after the first phase, if I can help land the aircraft to safety, in the second phase we are able to really understand why an affair took place. Understanding is not condoning, and it's also never an easy pill to swallow. It is a very deep, often dark yet illuminating dive that requires looking honestly at a couple's narrative.

Sometimes this reveals a terrible relationship—one we almost proverbially need to throw in the bin, cut the losses, and start anew. Sometimes it reveals the involved partner's narcissism or entitlement, and if so, then I need to know if that person is willing to change.

Much of the time, this process provides a profound springboard for transformation. There are many times, though, when the pain, the hurt, seems so big, so intense, and everlasting that the second phase remains a distant dream for as long as a year, if not forever.

The challenge with Rex and Serena was that she wouldn't admit to, and lacked the self-awareness for, what she could do differently in the marriage. She blamed Rex entirely and said explicitly that his transgression gave her 'full licence' to punish and keep him locked in what she would refer to as 'a prison of his own making'. While Rex was responsible for the choice that he made—to have an affair, he was also trapped in a marriage that didn't have space for him. Serena didn't care how he was feeling. She never did. And this was the fuel to care less and justify caring less. The affair emboldened her entitlement to fill the marriage with all things Serena.

Magical thinking

I listen to people's stories for a living, and I often say the way people tell their stories matters. There's the story and there's the way my clients tell the story. Are they the victim? Are they clear about the part they played? Are they willing to recognise the bare, naked and confronting truth of their marriage? Serena asked to pause the couples counselling until Rex could agree to preserving their flawless image and to keeping the family intact.

Once it became clear that Serena and Rex would stay married, and that Serena had no interest in making changes, Rex and I met to discuss how he could show up differently in his relationships. When Rex told me the story of falling in love with this other woman, it was as a passive character. 'I just fell in love,' he said. 'I had no choice. It just happened.' His words had a mystical tinge as many of these affair stories do, yet when we really dug into the details and choices along the way, I could see his passivity allowed him to dissociate from the pain of his marriage and the truth of having an affair. If he numbed his pain in the marriage with a narrative of what I dub 'mystical victimhood', then he could see the affair as something that not only just happened but also needed to happen.

I told him to take a deep breath. Warmly and directly, I said, 'This is going to sting. People don't bump into each other naked. If you love this woman, own it! You didn't just bump into her. This didn't just happen. *No affair ever does.* Regardless of whether you stay in this marriage, stay with the other woman, or go off on your own, how you're positioning yourself in the story of your life matters. Your wife erases you from the story of the marriage, yes. She grabs you by the throat, steals your words, and then kicks you in the balls on the way out. I get it. But with the affair partner, you're also presenting a passive setup as if this "just happened". She shows up, magically, and asks you on a deep yet basic level how you are as a human. She dares to see you. This work we're doing is, yes, about clarity regarding your marriage, and I always support whatever Serena and you decide. Yet perhaps the greater work is the way you write yourself into these relationships and how we could do that differently. This is a journey with truth. Not these other women.'

His eyes lit up.

In my work as a therapist, I do not make a distinction between sexual and emotional affairs for a couple of reasons. First, emotional connections can be deeply erotic, deeply meaningful, and can motivate physical intimacy. The second reason is I've come to learn that many clients, by the third session, will disclose that the affair has already become physical.

What is fascinating is how clients narrate their paths and choices when it comes to affairs, with the line, 'It just *happened*.' Many clients come in with some iteration of 'The connection was too strong to ignore' or 'It just happened'—both are what we therapists refer to as 'magical thinking'. I often point out that we don't just bump into people naked.

There are probably a million and one small or big decisions that lead to an affair. Telling the truth to yourself, or your therapist, is a way out of the delusion that *things just happen* and a profound entry point psychologically into exploring why it happened and making informed decisions post-affair.

Feng shui masters in the therapy room

Rex is actually a spiritual man. He told me he had sought out his family's feng shui master to consult on whether to leave his marriage. 'Look, I know you know deep down, I don't want to be in my marriage. I went to my family's fortune teller, and the master said, "You know what you want to do, yet the time to do it is not now."'

He looked at me intently as if waiting for me to say something. I was used to my clients bringing up their spiritual guides. In Hong Kong and many parts of Asia, it's de rigueur for people to be influenced by their fortune tellers or feng shui masters. Some of my Korean clients, for example, use shamans to help them decide on major life decisions, such as when to have a C-section, when to buy a house, and when to invest in a business. Serena and Rex told me their feng shui master had urged them, after sharing details of Rex's affair, to move their furniture around to change the energy, and they would sometimes bring up the 'chi' of their relationship.

Rex asked, 'Do your clients tell you about spiritual experiences?'

I've learned over the years that you don't pick up the spiritual tool with a client unless someone has one in the shed himself or is genuinely curious to explore that pathway. Over the years, the field of therapy has expanded to include psychospiritual conversations, yet they are often still coded as inferior to anything that is 'rational' or 'evidence based'. There are plenty of therapists who drape their therapy rooms with mandalas, statues of Buddhas, and yin-yang signs yet will often lean on science over spirit.

I replied to Rex, 'I believe we are all born with deep, spiritual knowing. For a lot of people, this gets pushed down, devalued, as the intellect, the rational, the big brain stuff gets privileged as opposed to the gut wisdom. I believe some people are even born with a longer, more refined antenna. If you're telling me that something the feng shui master says resonates deeply in your bones, in your cells, then there's something you're connecting with. It would seem like malpractice for me to suggest we ignore that. Let's explore what he touched in you. It sounds like he reaffirmed that you do want to end the marriage, yet the timing isn't now. What comes to you when I just said that out loud?'

Rex spoke so softly that I needed to lean in. 'That's it. That's the truth. I want to divorce her, yet the timing is not now. What I need to work on now is what you said—re-working how I tell stories and moving away from anything that smells passive.' Rex understood the risk he ran by becoming a passive character in this part of his story as well. If he leant solely on the feng shui master as the truth master, then he would give up his collaborative power to influence his path.

There's nothing I can or should say as a therapist to override spiritual guidance, and for good reason. I've found if people can connect with something deeper, something that transcends ego, then that is often a deep instrument and anchor. What's tricky is that sometimes people will try to use spirituality to do what's called a 'spiritual bypass' and move away from the growth or work that's needed, and an example of this is the 'mystical victimhood'.

But with Rex, I could sense his conviction in the feng shui master when he said divorce wasn't on the cards anytime soon. The greater point was Rex's newfound determination to position himself differently in relationships and in life. When we first met, he was in the passenger seat, watching the women in his life drive. He was finally able to see himself in the driving seat, make different choices, and ultimately narrate his relationships with depth and truth. Many of us work our whole lives to narrate our lives with a semblance of either.

Rex was terrified of Serena and of a life without real connection. She was weaponizing their children against him, though, and he was afraid to leave because of the thought of not seeing his three children every day. On balance, that was worth the potential torture he would endure with Serena. He wasn't truly willing to stand up for himself, and his only peace of mind was making the choice with his eyes open. Like so many people I've worked with in his position, he fantasized about leaving his spouse once the children left home, thinking maybe that's the right time.

Rex's revelation was that he was powerful enough to pen his own narrative. Some of our narrative, of course, we cannot control—and ultimately control is an illusion anyway. But with Rex, the priority was to encourage him to be proactive, rather than reactive. Therefore, if he wanted to tell his children a narrative of daddy respecting mummy, and if respect meant staying within the bounds of a contract, then he would do it. Like Rex, many people feel more motivated to make changes for their children than for their spouse.

The three of us regrouped for a few more sessions after Rex 'promised' Serena they would stay married, a requirement that Serena made clear before continuing the couples counselling. She wanted to speak about maintaining appearances, he wanted to address a dynamic between them that came up time and again to see if he could make the marriage more 'tolerable'. Rex felt Serena was nagging and criticizing him all the time.

In the couple's session, he was able to express himself more clearly, yet still in a limited way as compared with our individual sessions. He spoke about not wanting to do things as he felt Serena would criticize his way of doing them. Rex would organize 'date nights', and Serena would often criticize the evening as a 'total failure', and, in turn, he felt like a failure. He wanted to be appreciated for getting something done in his own way and stopped organizing anything. Serena, meanwhile, wanted Rex to take more initiative with the kids and organizing 'exciting' date nights.

I raised the concept of the Core Negative Image (CNI) by leading couples therapist and author Terry Real—the image each of us has of our partner at their most negative. We can never rid ourselves of this image entirely, but there are ways we can soften it. For example, if Rex's CNI of Serena was that she is a self-absorbed, criticizing wife, then every time Serena takes an interest in how Rex is feeling, she's working against the CNI. Serena's CNI of Rex was that he was a non-committal, immature, lazy 'boy'. Therefore, every time Rex reaffirmed his commitment and was proactive with planning 'exciting' date nights, he's working against her CNI.

Over the years, I have likely mentioned the concept to married couples from over twenty cultures. What's profound about this concept of CNI is that I have yet to meet someone from any culture with whom it does not resonate. I helped each of them to identify when they were triggered by the other, then to develop awareness of their CNIs. This was aimed at lessening the intensity of those images. CNIs can rarely be erased fully, but we can try to soften their edges.

Things improved just enough for Serena to feel Rex was committed and just enough for Rex to feel the relationship was 'tolerable'. Rex learned ways to take more initiative and be proactive, and to feel more comfortable with stating clearly when he would like to do something his way, rather than distancing himself because he feared his wife would be critical. Serena worked on voicing more appreciation for Rex and resisting attempts to correct him unless explicitly asked by him to do so.

I learned from this couple that just because people are miserable in a marriage, this doesn't mean they'll end it; often, they will settle for the status quo of dissatisfaction and little connection to avoid rocking the boat. Children, finances, and cultural stigma, especially in Asia, often still feature heavily in their considerations. On balance, it can be incredibly challenging and scary, whatever one's culture or context, to know whether to stay miserable and retain some stability or risk diving into the unknown.

I know of many couples who do not know how to be truly intimate and for whom the fights, drama, and chaos are the glue that keeps them 'connected'. These couples fear that if they tried to connect outside of the chaos, they would not know what to do.

In Serena and Rex's relationship, the chaos came from her sense of entitlement and his passivity. We worked on both and, over the months, succeeded in softening Serena ever so slightly and in the context of the marriage Rex becoming more proactive. But the breakthrough lay in empowering Rex, in teaching him to tell his own story differently, to realize that he had the power of choice, and that he could *choose* to leave the chaos behind.

Justifications for straying

Over the years, I've heard countless justifications for straying in a marriage. They go something like this:

'I had no choice. This affair chose me.'

'Given my unfulfilled needs, how could I not?'

'I tried to talk to my partner about our challenges, yet I didn't see any changes.'

'I was always a compliant, good child, and I don't know where this came from. I guess I wanted more in my relationships than I realized.'

'I wouldn't have done it had I not met Shirley. Shirley is everything my wife isn't. My wife never could get her career going and lives off my hard work. Shirley is ambitious and independent. I always end up wanting to pay for dinners knowing that Shirley works hard herself and could afford to pay if I let her!' (Said man returns to therapy two years into a relationship with Shirley and complains she is too ambitious and has no time for the relationship or him. Why does she have to be so cutthroat?)

'I wouldn't have done it had I not met Maria. Maria energizes me while my wife drains me. My wife is so ambitious with her career she doesn't have time for the relationship or me. She hasn't adored me in years. Maria works as a freelancer and can choose when she's working so she's able to give me lots of attention. Maria will always be able to follow my next career move, or hey, sometimes I just need a partner to follow me to a villa in Thailand for the weekend. Maria is flexible, adoring, and wants the best for me.' (Said man returns to therapy two years into a relationship with Maria and complains she is mooching off him and wonders what she's doing with her days. Why can't she be more ambitious?)

'My husband never paid any attention to the type of sexual pleasure that matters to me. Mike, though. Mike! He totally gets it. He gets that women's physiology is complex. I need complex. My husband rocks up and expects me to just satisfy him. Mike truly gets that a woman's pleasure matters. He touches me in all the right places. He talks clitoris. Female orgasm. For all these years with my husband, I thought perhaps there was something wrong with me sexually. Mike clearly confirms the opposite.

I'm alive!' (Said woman returns to therapy sharing all the reasons Mike really knows all things clitoris. He's penetrated many.)

'I couldn't believe that he also loves to read books on *The New York Times* best seller list (insert Leonard Cohen songs, TV shows…). My husband just doesn't pay attention to stuff like this. He feels I'm too intellectual and wants me to relax and sit on the couch watching Netflix dramas. I love the way I can converse with this other man—the intellectual intimacy is so intoxicating. I mean, how many people read books on *The New York Times* bestseller list? This must confirm we were meant to be together.' (Said woman returns to therapy and realizes not only do many people read books on *The New York Times* bestseller list but also this same man converses with many other intellectual women about these books after a shag and a cigarette.)

'It's not *natural* for me to be with one person. This affair reflected my true self, my most authentic being.' (Said man returns to therapy and shares that his 'true self' is lonelier than before, despite the many 'authentic' interactions he's had.)

We all justify our choices and actions to some extent. But if growth is going to happen in the therapy room or anywhere else, then it requires courage to name and face these justifications and make different choices.

There is a need to differentiate between honesty and transparency after an affair is revealed. I do not necessarily encourage couples to be transparent with one another but rather be honest. *Transparency* can risk really hurting one's partner. For example, if your partner asks, 'Am I getting fat?' and if you answer, 'Yes, you are, and I'm repulsed by you,' it may be exactly what you're thinking, yet it will likely deeply hurt your partner. It won't help the relationship. Honesty combined with sensitivity, meanwhile, with both one's self and one's partner, is fundamental to growth. Often my role as a therapist is to help people translate transparency into respectful honesty their partners can hear.

Therefore, a respectful and honest answer to the question might be, 'I would like us both to work on valuing health more as we have children to think of and take care of, and I want us to grow old together. How can we work as a team so we can both get healthier?'

At its best, therapy gives people space to be honest and tell the truth. The danger comes when clients become lost in the stories they tell about themselves and lose sight of their personal responsibility. So, while I encourage clients to understand the 'why' behind their actions, I sometimes need to intervene when that understanding starts morphing into justification.

That's when I sometimes use humour and say stuff like, 'We don't bump into people naked!' Humour helps lower the levels of the stress hormone, cortisol, in the body, and that helps some people to become open to discussing the truth.

Justifications are plasters. They cover deep wounds and bitter truths. They did for Rex until he opened his eyes, put himself in the driver's seat, and acknowledged that cheating doesn't just happen.

Chapter 6

High-Powered Affairs

Why know thyself when you can pay for whatever you want?

Amanda was dressed classically in an elegant, understated hunter-green suit and a tan leather handbag. Her greying hair was swept into a bun, and she had fine wrinkles around her eyes, yet there was a youthful quality to her fair-skinned porcelain face, a trace of naivete.

She told me she had been totally shocked when she discovered her husband, Jay, was cheating on her. And since their children were grown-up and married with children of their own, she wanted a divorce if he wasn't going to be faithful.

The man with slicked-back pepper-grey hair who sat in front of me wore a bespoke navy suit, tailored to perfection, like an impenetrable armour. In his late sixties, Jay was one of the wealthiest men on the planet. His platinum watch glistened as he checked it periodically out of habit.

Money gave Jay a very special power—the ability to do just about anything he wanted, in every area of life. It meant that nubile young women would throw themselves at his feet, hang on his every word and whisper what he wanted to hear. For Jay, life was a seductive cocktail he hadn't been able to resist for many years, and his wife Amanda had had enough. His entire being revolved around the love of power; she yearned instead for the power of love.

There is an unwritten contract in many uber-wealthy circles in Asia where wives turn a blind eye to their husbands' mistresses in exchange for the goodies and the jet-setting lifestyle. But that was not who Jay married. Amanda could not be bought off with that unwritten contract.

Sometimes having a lot of money obscures the need for self-awareness. A fellow therapist once told me that their clients' self-awareness was in inverse proportion to how much money they had. I wondered about this theory when I started sessions with Amanda and Jay.

High-powered love

Jay and Amanda were an Indonesian-Chinese couple who had been married for thirty years. I met them first as a pair, then individually—one session with Amanda and three with Jay—and then as a pair again. In the initial couple's session, we spoke about what they wanted for their future. Amanda was clear she wanted to build a second marriage with Jay if he could agree never to cheat again. Jay was ambivalent. We all agreed that I would work with Jay to see if he had enough commitment to work on the marriage. It was important that I hear from Jay that he wanted to change. He was stuck on this clause about monogamy yet wasn't able, when we first met, to articulate clearly what it was he wanted instead. He wanted to be free—sexually and geographically—to go jet-setting and bed-hopping around the world. Yet he also wanted to be rooted, able to return at will to a wife and a 'stable home'.

They were choosing, as so many couples do after years fly by and children leave the home, either to repair their connection and move forward or end the marriage and gracefully divorce.

To repair a connection in a marriage of thirty years is a challenge, yet so too is to end three decades of shared experiences and history. This was a decision that needed to be handled delicately and commanded respect.

For some couples, years together equates to depth of connection. Not so for Amanda and Jay. When I met them, they had a shallow connection, but not because they were shallow people—quite the opposite. Rather, like so many couples, they avoided emotional intimacy. Amanda herself came from a wealthy background and entered the marriage wanting emotional connection, depth, and to build a family. But for Jay, such intimacy felt too squishy, too intangible. Therefore, Amanda buried this need early on. How many of us do?

The question we faced was: could we honour Amanda's need for fidelity and emotional connection along with Jay's need for both stability and the freedom to continue his adventures? A tall order.

In our first individual session, Jay spoke about his guilt over his latest infidelity. He was used to being in control. Without his wife in the room, he was happy to give me a blow-by-blow account of how his philandering started. Around five years ago, when he was inebriated one night after a few drinks too many following a conference in London, he met a Russian woman through one of his business partners. They met in the elevator of the hotel, and the next morning he woke up beside her. He couldn't remember the details of the rest of the night but recognized it must have been a significant moment because bedding random women became a staple of his packed schedule from that point on. After that one-night stand, he felt comfortable basking in attention from young women aged nineteen to thirty-two, and they gravitated to his charisma and jet-setting lifestyle like bees to honey.

He told me that he thought he could have his cake and eat it by keeping his wife happy enough not to leave him while continuing to pursue the thrill of intoxicating interactions with gorgeous young women.

Such an idea is a fantasy, a farce, one that I often hear from men and, in more recent years, from women as well. People conveniently forget that opening a marriage to other sexual partners cannot be a unilateral decision. It requires a precise contract like any other decision in a marriage.

I wasn't surprised in the slightest that Jay was straying. He was an energetic, good-looking man who lived in a different city from his wife for six months of the year. He told me he placed little 'value' on monogamy. He believed marriage was a familial obligation, while having girlfriends and gratification on the side was a cultural mandate.

In fact, when I first met Jay, he saw everything in terms of its 'value' to him, as if lovers, experiences, and the institution of marriage could all be placed on a sliding scale of investment.

One of the aspects I find most fascinating in working with people is learning to connect with their language and to readjust my own so that I can pace and lead them to where they want to go. As the sessions with Jay went by, I would speak in terms of 'value' and 'investing' in his marriage—vocabulary familiar enough to Jay for him to listen. With each client, I am a different therapist. Just as no two children have the same parent, no two clients have the same therapist. I pivot throughout my days based on the client, their needs, their goals, their pace, and ultimately their own psychology. I need to understand their language, worldview, values, all of it before I can truly support them. With Jay, my pivot required me to dance delicately between the emotional and the rational. Eventually, I led Jay from 'value' to 'value system'—one step in our elaborate dance, but no seamless pivot.

I needed to dial in to all things Jay before I could support the man in front of me, and ultimately his marriage. Doing so was important for him and a humbling reminder to me. No client fits into a textbook, no session can be scripted. Regardless of the number of clients I sit in front of, I am constantly reminding myself to open my eyes and ears to who and what I am seeing and hearing.

As I listened to Jay, it became clear that Jay's emotional vocabulary was limited. He was a warm, likeable man, yet he did not value his emotions, so the language he used and the stories he told were mostly devoid of feelings. If I asked him how he felt in his heart, he would tell me what he thought in his head. Jay was a picture of all things rational. He talked numbers. He talked spreadsheets. He talked profits. It was all neck up.

This made sense given he had not been encouraged to express his feelings growing up. His parents had had an arranged marriage, both loveless and soulless. Empty. His father had had two other wives openly, and the constant in-fighting and power struggles between them meant Jay had grown up feeling bitter.

Jay adapted to all of this by trying to support his mother emotionally but had been unable to fill her bottomless tank— like all children who find themselves enmeshed—and found himself secretly siding with his father who wanted nothing to do with emotions. Jay had sworn to himself he would never care emotionally for another woman and admired his father for being able to 'manage' so many women. Now an adult, he admired friends who did the same and believed he was entitled to it, too.

Why was he seeking my support? What was his motivation to change this perspective? It is challenging to change someone's behaviour, however destructive, if they have modelled themselves on a parent they admire. Jay was also kept in business by a system of cooperation. He saw other powerful men just like him who did have unwritten contracts with their wives. I probed repeatedly, trying to understand whether he was truly interested in changing his ways. I asked him, 'If you sign this deal, what will it cost you?' In any agreement, it's critical to recognize the potential gains and losses and this deal was no different, however many zeroes in their bank account. He needed to see what lay ahead of him and Amanda.

Whenever I ask these questions of anyone, I am conscious to drop any agenda I may have and take them on a genuine journey of exploration. Clients can smell agenda ten feet away, and the moment they do, the session is no longer true therapy but a power struggle. So, when I asked Jay these questions, I genuinely needed to understand why he wanted to change, and what it would cost him to change. Equally, he needed to hear himself answer these questions aloud. He needed to smell his own bullshit and to bathe in what could be a radical transformation. He had to step out of his entitlement if he believed his marriage to Amanda was worth more than his other world of endless orgasms and flattery.

A lot of behavioural changes are first and foremost about identity—clients need to be able to see themselves as a different person who makes different choices. People will pledge endlessly to change or want to change. Getting them to articulate why they want to do so is important. It's also important to understand what they are actually prepared to do to make changes. Even early in my career, cathartic moments in the therapy room seemed less promising than someone with a plan and a will to execute it. For someone to viscerally shift his or her identity ultimately means being clear about a different value system. A different value system demands different choices, and Jay knew very well we were not there for empty proclamations. He would either choose to make the changes or not.

As we continued our sessions and dissected the affairs, he continued to demonstrate his entitled attitude. He listed off all the men who behaved the same—including his father—whose wives signed up for a life of goodies and looked the other way. He said that that *should* be good enough. That word 'should' was the psychological tip-off I needed to go deeper. To make a deal that would be acceptable to both Amanda and Jay, I would ultimately need to target his entitlement. If he believed he had a right to be unfaithful and was surrounded by a system that entrenched that view, then this truly would require a profound identity shift.

I asked Jay if I could be direct. He looked at me as if there was no other way. 'Jay, we've sat together now for a few sessions. You're a solid guy. You show up for sessions, ready to work, answering my questions honestly, no bullshit. Yet, what you're saying to me sounds utterly entitled. It's totally fine to shower your wife with goodies in exchange for her looking the other way while you live a life of gratification if that's the woman you married. But that's not Amanda. It's not the deal you made, and it's not the deal your wife is looking to sign. We can get you what you want—stability, freedom. Yet, there is a cost. That cost translates into the clause about fidelity, and Amanda wants that built into the contract in titanium,' I told him.

He wanted a stable marriage because it looked good and meant societal approval. It also brought a touch of stability for his business. His shareholders wanted the man at the helm to be a family man, even if he was surrounded by an old boys' club of other elite men who felt entitled to a bit on the side. But how could faithful stability compare with sex parties and endless praise? Wasn't a man entitled to both?

But the stability Jay sought was not just about his shareholders. He wanted a pillar by his side. When he spoke of her, I could sense his deep respect for her dedication to their family and the commitment they made so many years ago at the altar. Amanda had been an incredible, doting mother, and despite having several nannies, she changed the diapers of all of her babies, went to all the parent-teacher meetings, and emotionally supported their children throughout their ups and downs. Amanda was motivated by her value system, which revolved around family and faith, and her choices aligned with these values. Amanda understood Jay and loved him despite his foibles and his work addiction. Yet she had a red line.

I've seen in countless longer-term, ten- or twenty-years marriages that at certain points people fall in and out of love, and that is to be expected. That is entirely different from when one person wants a divorce or has no desire to change. Many people in long-term relationships may not realize how common it is to fall in and out of love over the years. People change, and challenges and joys vary across the seasons and cycles of life. This is sometimes when psychoeducation as a therapist is key; to let people know this is a normal phenomenon and that it is not the same as wanting to end a marriage.

No therapist, however flexible and creative, is a magician. If one wants to rebuild, like Amanda was willing to do if Jay changed, there is a chance to improve. What encouraged me throughout our sessions was Amanda's willingness to make changes in this 'second' version of their marriage as well. She wanted to be more expressive, more engaged with his interests, and to improve their sexual connection.

Amanda told me Jay had seen a couple of therapists but never went back. He had burned through several sycophantic types, she said. 'The difference with you is you were in his face and called him out. But you can still see his humanity,' Amanda said. And she was right. I figured out early in my career that nobody would go far if I tried to seduce them with endless flattery. What I seek to offer is both a space that allows for psychological safety along with *just enough* tough love that we can be truthful about what needs to change.

We regrouped for couples counselling as both Amanda and Jay were clear they did want to build Relationship 2.0 together. As a couple, they were tender, respectful and even loving at times.

What was his motivation? Sure, sex is pleasurable, but it couldn't be lust alone. Was he looking for validation? Had he fallen out of love with his wife? The passion had faded, probably due to his constant trysts with much younger women along with the self-made myth that he lived in—that a powerful man like him has what he wants and whoever he wants, whenever he wants them.

While Jay was chasing younger women, he still dreamed of retiring with his wife and holding her hand in their twilight years, into their seventies and eighties. He would also insist that he still found his wife attractive, but how could she compete physically with women in their twenties? Again, he wanted the best of both worlds—to hold hands into their dotage as he slept with women young enough to be his grandchildren. Jay was not unique in holding such a dream. Even outside uber-wealthy circles, there has been a rise in open relationships, sometimes lacking clear terms and no negotiation. Amanda was not willing to tolerate Jay's unilateral decision to open the marriage, regardless of how entitled he felt to experience the 'best of both worlds'.

Jay told himself a story that the impulse was too strong, that he was unable to control himself with women. Yet this was someone who could control his impulses all day long while negotiating deals.

I shared with Jay that if he's had a few drinks and another person is in a bedroom with you naked, then of course he will lose control, like the next person would. However, if he's able to exert control throughout the day, then the story that he lacks control is a myth.

I urged him, 'The only way your wife will trust you is if you can trust yourself to be honest. You want the freedom to travel and the stability of a solid wife. Your wife wants commitment to fidelity. Can you imagine yourself at a conference, the lights are shining brightly on you as the expert while some twenty-something woman tells you that you're a genius? That woman is seductive and adoring all at once. Could you hold your wife in your heart in that moment? That's the moment I need you to travel to, over and over again, and to be honest with yourself. Because if we are brokering a deal here that accounts for what your wife and you want, then during those travels of yours, you will need to lock your wife firmly in the vault of your heart. It will require reducing risk—drinking less, for example—and walking away at the first sniff of anything seductive. One bat of the eyelash that has you looking at a woman differently, you get the hell out of that room. Anchoring your choices in what matters, what you value, is ultimately the way you'll know your identity has truly shifted away from an entitled husband to a committed one.'

Jay was well aware he could find another wife to agree to the unwritten contract he wanted. He also was aware he could live a life of gratification and have his trousers unzipped each evening. He could easily lie to me, lie to his wife, and just agree to Amanda's terms. But that he was willing to delve this deeply in therapy told me there was more to him than met the eye.

Jay took my tough words on the chin. He told me he could trust me to be direct and supportive. I was not just calling him an entitled ass. What I liked about working with Jay was that he was a straight shooter and there were no pretences; he was the first to admit that he was a proud hedonistic guy and that he enjoyed the perks of his status.

I wondered how best to be a sounding board to a mover and shaker who spent his days making megawatt deals, surrounded by an army of support staff, especially since I had met Jay early in my career in Asia. I had to be discerning in how I reached him. In the therapy room with me, he was negotiating the biggest deal of his personal life, under very different circumstances, and his status mattered less because his wife was anchored in values, not pretence. Jay said he slept soundly at night with one exception— when he and his wife were fighting. And until he and Amanda reached a clear deal, one he could trust himself to uphold, he was having more sleepless nights than he wished to recount.

82

Rethink the Couch

I learned a valuable lesson from Amanda and Jay. In every marriage, regardless of how much money people have, negotiation is a critical skill. The fairy tale tells us that once we commit to a partnership, our souls, hearts, and heads should be totally aligned. In reality, all couples negotiate. Jay negotiated his sense of entitlement; Amanda negotiated her flexibility.

There are times when one person will give their partner a proverbial gift in a marriage. When I work with couples who give these gifts, I encourage them to have a conversation with their future selves to make sure there would be no potential resentment that could follow. Amanda was clear she would not give a blank cheque to Jay—she knew that it would lead to resentment and the end of the marriage. So, too, was Jay unwilling to give away his freedom and commit to staying with Amanda all year round. Their final agreement was Amanda would permit Jay to be out of Hong Kong for six months each year, and Jay agreed to no more cheating. If Jay cheated, then Amanda made it clear she would end the marriage.

And with that, they left the therapy room with a clear contract.

Mindful of assumptions, let's negotiate

Amanda and Jay taught me the value of understanding where my clients are at and paying meticulous attention to the language they use and their processing speeds. They also taught me that even couples from the same culture will speak different languages in the therapy room and the outside world. At the beginning of therapy, Jay's language was all about 'value' and with him I could zoom in on anything as long as it wasn't touchy-feely. He was high energy, all about the bottom line, full of wonderful ideas, super enthusiastic. Amanda's cadence was much lower, so I had to slow down with her. Grounded in family and faith, she was a deliberate speaker whose vocabulary was elegant and reflective of her values.

Like most Asian couples with whom I have worked, they were very shy about speaking of sex with me. There was so much abstract sex in the room with us in terms of the cheating, yet when it came to sex between Amanda and Jay, I could sense that I needed to slow down and respect their discomfort.

They both agreed they needed to decide soon about their marriage so they both could have peace of mind. Jay became more attentive to Amanda and constantly checked in with her, yet he often lacked understanding of her motivations and desires. She wanted an emotional connection, but he struggled to see the value in this, and his parents had not shown him how. Sometimes they disagreed on memories and 'facts' from the past but I would nudge them away from 'fact battles' and move them towards the meanings, feelings, needs, and dreams behind the clashes to help them align and discern the best way forward. I deeply admired that they were respectful in my therapy room and wanted to listen with both their ears and their hearts. They were always polite in explaining a misunderstanding.

One of the things I learned from working with Amanda was to be mindful of the assumptions I make about wealthy people who no longer have to work and to be more curious about their struggles. It was easy to think that as Amanda was set for life, she wouldn't have regular people problems. After learning more about her value system, her amazing wealth seemed more like a coincidence. She was motivated by faith, philanthropy, and her family, while Jay had a different value system altogether. To Amanda, unfaithfulness was valid grounds for a divorce and there was no deal in the world that could convince her to stay.

Beyond superficial qualities such as money and appearances, they taught me to be careful about the assumptions I make about any person I support. I must consciously shed all my preconceptions if I am to understand the many meanings people attach to their identities. The only way to truly support the person in front of me is through curiosity and presence.

Ultimately, Amanda and Jay wanted the simple confidence that I could hear and support them and speak to them as people, not numbers. They wanted me to witness the pain of their indecision and help them navigate this big decision.

Every time I worked with them, I felt more confidence in what I was advising, and I trusted my clinical gut more. I started to believe it was no coincidence we met. They could get on a plane and see any therapist in the world, yet they found me.

Years have passed since then, but I am yet to meet the client who feels like coincidence. This is the mystical privilege of my work that allows me to connect with and respect each and every client I meet.

Infidelity in Asia

Dating apps like Tinder and social media have made it infinitely easier for people to engage in extramarital liaisons, and perhaps nowhere more so than in the hyperconnected societies of Asia.

Data on infidelity in Asia is hard to find for a host of reasons, including sex still being taboo and not openly discussed in countries like Indonesia, where adultery is a crime. But from my therapy room, I have seen an exponential increase in affairs.

A survey in 2012 by Durex of 29,000 people in thirty-six countries found that the likelihood of someone cheating depends on where they're from, and the world's highest rate of adultery is in Thailand, where 51 per cent admit to having strayed. In Hong Kong, a 2017 survey found that slightly more than half of married people cheat on their spouses. The Pew Research Center's study ranked Japan as the seventh country out of forty nations where infidelity was 'morally acceptable'.

In 2020, around 20 per cent of Japanese people reported being unfaithful to their spouses. Compare this to Americans born in the 1940s and 1950s, who were reputed to have the highest rates of adultery because they were the first generation to come of age during the sexual revolution—33 per cent of men and 26 per cent of women were unfaithful to their spouses. Meanwhile, a recent General Social Survey says around 20 per cent of American men engage in extramarital sex compared to 13 per cent of women.

Changing marriage dynamics

In Asia, arranged marriages that joined powerful families together were the norm for centuries. It's an entirely modern concept altogether—around a few generations old—to have a love match for a spouse. Many of my clients with love matches had parents and grandparents with arranged marriages. Also common in this part of the world is the ancient concubine system of having a second or third wife, or more, which could explain the cultural and generational acceptance of infidelity.

There's a need for negotiation in every marriage. This one wants a puppy; this one wants to move to Uzbekistan; this one wants to holiday in Paris; this one wants to go back to MBA school; this one wants more kids; this one doesn't.

What was interesting about Jay and Amanda was that they presented two different versions of marriage. In essence they were negotiating what their marriage contract looked like so they each felt happy with what they were getting out of it. Many live for gratification and want that. Some, though, are totally unaware that a deeper connection is possible. Jay had never seen it being modelled in his own parents' marriage. His family supplied physical and intellectual nourishment, but emotional nourishment was absent, as it was in so many of my clients' homes, because it was devalued. People had feelings, yes. But did those feelings have value? Very little, if any.

I gently guided this couple away from their respective battle positions and moved them to negotiate power and sexuality by considering more deeply the meaning of their desires. For disagreements to evolve in a marriage, I have found that starting with something the couple agrees on can provide enough encouragement that people will stay at the negotiating table. In this case, the agreement was that the couple wanted to stay married. What I've noticed with couples is that if we can start with an agreement that brings down the emotional temperature, then I can help bond them over something they share. Jay and Amanda wanted to stay married. Why? It could have been the history they shared, the imagined future in which they enjoyed grandchildren and their dotage together, or simply the possibility of genuinely becoming more emotionally and sexually connected.

Many people fantasize that marriages are easy, that people are endlessly compatible, and that no negotiation is required. I've seen brilliant people brought to their knees in the therapy room trying to negotiate with spouses—men like Jay who can easily persuade the boardroom to share their vision, only to find their own spouse won't do the same. Regardless of how much money or status people have, there are often bottom lines that, if crossed, will signal the end of a marriage. Everything else, though, is fair game to negotiate.

Without a basic agreement, we can't go anywhere. Sometimes couples get trapped in 'winning' and get entrenched in their positions. I tried to steer Amanda and Jay away from these positions and onto meaning. Why does this matter to you? What's the meaning of it?

The necessity and power of negotiation was a huge lesson for me, as was the realization that no matter how much money you have, all couples deal with this many times throughout their relationships. Jay and Amanda's desire to be married to each other outweighed their combined desire to win and get 100 per cent of what each of them wanted. We worked towards dislodging entrenched patterns and moved towards creating Relationship 2.0.

I also realized that I could not sell past the close and that some people want very simple agreements and marriages. I had many ideas of how Amanda and Jay's marriage could be different, but I also realized I needed to listen to them say what they truly wanted and not assume that all marriages took the same shape. Instead of working towards a grand contract replete with deep emotional connection, intimacy, and time together, what Amanda and Jay worked on was a contract both could live with—some freedom for Jay, some peace of mind for Amanda.

Once the deal was closed, we were done.

Chapter 7

Gonorrhoea Tests Don't Lie

'Tell Allison, it's *your* fucking selfish choice that brings us here. I'd rather be getting my nails done,' Stephy ordered, as Billy turned crimson and looked down at the ground, visibly ashamed.

The good-looking statuesque couple sitting across exuded warmth towards me and thick tension towards each other. Stephy and Billy had lived together for five years and met at Alcoholics Anonymous. They were both soulmates and 'wound mates'. By looking at them, you wouldn't know that British Billy had given his Hong Kong Chinese fiancé an STD a month ago. Or that this had thrown a spanner in the works of their plans to get married—plans that had already been postponed due to the pandemic.

Stephy was desperate to have a child, even if that meant doing so before tying the knot. She was thirty-four, and in Hong Kong, any pregnancy past thirty-five is classified as 'geriatric'. Tick, tick. She knew her Chinese family already judged her for her past alcoholism and disapproved of her living with Billy before wedlock. Her plan was to get pregnant, then 'beg for forgiveness' from her family and marry Billy. She and Billy would live with her family after marriage, and it was assumed that Billy would give Stephy's family a generous allowance from his pay cheque each month. Many Chinese families do still collect allowances each month from their adult children.

It all seemed to be going according to a culturally negotiated plan.

One day, though, Stephy felt a weird burning sensation in her abdomen. She felt thrilled and thought she might be pregnant. There was a spring in her step as she went into her family doctor's office. She asked the receptionist for a cup to pee in and waited to see the doctor for ten glorious minutes full of giddy anticipation.

Once inside, sure enough, the doctor asked her to pee in the cup. But he also recommended taking a swab from her vagina to test for STDs. Stephy agreed as she was sure the pee would provide the answer she wanted. The swab test, she figured, was just about checking all the boxes.

A few days later, the doctor called and told her the pregnancy test had come back negative, but the swab was positive—for gonorrhoea. Stephy was shocked and horrified. She immediately called off her engagement and threatened to leave Billy.

And this is how they ended up in the therapy room with me. Often, it is a crisis that compels people into this room, even those resistant to therapy. Stephy wanted to address not only the infidelity but also Billy's apparent relapse with alcohol and the cocaine bender that had led to his encounter with gonorrhoea in the first place. Stephy wanted to get right to work and transact only in the truth. But Billy wouldn't admit to any wrongdoing in the first session. Even worse, he gaslighted Stephy.

'I didn't do it,' he stammered. 'You're the one cheating. Come on, Stephy, come clean.'

'Why do I have an STD!' she said, turning to me. 'I don't sleep around. He's the only one who could have given it to me. I'm furious. I will call off our engagement indefinitely unless he can admit it.' She looked at me then tearfully at Billy. 'I can't trust you anymore. You were with other women and put my health at risk! How dare you betray me. I don't know you anymore.'

Billy sat there like a lump.

I asked, 'Stephy, tell me about how you two met. Bring me back to earlier days in the relationship.' At this moment, I needed to ask about their history. When couples come to see me, I address first and foremost their current pain and challenges. Usually, I will then dig deeper and get to know their history. I look for any family-of-origin wounds that might be lying under the surface wound. In subsequent sessions, I will ask about their strengths and lives more broadly.

Still, working with couples is not like opening a cookbook. I must always keep my eye on what is in the room with me and attend to that.

With Stephy and Billy, the task at hand was addressing the substance use, infidelity and whether they would stay together. I needed to ask about the early days of their relationship because the pressure, the tension in the room was so high, I needed to break it, even if only ever so slightly. Hearing about their history would give me some insight into their connection. Once the psychological pressure reduced to a tolerable level, we could return to the wound and hopefully stop the bleed.

Part of what I need to keep my eye on with couples is emotional intensity. Once I can establish enough psychological safety, I can stress the system just enough that it will be open to shifting; then the couple can start changing. Too much intensity, too much stress, and the system implodes, the couple is overwhelmed. And when the system implodes, I sometimes have two adults having tantrums. This can look and feel like explosive fireworks in the room—call security! Or it can look like one putting up a metaphorical wall while the other is melting down. Or, I have two people who are stonewalling each other.

But no iteration of adult tantrums helps the process, or anything, really.

Over the years, I have become more confident in not allowing these tantrums to endure. Just like when the couple fight at home, we go nowhere when this happens. Working with couples requires the therapist to assume a leadership role even more so than when working with an individual. I will sometimes sit and breathe with couples, or we will take a break and resume once there are three adults in the room, or I will break the intensity with a question like I did with Stephy and Billy—oh, look, there's a bird! This is, in part, about controlling the intensity yet I am also modelling how to respond in a healthy way to intense emotions that all of us feel in our relationships. Therefore, whether it's breathing, taking a break or a healthy distraction, I do whatever is needed to get the train back on track.

Stephy mentioned the moment she and Billy met at Alcoholics Anonymous. She said they had a beautiful connection, strong mutual respect, adoration, and shared life goals and values, yet she finished that sentence with, '…until I found out about the STD result. It was a betrayal of my trust in Billy. I lost respect for him. He swore he would never drink again and never betray our love.' Her mouth twisted into a sad, confused frown. 'Every time I look in the mirror now, I wonder if I'm the reason he cheated. I have recently gained weight,' she said, morosely.

I'm still not sure whether Stephy believed in that moment, or any moment, that her weight gain was the cause or whether she was trying to poke Billy for a response. He was so wooden. Billy donned a poker face; her weight couldn't have been the reason he cheated because he maintained he never cheated.

We met for another couple's session and were going nowhere as it descended into gaslighting once again. The only leverage I had was Stephy's conviction that she would leave Billy if he didn't admit cheating. This meant that if Billy didn't want to marry her, he would likely maintain his position and continue to gaslight. If he did still want to marry Stephy, he might just crack. I needed to decide whether to sit tight and hope the gaslighting stopped or to take a gamble.

I rolled the dice.

At the third couple's session, I carefully and kindly confronted Billy and made clear what he stood to lose if the truth didn't come out. 'Billy, this woman in front of us, until very recently, wanted to have a baby with you and spend her life with you,' I said. 'She goes to the doctor, exhilarated by the thought that she is pregnant. She dreams of the baby you will raise together, imagines kissing that cute baby's feet, walking down the aisle, all of it. The doctor calls to tell her she is now infected with an STD that could threaten her fertility. She maintains that she has never had sex with anyone else while in a relationship with you. With the first two sessions, Stephy comes in hurt, disoriented, and uncertain about the future. You maintain that Stephy has cheated. I will not continue to take your money and waste your time if we are caught in this cycle. I don't believe you, but I do believe *in* you, Billy. Do you love this woman?' I looked him squarely in the eye.

He looked at Stephy, then held his head in his hands. Finally, the tap turned on.

Billy's tears could have drowned the therapy room. I could feel his remorse filling the room. I have witnessed the whole spectrum of remorse in the therapy room—from the performative 'Will this get me out of jail?' all the way to 'Oh, my soul cannot bear the pain I've caused you', à la Billy.

À la Billy was the exact salve this couple needed.

Stephy started crying herself, and she grabbed Billy's hand. They both stared at me, disoriented and looking to me for clear direction, as a team, wanting to head in the same direction.

'The therapy has now begun. Billy, let's start with the truth. Take a deep breath, and when you're ready, tell us what happened,' I said.

'My anxiety got worse after my workload increased during the pandemic. My boss had come in, a few days before the lockdown, and shared that my role might be made redundant. I was afraid I'd lose my job, and I wanted to save up for the wedding,' he said. 'Stephy's parents also expected that I would start giving them an allowance from my pay cheque, and quite a lot, given that Stephy isn't working right now. One night, the pressure, everything, just felt like too much. I was looking for a way to blackout from the pressure. I stupidly went back to my old coping mechanisms. Alcohol and cocaine were my former tickets out of all the pressure. I just thought I could control it. I never imagined that I would have sex with another woman, and I told myself, "Just this one time," with the alcohol and cocaine.'

There are two common ways I hear alcohol, cocaine, and other benders framed. 'Just this one time' and 'Only four times a year'. The latter is often said by people working in finance—only once a quarter! Usually, when clients do share about alcohol and drug usage, therapists can confidently multiply whatever comes out of their mouth by at least a factor of two, if not ten. It's truly terrifying for some people to hear the truth out loud, and so when clients do share, it's often drip, drip, drip. And then, boom.

Even long before the pandemic, Billy had struggled with anxiety, and it became even worse during the lockdown. Prior to joining AA, he and his expat buddies would drink and party every weekend at the girlie bars in Wan Chai, a neighbourhood in Hong Kong. The drinking took the edge off and eased the pressure to make small talk, as Billy's anxiety was linked not only to work but also social interactions. Drinking and cocaine provided a pathway out of the pressure while easing the pain he felt when interacting with others.

The night his boss told him he might lose his job was a few nights before lockdown closed the city's bars. Instead of sharing his feelings with Stephy or anyone, Billy told himself he could 'fix this pain' easily. He disguised his plans by telling Stephy he had a late-night conference call with a client in the United States, then texted his old bar buddies and asked if he could join the fun that evening. They were gathering at an apartment above a watering hole in Wan Chai. Billy had a few too many vodkas and several lines of cocaine. One of the Filipina bar girls wrapped herself around him, and then he claims to have blacked out. He said he couldn't remember the rest.

I challenged him about the evening directly. 'Were you so high and so drunk at that moment that you couldn't think of Stephy? Do you recall the last thought going through your head?'

'I can't remember anything. I swear on my mother's grave. I never meant to hurt her,' he pleaded.

This one line—I never meant to hurt her—was a tip-off the real work was about to begin. We were launching deep into the swamps of Billy's soul.

I don't believe you, but I do believe in you

It's a line that the writer and speaker Caroline Myss refers to as 'the pain of the lie'.

According to Myss, people often reflexively lie to themselves and others by saying, 'I never meant to hurt you.' The only way to truly heal, she suggests, is to stop lying to ourselves and others. This happens only by being honest: 'I knew what I was doing, and I knew it would hurt you. I chose to do it anyway. I chose me over you. My actions redirected the course of your life.'

I've lost count of people in the therapy room who say to their partners, 'I never meant to hurt you.' This is against a backdrop of people who have had affairs, financial infidelity, you name it. People will often try to connect with a psychological alibi, that they never had intent to harm another.

I said to Billy, 'You had no awareness that cheating would hurt your partner? If that's true, then we're no longer talking about the possibility of repairing this relationship anytime soon. Instead, we are speaking about a lack of empathy. Is that really true—no part of you thought this would hurt your partner? Please take your time to respond. Because if it is, then a lack of empathy will take us down a much, much, much, longer, way more intensive path, and there is little to no hope this relationship will heal.'

Billy looked like a shell of himself and sank deeper into the chair, his downcast eyes glued firmly to his shoes. He took about a minute to respond and then said, 'I must have known on some level. I guess I deluded myself like the next guy would.' Billy's usage of 'I must have', 'I guess', and 'the next guy' told me he was not fully owning up to knowing, on some level, that his actions would possibly damage the relationship and hurt Stephy. Yet, this was a time when, as a therapist, you take what you can get. Billy had already demonstrated through his profound remorse and willingness to stay present in the session that this relationship mattered to him. Thou shalt not torture thy client.

I looked at Stephy and Billy, and after a beat, I said to them, 'If you are both willing to put in the work, I do believe you two can heal from this. It doesn't mean the trust will ever be back to 100 per cent. We may get to 97 per cent or 98 per cent but unlikely to be 100 per cent. Some wounds never fully heal. This will take consistency with the couples work, and I also want Billy back in AA and seeing an addiction specialist.'

They were holding each other's hand tightly; their eyes didn't meet. Sometimes the convergence of truth, pain, and hope is so intense we need to bear it alone in the safe space of others. There is always a part of us that yearns to tell the truth. And when we do, it's often a massive exhale, even if there is a massive mess to clean up.

Confronting addictions

While there can be a real cathartic element to telling the truth, there is often a more practical, demanding component. With Billy, for example, it wasn't enough for Stephy to know the truth. For the therapy to really support their relationship, she would need to know he was taking concrete steps to reduce the risk of this happening again. This would happen only when Billy could trust himself, and he could trust himself only when he could trust his own judgement.

Billy's previous commitment to AA had waned due to work demands, yet I made clear he would need consistent support—support that I could not provide. As much as I could sit with Billy and talk for endless hours about the history of his addiction, why it came to be, and piece together an elegant narrative, what he needed was a clear plan, not endless cathartic moments. As the years go on, I have become more confident in making clear that certain treatments are needed before any valuable therapy can be done.

Once Billy was back in AA and seeing the addiction specialist, I had an individual session with him to speak about reducing stress and taking care of his physical and mental health. We spoke about nutrition, exercise, sleep, cultivating strong connections with others, and setting boundaries with his social media usage. Although I don't use the label, I see myself as a 'holistic therapist'. My bachelor's degree is in nutrition, and I have long known about the strong connection between food and mood along with the power of sleep, exercise, and connection. Many people are in vicious lifestyle cycles—not eating well, not sleeping enough, not connecting enough—and this sets them up to have impaired judgement. I try to set people on a different path, a virtuous cycle, to help them become more confident of the agency they have with their mental and physical wellbeing.

With couples, especially after a crisis, resetting lifestyle choices, getting them on schedules that are more synced and healthier, can be a powerful way to help connect them more. Think more regular, healthier meals together. Pillow talk. Protected time together. While these alone are not going to sustain a partnership, I have yet to meet a couple who are in sync, with clearer rituals, who don't reap some benefits.

Amplifying commitment

When a client commits to something like couples therapy, individual therapy, AA, lifestyle changes, any kind of change, I try to amplify the verbal commitment by asking them, 'Why do you want to do *this*?' It helps solidify why this is important and, if I'm working with a couple, it helps for the partner to witness the response and hear what is really driving change. With couples, I often ask each partner, 'What do you love about this person?' It's extremely revealing when someone says for instance, 'I love that they support me and make these decisions to help me.' I then ask, 'What you love about them is not about how they helped you. Let's try again and don't bring it back to you. Speak about them.'

In Billy's case, when I asked why he wanted to make these changes and what he loves about Stephy, he said, 'I don't want to end up dead in a ditch. I love the future we agreed on. I love her humour, warmth and heart, and want to have kids with her. I love her beautiful heart the most.'

It was a beautiful, forgiving heart.

Restoring trust

As we continued with the sessions, I brought in the Gottman concept of an Emotional Bank Account—an imaginary bank account that each couple shares, one that is reflective of the emotional investments and divestments they've made over the years. I reiterated with Stephy and Billy that after a breach of trust, we needed to be very mindful of this account. Healing trust takes consistent, conscious choices—how they interact, respond to each other, all the efforts they do or do not make, and so on. I explained that each choice we make in a relationship is either an investment or a divestment.

Turn away from or stonewall your partner when they want to connect? Divestment.

Act entitled or grandiose with your partner? Divestment.

Argue with your partner's feelings or meet your partner with defensiveness? Divestment.

Turn towards your partner and work to connect? Investment.

Express respect and adoration? Investment.

Be compassionately curious about your partner's experiences? Investment.

I tailor these examples for every couple. Most important is for people to open their eyes to their choices, make consistent investments, and become aware of how all this affects the other person (building empathy) and the relationship (strengthening the connection).

Billy made some serious investments by displaying remorse, sharing with his friends that he was no longer drinking and not going anywhere near a bar, going to AA, seeing an addiction specialist, coming regularly to couples therapy, being more open with Stephy and curious about her feelings as well. Stephy invested by being clear about her needs and welcoming Billy's efforts when he made them.

This did not mean, though, that Stephy did not have moments when she questioned Billy's motives or whether this would all lead to change that was both sustainable and trustworthy. I reassured Stephy that doubts were normal, that, indeed, I would be a bit concerned if she just swooned into Billy's arms and forgot the betrayal entirely. Of course, she would have moments where she questioned things. Who wouldn't? Nonetheless, overall, Stephy was receptive and believed in Billy; she did not want to lock him in a 'Prison of Shame'.

We talked about how some investments might feel 'messy' or 'negative'. After a betrayal, some conversations may not be 'positive', I explained, and it's important to be comfortable with that. 'With any kind of betrayal or really any challenges the two of you may face if you decide to marry, there will at times be a messiness to the conversations—emotions and thoughts may not be coherent, or you may not get something on the first attempt, and that's OK. We are keeping our eye on teamwork, respect, curiosity, and kindness in these conversations. There may also be times when the conversations are about the past. As time goes on, I expect less of that, and I imagine the two of you could get to a place where you're both enjoying the present together and looking forward again to your future.'

Healing is rarely a linear path. On a good day, we take a step forward.

Once there was *enough* healing from the betrayal, enough good days, we spoke about whether they still wanted to marry. Unwaveringly, they both said yes. They had a strong foundation and connection to begin with, and unlike a lot of couples, the infidelity didn't reveal even more fissures. There was a generous overlap in their values and vision for life. Billy became willing to talk about his anxiety and his drinking to mask it. More than just talking, he would take clear steps to show Stephy how he would reduce the risk of a repeat and strengthen his judgement around decisions.

We met for a few more sessions to discuss their life ahead—about having children and living with Stephy's family. We had direct, honest conversations about cultural clashes between Billy and his traditional Chinese parents-in-law. Initially, he was reluctant to pay them a monthly allowance, yet he subsequently accepted it as part of his wife's filial duty to support them in their retirement. Billy and Stephy were also able to discuss which cultural values were most important to impart to their children. They planned to stay in Hong Kong for the foreseeable future. Stephy was clear she wanted her children to learn English, Cantonese, and Mandarin; for Billy it was important they spend the summers in the UK with his family.

Billy and Stephy married in early 2022 in a traditional Chinese wedding. After three rounds of IVF, Stephy gave birth to a daughter whom they adore deeply. Stephy's parents have embraced Billy and honour his efforts.

This is a story not only about remorse but also forgiveness. Fold both into a relationship with enough connection and commitment to work as a team and maybe, just maybe, the relationship transforms.

Pandemic cheating

The Hong Kong government made it difficult for people to cheat. I sometimes say this to be cheeky, yet the reality is that its commitment to a zero-Covid environment really did make it more difficult.

High-flying businesspeople were grounded due to Hong Kong's requirement that travellers undergo twenty-one days of quarantine on entry. Contact tracing meant there was no guarantee secret meetups would remain secret. More people were working at home, so unexplained absences became more noticeable. There were fewer women being trafficked into the city, so fewer prostitutes, and anyway, authorities were keeping a closer eye on the kind of vices that could spread disease.

Many clients complained that they couldn't see their mistresses overseas, that their favourite brothels had been shut down, that they were now terrified of catching Covid and being traced or getting caught by the increased surveillance.

But where there's a will there's a way.

Many turned to virtual sex instead. Others simply learned more stealthy methods. I saw countless couples dealing with one-night stands, 'virtual' affairs, and STDs. People took risks and chose thrills and orgasms over the risk of getting Covid and sent to hospital or quarantine. The world's most well-known dating site for married people, Ashley Madison, saw a rise in subscribers.

People often ask me what makes someone cheat and whether these factors changed during the pandemic. I usually respond that we are all vulnerable, some more than others, and that the pandemic was a humbling reminder that if we are not clear with what we truly value—and take steps to fiercely protect it—it becomes far too easy to cross the line.

Even in open relationships, people can cross a line. Every relationship needs boundaries that, ultimately, reflect a set of values. No values, no boundaries, no relationship.

So, what *does* make some people more likely to cheat? Below is not a scientific gathering of data, more a reflection of what I've observed over many years.

- Narcissistic or other personality or character 'challenges' such as lack of empathy
- Unclear value systems—either by having undefined values or making choices that do not reflect those values
- Victim mentality and/or entitlement—believing that they did bump into someone naked! It just happened. How could they not? They deserved it.
- Porous boundaries—feeling an attraction and not taking action to remove oneself from interaction or lack of clear boundary setting

- Impulsive behaviour—due to substance usage, certain pathology, or a desire to be 'high on life'
- Unwillingness to reduce risk, to reduce or eliminate substances, putting oneself in risky situations and being surrounded by others who are cheating

Many psychologists believe there is a link between the severe and unusual social, economic, and emotional circumstances people experienced during the pandemic and the rise in infidelity, especially in virtual affairs.

For relationships already under stress—for example, over who watched the children, or who made the money—the pandemic added extra pressures. It also magnified the cultural differences and shifted the power dynamics in many relationships.

And it did not help that tiny, cramped apartments of a couple of hundred square feet are the norm in this part of Asia. Living alone in lockdown meant isolation; living with others meant suffocation.

But blaming the pandemic risks its own form of dishonesty. Not all relationships suffered. Some got stronger. Some couples took the chance to reaffirm their love, brought together by the enforced closeness and a sense of 'being in this together'.

When couples tell me about the impact the pandemic—or any external stressor—has had on their relationship, my thoughts often turn to the group of men I met a handful of years ago, when I started Hong Kong's first therapy group for male refugees and asylum seekers.

These men were Coptic Christians who had fled Egypt because their houses were being burned down, trafficked Rwandans facing persecution for being Muslim, former boy soldiers from Somalia, Yemenis fleeing a civil war who had watched their grandmothers being raped.

I would meet them once a week for a couple of hours, and they would tell me their stories honestly and openly. Many of these men had not even heard of Hong Kong before touching down with their wives and children. They had paid money to someone to help them escape their own homes and expected in return only a promise to land *elsewhere*. They had been forced to choose between life and death and knew they could never return. No home country. No safety net. A suitcase at most. And yet, many had strong relationships with their wives.

Blaming the pandemic is easy—in part because living through it was so damn hard. So hard, and for so many reasons. It is also easy because it offers us a scapegoat, a narrative for the unravelling of a relationship that leaves us looking outwards, rather than within.

It's an appealing story to both those who tell it and those who hear it. Like Billy and Stephy, we have all had our own run-ins with Covid, the supposed villain of this piece. But it's not an entirely honest story. There's no simple answer to whether the pandemic rotted a relationship away, no easy test like there is for pregnancy, or gonorrhoea, or even Covid-19. The truth is far more complex. The truth is that the pandemic did influence how and when people cheated, and how and when their relationships broke up.

It also reinforced tales as old as time.

Part III

Marriage, Divorce, and Revenge

Chapter 8

Sexless Marriages

The Cold War winds were blowing frigid from the start.

Putri and Ahmad could barely look at each other and sat on opposite sides of the room. The physical space between them mirrored their emotional distance—it looked painful for these two to be in the same room together.

For the first part of the session, I couldn't sense any kind of connection from this elegantly dressed couple in their late forties, married for eighteen years with two kids. They both worked in finance, both Indonesian. She was in the C-suite, wheeling and dealing in the world of mergers and acquisitions; he was an accountant for small and medium-sized enterprises. In his spare time, Ahmad worked on charitable projects and found 'lots of meaning' in it. Putri 'hated' her all-consuming job, which she described as a 'golden coffin'.

Putri cut straight to the chase. 'We have a family trip back to Indonesia, and I don't want our family to think something is wrong with our marriage. That's what we need your help with.'

'Yes, we need to maintain the façade of a good marriage,' Ahmad replied without skipping a beat.

'At least during the trip,' Putri interjected. 'Otherwise, I really don't want to have anything to do with him.'

Ahmad looked at me over his silver-rimmed spectacles and said, 'She doesn't have anything to do with me anyway. We don't even have sex anymore.'

This launched us into the heart of why they were really here.

'Look, I'm home most nights at 11 p.m., and my sex drive is pretty much non-existent. I think I've hit menopause, so what do you expect? I resent the fact that the household and childcare are not done well enough,' she said to Ahmad.

She crossed her arms and turned away from him, then spoke directly to me. 'If you're wondering how long we haven't had sex, I'd say around three years.'

'It's been three years and three months. We don't even sleep in the same room. Putri is convinced because she makes more money, she gets to control how I am with the kids. I have a lot of pent-up frustration,' Ahmad said as if he had just unpacked one of many suitcases he'd been carrying.

Though they couldn't pinpoint when they fell in love and knew the other was 'the one', they recounted meeting through work friends in Singapore and quickly moving in together, then marrying within a year. From the start, their relationship was unconventional compared with most of their friends in Indonesia. Ahmad had more time to cook and take care of the cleaning, and he organized their weekend activities.

When Putri's work in mergers and acquisitions required her to travel more, her resentment at the long hours began to rise—and so too did his anger at being 'abandoned'. He felt most connected and valued through sex, like many men are conditioned to feel, and kept referencing the sexlessness throughout the session. Putri on the other hand spoke about the sexlessness almost like a footnote.

As their physical connection dwindled to nothing, Ahmad began to sleep on a mattress between his children's beds from the time they were six and nine. A doting father, he would wake in the middle of the night to make sure their blankets were still on and just to gaze at their sleeping faces.

He wielded his love for his son and daughter as a weapon like 'I'm going to do this to punish my wife—they will pledge their love and loyalty to me', yet on the surface, it all seemed very genuine and loving. The children were very close with him. In response, Putri became more controlling over how the household chores were executed and how the children were cared for.

'Allison, we are basically just tied together by the kids, and since I'm paying for most of the things in our home, I should have a say,' Putri said flatly, as if sharing a risk factor with an acquirer's board of directors. 'When they're out of the house, we'll get a divorce.'

Ahmad nodded in agreement and said, 'If we're not having sex, then we will.'

The room was silent for a few seconds. It felt like the dust cloud needed to clear. I said, 'If you two agree that you're working towards a divorce in at least eight years, then what do you want our work together to look like now? Do you want to work on the sexlessness or is it just being civil during the trip?'

'Well, first, it may be longer than eight years if our kids live with us before they get married and possibly even after,' said Putri. 'That's very common in our culture. And we may not even get a divorce because . . .' She paused, turned to Ahmad and said, *Jaga nama baik.*' Then she looked back at me. 'That's Bahasa Indonesian. It's about saving face. Do you know what that means? I probably should have asked when we spoke earlier about preserving the image of our marriage to our family,' she said.

I am endlessly amazed by how many terms exist in Asian languages for 'saving face'—not bringing embarrassment or humiliation to the family name and therefore making choices that maintain and protect the family's reputation. I have had countless clients reference this idea, which runs counter to the idea favoured by many in the West of 'speaking your truth'. This difference is a neat illustration of how Asian societies tend to prioritize collective duty, while Western ones prioritize the individual.

'At this point, even if we don't fix the sex stuff, I just hope to be civil and feel trusted with household decisions,' Ahmad said. 'Right now, all I hear from her is a nightly litany of what I did wrong. She was angry I ordered chocolate cake with chocolate frosting for our son's birthday instead of chocolate cake with vanilla frosting. She didn't like that I sat with our daughter for twenty minutes instead of fifteen to help her with her homework.' He sighed and continued, 'Best case would be that we could have sex again.' Then he inched towards Putri to take her hand.

She recoiled, disgusted. 'I would rather walk on hot coals than have sex with you. And yes, our son prefers chocolate cake with vanilla frosting, and yes, if you sit with our daughter for too long, then she'll never be able to do homework on her own.'

There was clearly more to this conversation than chocolate cake, yet like so many couples, they felt the need to engage first with familiar distractions before they could tolerate a real conversation.

'Honestly, I try. But she can't even honour my sacrifice for her and our family. That should at least award me a little respect and some closeness. I feel like she isn't even open to touching me. I get no emotion from her,' Ahmad said, a dash of vulnerability in his voice.

'You get it from our kids,' she said sarcastically.

'How long has this Cold War been happening between you two?' I asked, looking them both squarely in the eye. I was curious how they would respond to this idea of a Cold War. If they rejected it, then I would back up and steer the boat elsewhere. If they accepted or embraced it, then we would keep going with it.

'Ha. Cold War. I'd say since we started arguing about sex. He's absolutely insane to think that I would want to have sex given my workload,' Putri said.

'Yeah, Cold War indeed. That's what this is,' Ahmad responded.

'Now that we're all in agreement with what this is, I would like to ask each of you a question. Ahmad, I want to ask you to tell me about Putri, and then I'll give Putri time to respond. Once Putri responds, then I'll ask her about you and give you time to respond, Ahmad. Are you two OK with this?' I asked and watched them both nod yes. 'Keep in mind, this is your partner's opinion of you, and you will have time to respond after they are done speaking. The point of doing this is for me to understand a bit more about your dynamic.'

I engaged in what some family therapists call 'circular questioning', whereby the therapist asks one member of a relationship to describe the other and vice versa. I decided to try this with Putri and Ahmad because I wanted to take their emotional temperature and see if I could get anything warmer than the frigid Cold War winds.

'Putri is a star. I remember looking at her back when we met thinking she was super capable and just an overall star. I still feel attracted to her except when she is controlling. Then I just want to shrivel and feel like I'm not a man. I feel like a kicked dog if I'm honest. But anyway, Putri is a good person. She's always cared about family, and that's certainly a value we share. She's very good to her parents and mine and has always worked hard. I know she hates her work, yet she's a star, Allison,' Ahmad shared.

'Putri, do you want to respond?' I asked, and she shook her head no. I noticed a slight thawing and could see she was a bit surprised, and delightfully so, by Ahmad's response. 'Your turn. Tell me about Ahmad.'

'Ahmad is a good guy. I wish he made more money because I hate my work, and I hate that I have to carry our lifestyle. But he's a good guy. Solid guy. He cares so much about our kids. I remember dating him, and after a few months thought I wanted to marry this guy. He always made me feel safe, like I could count on him.

And we used to laugh. I know we are showing up here fighting, but believe it or not, we used to laugh and a lot,' Putri said.

I also saw Ahmad thawing, just a tad, yet they still wouldn't make eye contact, and after listening to each other for a few seconds, they uncrossed their arms and legs, and assumed their battlefield positions once more.

I ended the session and said, 'I want you two to go away and reflect on whether we are working towards a "tolerable" trip and marriage or something else. Either will require an end to this Cold War—it feels anything but tolerable between the two of you right now. I sense you've been trapped by a pattern in the marriage whereby the relationship hasn't evolved with all the changes and responsibilities.'

And, like a good Cold War general, Putri looked at Ahmad and said, 'You need to change first.'

I wondered if we would tear down this wall.

Erotic load

The concept of 'mental load' refers to the person in the household, often the woman, who carries the cognitive burden of running a household along with the family relationships, often in addition to her own work outside the home. This often translates into what some call 'worry work'—carrying out endless tasks for the children such as making lunches, ordering extra supplies, arranging activities, and so on. This differs from the idea of a 'second shift' for women, as unlike a shift, which has a start and an end, mental load stays with the person throughout the day.

Although there are many countries in Asia in which hiring a domestic worker to assist with the household work and children is common, in my experience, women in Asia often report carrying the mental load. Typically, in a heterosexual couple, whether the woman has a job or not, she will be the one thinking about what the children will eat at lunch, what birthday gifts need to be ordered, and so on. The husband usually doesn't think about these things at all.

My best guess is that this has been socially conditioned, and it will take at least one or two more generations to profoundly change the idea that the woman is the go-to caregiver.

I've noticed, though, there's often another load carried in relationships—what I have coined the 'erotic load'. In a heterosexual couple, I have observed that most men carry this, albeit less and less with each year that passes. With gay couples, I have observed that one will carry the erotic load as well. The one carrying the erotic load is often thinking about sex or eroticism when their partner is often not. For instance, I sometimes hear one person fantasizing or planning for the next sexual encounter when the other is thinking about the kids' lunches and has no focus on the bedroom.

I imagine that the mental load and erotic load are not only socially conditioned but also a function of what is often referred to with couples as the 'minimizer–maximizer dynamic'—one is minimizing the significance, responsibility, or emotion of something, and therefore the other 'turns up the volume' and maximizes the significance, responsibility, or emotion.

With Putri and Ahmad, he was carrying some of the mental load with caring for the house and children along with all the erotic load. Putri had some of the mental load, juggling the household while working all day, but seemed to be carrying none of the erotic load.

Beyond frosting and defrosting

'It was nice leaving the session last week, Allison. I think we were both genuinely shocked to hear anything nice said about the other. We even held hands in the taxi ride home. But, somehow,

Ahmad thought that momentary closeness was an invitation for sex,' Putri said.

Ahmad lamented, 'Yes, I felt like a man again for a moment, and she just shut me down.'

Putri hemmed and hawed for a bit, and then finally said, 'OK, let's focus. I have a meeting right after this. We thought about your question about our goals for this work together. As much as I think Ahmad needs to listen more—he does—and just follow what I say about the kids and house, I can't deny that I do want to reconnect. Just like he hasn't felt much like a man recently, I haven't felt much like a woman. I go to work, I'm a spiteful robot executing these deals, then I come home and am exhausted, and now there's the delight of menopause, which means I'm dealing with hot flashes and, sorry to say, vaginal dryness.'

'I'm glad to hear you reflected. When you say "reconnect", Putri, do you mean sexually only, or do you mean emotionally as well?' I asked.

'Both. But I want him to listen more,' she said unapologetically.

I sensed Putri's need to win would likely show up for a while, even if the Cold War ended, even if Ahmad did put vanilla frosting on the chocolate cake or sit with the daughter for only fifteen minutes during homework time. I noted it, and I'm not sure how Ahmad felt about it, yet I wanted to focus on Putri's desire to reconnect. I also noted the tiny shift in body language this session—no arms folded and no legs crossed in the opposite direction.

Before I became a therapist, I once had a boss who told me, 'When you get the answer you want, get the hell out!' I was reminded of this listening to Putri imperfectly share that yes, she wanted to reconnect.

'Ahmad, what comes to you when you hear Putri saying that she wants to reconnect emotionally and sexually?' I asked.

'Finally,' Ahmad said with some relief.

'Time to roll up our sleeves all together as a team,' I said.

With Cold War couples, rolling up our sleeves means figuring out how to end the Cold War, and for some couples that's enough. Wave the white flag and surrender, you both lost.

With Putri and Ahmad, to end the Cold War, we would need first to work through some of their battles, in particular Putri's desire to control and Ahmad sleeping in the same room with the kids. I also had my eye on some other challenges—menopause and stress, for example—yet I felt this couple first needed to sense the other changing before they would be receptive to any trips to the doctor or conversations on stress. This is not always true with sexless couples; I do sometimes first address the practical or physical challenges.

I decided to start with Ahmad, then moved on to Putri, and then went through some ideas I've put together over the years with sexless couples. I imagined I would get more buy-in from Putri with her controlling tendencies if she first witnessed Ahmad making changes.

This is a judgement call I make with couples. With Putri, I imagined she would do the work as she struck me as someone who did not want to waste time once she had committed to something. Yet, she would be unwilling to do anything unless Ahmad made the first move.

Into the bedroom

We met again two weeks later and got right to work. Time to reclaim the bedroom.

'As a first step, can we speak about getting you two back in the same bedroom?' I asked.

'That would be a necessary step, yet I don't know if Ahmad is up for that. Every time I've mentioned that sleeping in the same room as the kids isn't healthy for them or us, he goes on and on about how "secure" it makes the kids feel,' Putri said.

'Ahmad, do you see this as a necessary step? Are you up for moving out of the kids' bedroom?' I asked.

'Well, I am. But they're so used to me being there that they might anyway come and find me back in the bedroom,' he said. That was what he said out loud. But his tone was saying something more like, 'Yeah, I see it, yet I don't see how this could change.'

In therapy, sometimes people will put themselves in a bind like Ahmad—I want sex with my wife, but I don't sleep in the same room as my wife. Ahmad knew, on some level, that these two truths were incompatible. When clients put themselves in a bind, I explicitly put the bind out on the table first for them to see it clearly and let them decide what to do about it.

'I'm going to hand you this bind. You want to have sex with your wife again, yet part of the challenge is you don't sleep in the same bed. She is clear that to have sex again, the two of you need to reclaim the bedroom, and I agree. And yet, you don't want to give up sleeping in the kids' room because you think they need you to or will come to find you anyway at night. What would you like to do? Staying in this bind won't move you any closer to connection with Putri, so you need to make a choice—live in the bind or work on the marriage,' I said.

'I want the marriage. But Putri, are you willing to try with me?' he asked.

Putri didn't respond. She was trying to keep her mouth shut, pushing down her lips as if someone had sealed them shut.

Silence flooded the room. I needed to focus on how to break through the bind inhibiting their connection. I told them that in my professional opinion, this would require both committing and not *trying*. Ahmad would need to commit to moving out of the children's bedroom, and Putri would need to commit to reducing her controlling behaviour and critical words. While this was not all that would be required to move the needle, it was a necessary first step—changing from 'trying' to 'committing' for many couples is a huge step. 'Trying' too often translates into endless excuses, years lost.

'Fine. I'll commit. How do I reduce this behaviour?' Putri asked.

Sometimes it's difficult to discern potentially controlling behaviour in certain Asian families. People will endure and excuse it by saying, 'But I'm a success story and I turned out so well. That's what I'll do to my kids. If I need to scream or hit my kids, and that's what will motivate them, that's what I'll do.' Or 'My parents have made it fifty years with being married and one or both are super controlling or critical.'

I broke the silence and asked Putri as a first step, 'Who was the controlling one in your family?'

'My parents ran a restaurant outside Jakarta in Indonesia and had to deal with a lot of crap. My father drank and gambled away their earnings and ran into some trouble with thugs when he couldn't pay back a debt. My mother felt ashamed by my deadbeat dad and ran the restaurant singlehandedly behind the scenes. She always made it seem like my father was the boss, but at home she verbally abused him and called him a failure. My mother always told me that she wanted to divorce him. My father was a great dad, and he doted on me. I don't know why I just can't appreciate how Ahmad is towards the kids.'

Putri was able to respect her parents and understand that by continuing to be controlling and criticizing, it was eroding the connection in her marriage. It might have been 'fine' for her parents to continue this dynamic, yet it wasn't fine for the man she married.

That's all that mattered if her marriage mattered.

Sexless checklist

Below is a general checklist of what I consider when I meet a sexless couple. Not all of these apply for every couple, and the

order in which I explore each point differs with each couple. I
went through this with Putri and Ahmad.

1. Physical issues: These are often overlooked. Sometimes
    sexlessness is rooted in a health problem, so I will
    often send people to see a doctor to rule this out or
    get treatment. Putri eventually saw a doctor to discuss
    her menopause symptoms, specifically for the hot
    flashes and vaginal dryness, and eventually went to see
    a traditional Chinese medicine (TCM) doctor to manage
    the symptoms. With men, I often hear about erectile
    dysfunction, and I never assume this is just an outgrowth
    of an emotional disconnect. I make sure they get a doctor
    to rule out any physical cause first and also work through
    lifestyle choices, such as smoking, that could be causing
    the erectile dysfunction.
2. Mental health: Sometimes mental health challenges can
    also contribute, and if that's the case, then the person
    needs to get treatment. For example, if someone is
    depressed, then it's challenging to feel sexual at the
    same time.
3. Life stage: I often look at where a couple is in life. Trying
    to get pregnant, adopting, pregnancy, and caring for
    young kids and/or elderly parents can all shift sexual
    connection in a marriage, yet each relationship is different.
    For example, when I worked at a midwives' clinic, I recall
    many women feeling turned off by sex during pregnancy
    and others were never more turned on than when
    pregnant—they weren't trying to prevent a pregnancy nor
    were they trying to get pregnant. Some men are turned on
    when women are pregnant, while others are not.
        Taking care of elderly parents is still very much the
    norm in many places, particularly in Asia, and this can often

be taxing on the marriage. There's often a sense of filial piety—an obligation to give back to parents—and therefore the marriage is sometimes sacrificed, at least in part or for a period, for caretaking of parents. This is in stark contrast to what people in the West are often told: to choose the marriage or your parents. I wouldn't say this to someone in Asia. There is also the sandwich generation phenomenon, in which middle-aged couples find themselves taking care of both elderly parents and young children.

4. Stress and stressors: Stress is part of every marriage and everyone's existence, and it often sucks the energy out of the bedroom because it's nearly impossible to feel both stressed and sexual at once. I work with couples to identify their stress, stressors, and what to do to manage the stress differently. With Putri, she was experiencing a lot of pressure from work. We eventually spoke about reducing her work hours and transitioning out of mergers and acquisitions towards something less time-consuming. Ahmad also agreed to look for higher-paying work. As the sessions continued and their connection improved, it became clear that Ahmad wasn't quite leveraging his skills or network to full capacity. Putri also started carving out time for herself each Sunday morning to walk with her friends and one night during the week to see her TCM doctor.

5. Marital injuries: There are many couples who are carrying around injuries from the past (or even ongoing ones in the present) that make it very challenging to feel close sexually. For example, I work with a lot of couples in which there's been an affair, and until that's been properly dealt with, it's challenging to work on sexual connection. With Putri and Ahmad, we worked on re-engineering their dynamic, yet they didn't have any major marital injuries.

No long-term relationship goes completely unscathed. What matters is whether these injuries are healed *enough*— that determines if they're necessary to discuss in the context of sexlessness.

6. History of sex: With couples, I try to hear enough of their sexual history to understand if there's been any sexual trauma and to get a sense of their sexuality overall. With Putri and Ahmad, there was no sexual trauma in their past, and they both, for religious reasons, waited until marriage to have sex. Their sexual history with each other was quite adventurous and robust. If there is a history of trauma, then this often requires that the trauma be treated before the couple gets closer sexually.

7. Sexual goals: I work with couples to understand what their goals are sexually. For some couples, this is relatively simple. For instance, they may want to have sex more frequently or try something new sexually. For others, this can be more complex, such as opening the marriage sexually to other partners. Most of all it needs to be about moving sex beyond just doing it to check a box. Many women, for example, view sex as a form of caretaking, and I have lost count of the female clients I've had who tell me they engage in what's referred to as 'the maintenance shag'—just often enough to keep their spouses off their backs about having more sex. Therefore, some women (and yes, sometimes men) need to explore a sexual identity beyond anything to do with checking a box or caretaking for there to be true sexual vitality in a marriage.

8. Reconnecting: I often work with couples to see if we can inject enough spice to get their sexual engine going again. Even speaking about sex can help to build up some eroticism. We work on various strategies, such as building up enough sexual tension by sending each other racy texts, or writing notes, or having 'his' and 'her' nights (his

night = do whatever he wants; her night = do whatever she wants). Reconnecting sexually never just happens. It requires energy, time, and presence like all aspects of a relationship. With Putri and Ahmad, they both wanted to work on exploring different fantasies each had, and they took very much to the idea of his and her nights. They also booked a night each month at a different hotel and were able to build up sexual tension before then.

9. Sex therapist: I am not a sex therapist, and therefore there are times when I run through this whole list and work with a couple to try to restart the sexual energy only to find that they need to see a sex therapist. It's sometimes obvious at the beginning of the therapy yet other times reveals itself only later. Putri and Ahmad were able to re-engage once we ended the Cold War, re-engineered the dynamic, worked on their stress, and reconnected them as sexual beings (not just workhorses and caretakers). Not all couples, though, are like this and some need the support of a sex therapist.

In the end, once we could rejig their dynamic and agree that both were making choices to zap sexual energy—Ahmad by leaning on the children for connection, Putri by criticizing and controlling—we redirected their energy towards the marriage. For most, sexlessness is multifactorial, yet often it's like a logjam, and if I can move one big obstacle out of the way, then there's a chance we can flow more easily with the other obstacles. This was true with Putri and Ahmad. By re-engaging sexually, they were also able to break the logjam in other areas of their relationship.

Sexless marriages, a global issue

There are 4.4 million search results on Google for 'sexless marriage'. It is one of the most common challenges couples faces, and this is true in many cultures, if not all. The definition of a sexless marriage is one in which there is 'little' to no sexual activity taking place. Of course, what counts as 'little' is subjective.

There is a huge range in how often married couples have sex. I have also worked with many couples from various cultures who are not married and have a sexless relationship.

Even though it's a common challenge, it often goes unaddressed, especially in Asia, where speaking of sex openly is still taboo and so too is seeking treatment from a sex therapist. There's another cultural layer in this part of the world as it is more common for grown-up children to remain in their parents' home, even after getting married, and many feel they lack the privacy needed for sexual intimacy.

Although sexless marriages are often thought of as something affecting older couples, one survey reported by the BBC found nearly 26 per cent of British people in their twenties and thirties—their supposed sexual prime—were in sexless marriages.[2] Another report found around 15 to 20 per cent of Singapore's married couples had sex less than ten times a year.[3] A 2017 survey in Japan found record numbers of married couples, especially those in their forties, were in sexless unions thanks to long working hours and the demands of raising a family.[4]

A 2009 study on married Chinese adults in Hong Kong, in the *Journal of Sexual Medicine*, found that unhealthy marriages and

---

[2] Jessica Klein, 'The millennials in sexless marriages', *BBC* (20 Oct, 2022) https://www.bbc.com/worklife/article/20221019-the-millennials-in-sexless-marriages (accessed 15 Feb, 2023).

[3] 'Experts Reveal Foolproof Ways To Repair A Sexless Marriage', *The Singapore Women's Weekly* (25 July, 2019) https://www.womensweekly.com.sg/gallery/family/repair-sexless-marriage/ (accessed 15 Feb, 2023).

[4] Justin McCurry, 'Record numbers of couples living in sexless marriages in Japan, says report', *The Guardian* (14 Feb, 2017) https://www.theguardian.com/world/2017/feb/14/record-numbers-of-couples-living-in-sexless-marriages-in-japan-says-report (accessed 15 Feb, 2023).

older age were the main reasons for sexlessness among women.[5] Older age, a lack of interest in sex, and even lower levels of formal education were the reasons it cited for men.

Often, the temperature in the bedroom reflects the temperature in other rooms of the relationship, though not always. I have worked with couples who have very passionate, connected sex only to struggle to converse or connect outside the bedroom. Some of these couples may be compensating for the lack of connection by ramping up the sexual activity. Many others may simply find they are attracted to each other sexually, but not intellectually or emotionally.

I have also worked with couples who have a sexless bedroom yet plenty of emotional and/or intellectual intimacy in other rooms.

When a couple agrees on the lack of sex and adapts to it, then it can work for them, and some couples are fine with this. I worked with a man who'd had surgery for cancer and afterwards experienced erectile dysfunction. He no longer wanted to have sex, and his wife was fine with this. They both agreed their marriage was strong and close enough without the sex, and they didn't want to work on the sexlessness, so we didn't.

Yet, when sexlessness is not agreed upon, there is often tension, and I will often wonder if one or both are having sex outside the relationship. Sometimes people ask me, does sexlessness cause cheating? It can certainly contribute to a 'bad' marriage and therefore make someone *more likely* (yet not fated) to cheat. However, the reverse can also be true—that many people who are cheating will have sexless marriages.

There are two main therapy camps when it comes to dealing with sexless couples. One camp believes that if you connect a

---

[5] John H. Kim, Joseph Tak-Fai Lau, Ka-Kin Cheuk, 'Sexlessness among Married Chinese Adults in Hong Kong: Prevalence and Associated Factors', *The Journal of Sexual Medicine*, 6(11) (Nov 2009), pp. 2997–3007, https://www.sciencedirect.com/science/article/abs/pii/S174360951532333X (accessed 15 Feb, 2023).

couple emotionally then the sexual connection will come back. I agree that *sometimes* sexual connection can be an extension of an emotional connection, and for some couples more than others.

However, I resonate more with the second camp, which believes that sexual connection often needs more than just an emotional boost. There are often overlooked reasons for sexlessness, some of them simpler to treat than others.

Sex is complicated, indeed.

Chapter 9

Loveless Marriages

'I think I killed my baby.' Cybil came to me under a dark cloud of mother's guilt, convinced she was to blame for the death of her unborn child.

Behind her thick, black-rimmed glasses, her eyes appeared vacant. She was dressed in a navy power suit accentuated by a gleaming large white pearl necklace and was unfailingly polite and kind. She looked uncomfortable throughout our first session, though, as if at once she had a lot to say and nothing at all. She spoke in a soft tone and hesitated often as she explained she was in a loveless marriage.

Cybil and her husband Ron were an Australian Chinese couple in their late 30s. They had been together for eleven years, married for nine, and had a five-year-old daughter called Charlotte. Yet for the past decade they had worked long hours in Singapore's notoriously competitive banking industry and lived virtually separate lives.

A few months before she came to see me, on a rare late night when they were both at home, they had drunk a bottle of wine and had sex without protection for the first time in years. Soon after, Cybil had begun suffering morning sickness and nausea. A sinking feeling of dread had filled her—she wasn't ready for a second baby. She had just been promoted to a regional

management role and wasn't eager to co-parent another child
with her 'absent' husband.

After taking a dozen pregnancy tests and getting a dozen
positive results, she had gone into denial for two weeks and
started to drink excessively every night, as soon as her daughter
went to sleep. When she told her husband about the pregnancy,
he showed little emotion.

'You know what he said after I told him? He said, "OK, I
guess we'll have another kid,"' she recalled.

In her eleventh week of pregnancy, Cybil had gone to see
the doctor by herself as she had noticed that her once intense
nausea had stopped completely, and she didn't know whether to
feel delighted or concerned.

When the ultrasound found no heartbeat, an overwhelming
sense of guilt and shame washed over her, and she wept bitterly in
the bathroom stall of the doctor's office. She was unable to face
returning to work that afternoon and sent Ron a text saying, 'I'm
so sorry. I killed the baby.'

This was the moment she decided to give Ron an ultimatum:
to face up to their 'broken' marriage and decide finally whether to
stay together or not.

To her surprise, Ron rushed home and asked her to speak.
He was saddened to hear their baby had died and, again to Cybil's
surprise, didn't blame her. She sensed in his reaction that there
might yet have been a tiny spark left in their relationship—and
that had made her feel even worse.

'It was a bit confusing. I thought when I texted Ron, he would
ignore it or blow up. I would have taken either response as the nail
in the coffin for our marriage. And yet, he did neither. He came
home from work and cried when he heard the baby died. I told
him I must've killed the baby by drinking so excessively, but he
didn't blame me at all and said it was unlikely that was the cause,'
Cybil shared.

Cybil had a very kind disposition, yet she was a woman of few words in the therapy room. She told me at the beginning of one session, 'I am not used to this kind of talking. It's my first time in therapy, and I'm not a big talker, so please ask me questions or something.'

With some clients, they talk a mile a minute and I fashion myself a traffic cop. Please pause! Turn to the right! Traffic ahead, please slow down! With others, though, like Cybil, I operate more like a dentist, using all the tools at my disposal to extract their words and thoughts.

I asked her about her confusion at her husband's sadness over their baby's death and—what sounded like—his compassion for her. (I used the word 'baby' deliberately, to match Cybil's language. Had she referred to a 'foetus', then so too would I have done.)

'I was so convinced the love between us had died that when I started drinking, I must have thought that my husband would be relieved to know we wouldn't have another baby. We never discussed this, I just assumed,' she said.

'Cybil, do you want to speak more about your feelings about the baby or your marriage?' I wondered out loud. I felt a heavy sadness, a disoriented sadness about what this all meant for her.

'I basically need more support in my marriage and for our daughter, Charlotte. I have none,' she said as her eyes welled up. I could see the tap dripping and knew it was one turn from flowing out of control.

She hinted at how sad and lonely she was in her marriage.

I see many clients who have a partner and yet still feel lonely. They feel ignored. Unheard. Not seen. Taken for granted. Rejected. They wonder if their partner loves someone else, or whether they have just checked out, or whether it's all too late to do anything about it anyway. Sometimes both partners are feeling and wondering a lot without the other knowing. I've lost count of the times one person has expressed utter despair about the marriage and the other looks at them and says, 'I had no idea. I also feel that.'

With lovelessness often comes distance, and with distance often comes a painful sea of emotions, torturous wondering, and countless assumptions. These assumptions often lead people to act as if they're true and thus further the distance.

In some relationships, one day, one partner will dare to say something and dare to breathe new life into the relationship. For others, this day never comes, and the lovelessness sinks the relationship.

Even in these cases though, with proper support, there is often much that can be done. But because love is a two-handed game, what can be done depends on the willingness of both partners. I have worked with loveless couples who have ended up separated or divorced, those who have broken the ice before retreating into their respective caves, those who have ended up reconnecting with their love and each other, and those who construct an even more loving relationship.

In addition to the assumptions Cybil had started making, she did what many do in loveless marriages and set the bar low. 'I'm not shooting for the moon. I don't feel this marriage is going to last. It's been years—we basically don't talk with each other. We don't have sex,' she said in a respectful tone without denigrating her husband.

Setting the bar low is not what helps couples reconnect and often leads to a self-fulfilling prophecy: the bar is low, so little effort is made, and the lack of effort becomes proof positive the relationship is done.

I did not share this with Cybil, as I wanted to see if she wanted to work on her marriage. I wanted first to let her know that most couples experience lovelessness at one point or another and see how she would respond to this. Many people walk around wrongly believing that the moment they're out of love, boom, the relationship is done. If you buy into the fantasy that marriage is a fairy tale, smooth, or linear, then this makes sense. It *is* just a fantasy.

'Cybil, I hear you on all this. In most long-term relationships, many people fall in and out of love multiple times throughout the years. That's different from wanting to end the relationship. Do you want to work on your marriage? I suggest bringing your husband in for couples therapy, if so. If you don't want to work on your marriage, then please tell me what support you need,' I said.

She responded, 'If he agreed to see you, would you see him first individually? He's never been to therapy before, so I think coming in the room all together might be a bit intimidating for him. But if he's open to seeing you first individually, then I'd be open to couples therapy eventually. But I don't know, maybe he just wants to divorce. Maybe he's already done.'

I could sense there was trepidation about her husband not wanting to work on the marriage, and this is often a healthy sign that there's still emotion about the other person. When I ask people if they want to work on their marriage, and I get contempt, something that sounds like 'they will never change', or fatalism, or a lack of care or willingness to change, then that is often a sign that the person is not just out of love but has both checked out and wants out.

'That sounds like a solid idea, if he's willing,' I responded. 'Maybe he is done. I don't know, and it sounds like you don't know either. That we can't control. However, if you do want to work on this, then it would be helpful to check out some of the assumptions you've made and see if your husband has made assumptions of his own. I call this a "Wall of Assumptions" in a relationship—when one or both people make so many assumptions about the other, a wall comes up, and you can't even see the other person anymore, just the assumptions.'

'Let's try that,' she said with a teary smile.

Assumptions abound

Ron came to see me the following week and soon into the session shared, 'Cybil and I used to be more connected. We used to have sex all the time. But it really wasn't just the sex. We used to be a ten out of ten.'

'Where are you now on a scale of one to ten?' I asked.

'A three,' he said, eyes welling up.

'What are you feeling when you say that?' I asked.

'Just awful. I can't believe we've gone from a ten to a three. I miss those days when we were a ten,' he said wholeheartedly.

Ron then rolled back the clock to bring me into the ten out of ten.

He told me a story of two children born to Chinese immigrants, whose parents had struggled to make ends meet by running grocery stores, and how those children grew up to win the intellectual lottery by getting into top Australian universities. He told me how those two met at an internship one summer before graduating. How they would go on long trail runs together, cook together, laugh together, and be 'best friends with each other's best interests at heart'. He told me how they shared values and goals, passion and friendship, commitment and respect. He was right; it was a solid ten out of ten.

He also told me how their parents had never taught them about the possibility of love in a marriage. Both sets of parents valued marriage highly, but love? Love was a potential bonus in a relationship—not a necessary ingredient. In fact, their parents modelled loveless marriages.

When Cybil and Ron got together, they had both pledged to uphold some of their family traditions, such as having a Chinese wedding and giving any children a Chinese name in addition to an Anglicized one.

However, they had also both wanted to embrace love as a necessary ingredient in a marriage. They felt they could embrace both tradition and love—and 'treasured' the fact that they both felt the same way. This is a question I hear a lot with my clients who have grown up with Asian parents yet have come of age, studied, and/or lived abroad: Can we as a couple be in a relationship that honours (at least some of) our traditional family values while also integrating some of our own?

'I used to leave work really excited to go home. We would share about our days, go for walks, and really take an interest in each other's lives. Now, I dread going home because she's usually asleep or ignores me. I feel like I'm sleeping with a stranger,' he said.

'How about seeing your daughter at home? How does that make you feel?' I asked.

'I'm thirty-eight years old, and the only regret I have is not being there for my daughter. I hung out with my buddies and watched sports when she was a baby. Because I wasn't there when she was young, I don't think she feels that close to me. It's a terrible feeling. I love her so much. My wife put her career on hold at the time Charlotte was born, and they were together all the time. Our daughter seemed so attached to my wife. I was a crap dad when she was a baby. I wasn't even present at the birth—I was with my buddies. Throughout the first year of Charlotte's life, Cybil and I basically stopped talking to each other. We stopped having sex. Our communication went out the window. We used to text and call each other all the time, but we don't have a marriage anymore, and there are basically no texts or calls unless it involves Charlotte,' he responded.

'Ron, I believe you that it feels like you don't have a marriage right now. Cybil has shared that she's willing to do couples therapy to see if we can reconnect you two. Does that sound like something you would want?' I asked.

He bawled, 'I am in. But I really don't know if Cybil loves me at all anymore.'

These two were loveless, but their love wasn't dead.

Behind the wall

Cybil and Ron walked in later that week together, and I could tell there was a Wall of Assumptions between them yet also lots of emotion and an eagerness to connect. They kept looking at each other and then down or away. Ron looked at Cybil, and very delicately, with a soft tone, said, 'Thank you for bringing me here today, and thank you for showing up, Cybil.'

Cybil pressed her lips together and took a deep breath. 'Thank you, Ron, for coming, and thank you, Allison, for your time.'

It was a very cordial, positive start. It had been years since they had felt that 'ten out of ten' kind of connection.

'It was a big step for you both to be here today,' I said slowly. I could sense that breaking the ice was the immediate goal. With couples, that sometimes means sitting all together in an awkwardness commanded by years together and years disconnected. With Cybil and Ron, it was exactly this kind of awkwardness. They both fidgeted in their seats, glanced up at one another, then right back down, looked at me to say something, and then made some chitchat about Charlotte's after-school activity later that afternoon.

'How would you two feel if we focus today just on you two and your marriage?' I asked very calmly. I could sense they both wanted to and yet were terrified of doing so. I then said, 'I can still feel quite a strong connection between you two, for what that's worth.'

I share this with a couple only when I genuinely feel and sense a connection, and it is always telling how they respond.

'Do you still love me, Cybil?' Ron said, swallowing and fighting back tears.

She looked down at her hands, folded in her lap, with her eyes welling up. Her lips were moving, with neither sounds nor words coming out. She started to weep, as did Ron. This is often one of the scariest questions a partner can ask the other in a loveless relationship, and I have witnessed a whole spectrum of responses.

'Yes. I just have felt so alone since Charlotte was born,' Cybil said with her hands now over her tear-drenched eyes. 'I thought you enjoyed drinking with your buddies more, and you didn't want kids and resented Charlotte and me.'

'Not at all. I still am not sure why I kept going out or ignoring you. It was some kind of escape, I imagine,' he said. 'I deeply regret not being there for Charlotte. I've missed her major milestones. And I deeply regret not being there when she was born or helping you at all.'

'I didn't even know you had any regrets,' she said.

'I am so sorry,' Ron responded.

'I am too. I am sorry that I have just allowed the distance to keep growing,' Cybil shared.

I sat in silence to allow their words to sink in as they continued to run their assumptions past one another—assumptions that the other was not in love, or did not want to be married, was in love with someone else, or resented Charlotte. The list went on and on. It always does.

Assumptions in a loveless marriage have a way of snowballing. It usually starts with something innocuous. For example, he's not taking out the rubbish anymore, so perhaps he doesn't care? That then snowballs into maybe it's not just the rubbish, maybe he doesn't love me, maybe he never loved me, maybe we never should have married, maybe I should have seen the red flags earlier, maybe this marriage is over. The snowball just keeps going.

I let Cybil and Ron empty the contents of the rubbish bins in their respective minds as they were both doing so respectfully and curiously. It was important to give them space to share these assumptions for a couple of reasons. Firstly, this was the only connection that they'd had in years. Secondly, it would give each of them a chance to respond to the assumptions, and for us all together to figure out why they were making them.

Once they had exchanged assumptions—and they looked genuinely surprised by most of them—Cybil turned to Ron and said, 'Can I just ask, why did you not want to be with me during the labour or with Charlotte and me when she was a baby?'

'I didn't know what to do, so I avoided being a father. I thought when you were pregnant, being a dad would just come naturally to me. As it got closer to the time you gave birth, I got scared and just avoided sharing this with you,' Ron responded.

In that moment, I could sense that avoidance would be, as it is with most loveless couples, a topic for us to explore at another hour. This hour was about something more immediate, the chance for each of them to witness the other's loneliness and longing and, perhaps, to feel a momentary sense of reconnection.

Cybil had tears streaming down her face. 'I know this is just the start, but it's so meaningful to hear him express regrets. I felt so alone thinking he felt nothing,' she said.

They ended this session both in tears, holding hands, and committed to regular couples therapy for the next few months.

Yes, regrets

When Ron was talking about his deep regret that he wasn't there for his first child's early years, I thought of the regret I experienced having been away for a few months from my first child when he was about five years old.

We were living in Hong Kong at the time, and I was convinced I needed to go to the United States to pursue my clinical doctorate. It was a five-year programme, and I knew this would eventually mean my husband and son moving to the United States too, even though not one of us had any desire to live there again. We were strapped financially, and logistically it made no sense to keep flying from Hong Kong to New York and vice versa.

I remember once flying back to Hong Kong from New York to make my son's birthday party. I had handed in a paper that morning, took an exam in the afternoon, rushed to the airport that evening, and cried much of that long plane ride, wondering, what is this costing *us?* I got off the plane and into a taxi in Hong Kong, only to ask the driver to pull to the side of the road. All of a sudden, I had begun to feel incredibly dizzy. I opened the door and vomited.

Indeed, my selfish choice had been making everyone dizzy.

I knew on some level my decision was me choosing what I thought was necessary over what was actually necessary: being with my son and husband, staying in Asia where we all wanted to be, and conserving finances. I conflated what I thought was necessary over what actually was at the expense of my family, and it haunts me to this day.

After the first semester, I realized moving to New York wasn't working logistically or spiritually, so I came back to Hong Kong and ultimately left the programme. I remember telling some friends at the time that I regretted my decision even to join the programme in the first place and often being met with a 'No regrets!' kind of response—as if expressing regret was repellent.

But I used my regret to fuel a stronger commitment to being a present parent. Surely that's a positive thing? At the same time, I am aware there are no psychological erasers. I always feel a dull pang of regret whenever I see a photo of my son around that time or when he asks me sometimes, 'Remember, mom, when you were in New York?'

I use that experience to connect more deeply with my clients. I don't believe in talking other people out of their regrets or anything they are feeling. I may hope to reframe a situation, look at it from another angle, see the potential for growth, or chart a pathway out of the intensity of the experience.

Yet, I've learned not to kick into action mode when something like a regret is in the room, until there is a clear invitation to do so. Most people don't have space to share what they truly regret, and having regrets is part of the human experience.

Coming back together

We met together two weeks later and every following two weeks over the next few months. We were able to cover a lot of ground as both Cybil and Ron wanted to work on their marriage and embraced the other's changes.

Ron reported, 'Cybil and I had a really nice week together. We took our daughter out a couple of times for activities and had a date night. We were able to reflect on how lonely both of us had been and started to laugh again and feel like we were in the marriage together.'

They both smiled cautiously as if they wanted to hold onto this connection forever yet were concerned at how fragile it was. And, in truth, it was. Working with loveless couples has taught me just how fragile love can be.

Couples with the most compelling love stories have turned up in my therapy room loveless. So too have couples whose love has been chipped away over the years by a marital injury here, another there, or been taken for granted and ignored. The couples who end up restoring their love are those that lock this fragility firmly in the vaults of their hearts, knowing how painful it is to be on the verge of loss.

Here are some of the ideas and questions I explore with loveless couples like Cybil and Ron:
Loveless checklist:

1. Normalize: This is often a first and necessary step. The idea is to get across to the client just how many couples, at one point or another, in a long-term relationship, will identify as loveless. Many people exhale just on hearing this as many mistakenly believe that *other people's* marriages are fairy tales. Social media has made this worse, in my experience, feeding the image that *other people's* marriages are vacations in Fiji and Mai Tais all the time. Cybil and Ron both watched their parents model loveless marriages and were told that marriage is about family obligation and perseverance, so both were afraid that their state of lovelessness meant they were becoming their parents.

2. Check for assumptions: Is there a Wall of Assumptions? Cybil and Ron certainly had one. And, with this wall, there's often an aversion to, and inexperience with, having difficult conversations. With Cybil and Ron, they were able to share their assumptions, respond to these respectfully and constructively, and work on how to have difficult conversations. For example, Cybil being truthful about how she felt about Ron being with his friends in a bar while she was in labour with Charlotte or Ron discussing his feelings of being ignored and shut off.

3. Check for injuries: Every long-term relationship has some injuries, and some of these can contribute to lovelessness. An injury may be something like an affair yet can also be emotional neglect or financial betrayal. There are many examples of injuries. With Cybil and Ron, one of the injuries was Ron being absent from their daughter's birth. We needed to work on not only how to have the

difficult conversation around how this made Cybil feel but also how to heal it, which required Cybil witnessing a profound sense of remorse from Ron. Just like physical wounds, not all emotional wounds can fully heal, and sometimes repairing a marriage requires an ounce of acceptance of this.

4. Explore their plan for the lovelessness: Do they want to accept it, reconnect, build something new? Many couples can get to the *why*—why they are loveless; yet the next steps of the *what or how*—what they want to do about it and how—are not always clear. I have worked with many couples who decide that they want to accept the lovelessness and feel they are getting enough from the marriage and don't 'need' the love. I've worked with couples who have had arranged marriages and are loveless from the beginning. There are also couples whose love has faded over the years for various reasons, yet due to family obligations decide to focus on other priorities and don't want to invest in reconnecting. Cybil and Ron were very clear they wanted to reconnect and deepen their love. The key with this type of couple is whether they want to focus on a past connection—and try to evolve it—or whether they are looking to build something new, or what I call a new 2.0 version of their relationship.

5. Tell the truth lovingly: People are often allergic to asking for change and lean more on passive acceptance only to find that the emotional and sexual distance in the marriage widens. Learning to discern what you want to change, what you can learn to accept, and how to have the conversation about what is possible is paramount to transforming a marriage at any stage of life. Many people will clobber their partners with demands without speaking like a team or making the changes work for both people, or they will go to the opposite extreme and

swallow their feelings and desires for change. Both Cybil and Ron were in the latter category and wanted to ask the other to change yet thought they 'shouldn't' and were scared that the other would reject this need for change. In therapy, we worked on how to lovingly ask your partner to make changes, and Cybil and Ron were able to do this after they were clear both valued growth and were willing to make changes.

6. Check for value conflicts: With some couples, lovelessness can result from a conflicting value or values. For example, I worked with a couple in which the husband, an American expat, refused to provide a financial allowance and care for his Chinese parents-in-law. He saw this as 'not his responsibility' and valued independence whereas his wife valued filial piety. This, in part, eroded the love between them as the wife saw taking care of her parents as a way for them to work as a team and value their family together. With Cybil and Ron, at their core, they had a strong overlap in values. Ron was ultimately willing to shift his relationship with the daughter and take on more of the responsibilities with her. Once we worked on telling the truth lovingly, they added growth to their value set.

7. Any dreams ignored? In loveless relationships, people often tell me their dreams and desires seem ignored by their partner and therefore they don't feel loved and supported. Cybil shared that because she came home each night after work to care for Charlotte, she had neglected her dream of getting an MBA degree. They agreed that Cybil could start her MBA programme and that Ron would be home each night she had classes. This would also help Ron invest in his relationship with their daughter. It turned out both had a dream of having another baby yet were terrified to tell the other and terrified their marriage

couldn't sustain it. We worked on how they could plan on having another baby and how the experience this time could be different.

8. Misery stabilizers: In many relationships, people start leaning on what author and therapist Terry Real calls 'misery stabilizers'—what a couple will turn to instead of each other. Cybil was turning to her daughter and too much alcohol while Ron was turning towards his friends and partying. The more they leaned on these misery stabilizers, the more the distance and assumptions grew, and their connection dimmed. This led to avoiding difficult conversations, and that's something we worked on together. Misery stabilizers can be in the form of substances such as drink or drugs but aren't always just that. They can also be in the form of shopping, cheating, only speaking with a friend instead of a partner about a marital issue, exercising too much, workaholism, or a whole host of other activities or relationships that temporarily bring relief from the pain, misery, or challenges in a relationship yet ultimately detract from a loving connection in a marriage.

9. Demarcate and re-prioritize: Instead of engaging in toxic blaming and perverse communication, can a couple start afresh and say that was then, this is now? It's quite difficult for couples in loveless marriages to do this because, usually, at least one person is trying to hold the person in the history, often contemptuously, thinking, 'You'll never change.' Or they will battle endlessly over the 'truth' or what *really* happened and who is *really* to blame. Cybil and Ron were able to demarcate the past from the present, and this is often one of the most challenging steps in helping couples to share love again. They were also willing to spend more time together. Sometimes couples resist

doing this, claiming they are 'too busy', which makes it very challenging to connect.

A year later, Cybil and Ron were preparing for their second child and their love felt alive again. When Cybil was around twenty weeks pregnant, we worked on ways to 'rescript' the experience with the second baby. We couldn't turn back the clock and have Ron be present for Charlotte's birth, but we could make things different for baby number two. Too many couples get stuck on this point, wanting desperately to rewind and redo.

We worked on ways for Ron to be more present, Cybil to be more expressive of her needs, and for them both to be clear about the experience they wanted to share.

After their son, Myles, was born, they sent me an email. Cybil wrote, 'Ron was a total star. He was present during the labour and delivery, and we're now settled at home as a family. The best part is we no longer make assumptions, and we no longer feel alone in the marriage.'

I still have a warm feeling in my heart about them. Every time I hold myself, my husband, or another in history, I think back to the grace they gave each other, the grace that allowed them to be different and do differently.

That was then; this is now.

An Asian cultural stamp

There are loveless couples in every culture, and many common themes that link them, but I've learned through my work that there are also unique cultural factors at play here in Asia.

Love matches are a relatively modern phenomenon compared to the ancient tradition of arranged marriages that has long united and formed alliances between wealthy East Asian families, including in imperial China where a matchmaker would look for suitable candidates and do background checks on their family's status, character, and reputation. Since the 1950s, arranged marriages have been illegal in China, but parents still factor heavily in their children's decisions. In South Asia, arranged marriages are very much a live tradition.

In many cultures in Asia, there exists a strong principle of respecting one's elders and an obligation to care for them in their old age. Giving allowances to parents, taking care of their needs and having the in-laws live under the same roof are part and parcel of marrying two families. A marriage, unlike in many Western countries, is not about two individuals coming together but rather about family commitment and responsibility. This can often be an incredible investment in the family unit, and for some families this works harmoniously.

I once had a Singaporean client, Clara, who was married and living at home with her in-laws. She was educated in the UK for secondary school and university and had one foot firmly in the West and one in the East culturally, as she herself put it. Her parents made clear that when Clara started working, she would need to give them a generous monthly allowance even after she got married. It was highly conflicting for her to do so because of the influences Clara felt from living in the UK during a formative time—she described it to me as, 'My head was spinning about it.' Clara wondered whether she and her husband would want their own children to do this.

Clara lost her job at a bank and a few months later found another role in consulting with a reduced salary—50 per cent of what she made at the bank. Yet out of a sense of shame and filial piety, she still gave the same allowance to her parents, which meant she could no longer save money or help pay for anything for her in-laws. This caused stress in her marriage, which ultimately became both sexless and loveless. She explained, 'This pressure to provide for our families drained us, and we had no privacy and time for each other.'

Another thing I have learned is that Asian couples will often hide their marital problems to save face with their communities and families. Many clients told me this was one of the reasons they had chosen an expat therapist. They didn't want to tell their problems to their parents and families because they would be told, 'Marriage is hard. Stick with it. That's what I did.' It's common for parents to tell their adult children to push through rocky marriages and affairs. This is in part because residual or generational stigma towards divorce is widespread—as it is towards getting therapy.

The 'solution' is not to copy and paste what people are doing in the West, which sometimes translates into oversharing, over-emoting, self-obsession, and a commitment to telling 'one's truth' at all costs.

Rather, it lies in striking a balance between the values of the individual and of their cultures, in a delicate fusion of family, harmony, and filial piety with connection, love, and intimacy.

Chapter 10

Revenge is Rarely Sweet

'I *could* work on this. But, Allison, the thought of *this* staying with us forever? I don't want that, this all has shaken me and made me realize how fragile life is,' Ming said.

Ming, a Hong Kong–Chinese man in his late forties and a law partner at a local firm, with jet-black spiky gelled hair and a boyish face, came to see me in Hong Kong, with rage pulsing throughout his whole system. He took his suit jacket off at the beginning of the session and threw it on the chair next to his. I watched his heart and biceps pulsating from inside his spiffy white work shirt as he told me the story of his Hong Kong–Chinese wife, Yan, of seven years.

Yan had slept with Ming's boss during a drunken night out. They had kept on with the relationship behind his back for months, replete with racy 'quickies' during lunchtime and a long list of WhatsApp exchanges. What deepened the traumatic double betrayal was he found a cache of their text messages, tearing him down as a husband. Ming always loved painting as a hobby and would often share his paintings with Yan. In the text messages, Ming found a slew of exchanges between his wife and boss that humiliated him. 'Look how pathetic my husband is—he wastes so much time on the weekends painting these ugly paintings. Uh, soooo lame. That's why I'm so turned on by you. Finally, a real man,' Yan wrote with racy emojis. Ming's boss would respond with a laughing emoji or some hideous comment.

There's nothing like humiliation to enrage us. I felt protective of Ming and a deep reservoir of empathy. Ming was an extremely kind and gentle man, a truly solid person, yet the adultery gave him an uncontrollable urge to hurt this boss physically, and he started having intrusive thoughts. He fantasized about meeting his boss in an empty lift and throwing him against the wall. In the middle of eating lunch, he would be distracted by the thought of running down the hall in his office, closing his boss's door, and beating him up. These dark fantasies hunted him down while he was trying to do his work, at 2 a.m., any hour the rage could find him; 2 a.m. is the unfavourable hour the betrayed of the world know well, also the hour the anxious of the world know well.

During this first session, he was hyper-focused on these text exchanges and how his boss had betrayed him. The boss was in the room with us, *energetically*, almost the whole hour. I always pay attention to who is in the room *energetically* with clients—it's often a reflection of who is in their psychic space. Today, there was talk of humiliation. There was talk of rage towards his boss. Yan? His marriage? Nowhere to be found.

There was plenty of rage to go around, though. In subsequent sessions, I suggested we redirect the conversation to how Ming was feeling, how he felt towards his wife, and what this all meant for his marriage. I understood why Ming was avoiding speaking about her—we all try, to varying degrees, to avoid the pain we're swimming in. He told me he wasn't sure what he was feeling; that the humiliation and rage eclipsed everything.

When I asked about Yan, he said she had shown no remorse and even kicked him, metaphorically, when he was down. One day he was crying, and Yan turned to him with a self-righteous tone and said, 'How can I even pretend to be turned on by you anymore? I mean, I guess I should be sorry that I chose your boss, but come on, Ming, you haven't done it for me in a few years.'

When I asked whether he wanted to work on his marriage, he was too numb to respond with a yes, no, or even a maybe. He said that he had asked Yan if she would consider couples therapy, and she flatly refused. When Ming tried to stand up to her, express his pain, and speak about boundaries in their relationship going forward, she didn't bat an eyelid.

They had no children, and he was at a crossroads. Ming knew he was potentially looking at the rest of his life alone with his humiliation and alone with his sadness as Yan had shown no interest in change and told him point blank he was to blame. He could go along with his days, maybe dance a bit with delusion and tell himself a terribly toxic tale that he deserved this. Or he could be courageous and leap into the unknown.

Ming became clearer with each session that he was leaning towards a divorce and realized he was more upset about the idea of telling his parents about it than actually leaving Yan. His parents, especially his father, had always sent a strong message to avoid divorce at all costs, telling Ming that marriage for everyone is 'mostly hard' and 'divorce will bring shame to the family's name'. Ming could do hard. He couldn't deal with a soul theft, though.

We worked on how to respectfully bring up a possible divorce with his parents that honoured their Chinese value of marriage and saving face yet also made space for his likely decision to leave Yan. He knew deep, deep down that his family would ultimately support him.

I often help clients respect and uphold what matters to their families and culture along with the decisions they make. Part of what drew me to Asia were the collectivist values—harmony, honour, family, to name some—and I feel most of my Asian clients do want to at least respect their family members' feelings on these issues. Even my clients who have studied abroad are typically allergic to pushing what I have come to term 'Authenticity at Any Cost' on their families.

'Allison, it's very important I show respect to my family when I share this news. I don't want to bulldoze them with some speech about being an individual or authentic or anything like that. Ever since I went to law school in the USA, my parents have been concerned my values have shifted and that I've become focused on myself. The truth is they have shifted slightly, yet my family is still my most important value,' Ming said.

Ming and I role-played over a couple of sessions how he could share the news with his family and make sure he did respect the values they held dearly. He would tear up each time we did. The times I would role-play his mother or father, his eyes would well up.

We also worked a lot on building Ming's emotional vocabulary and ability to express his needs. I came to know through the stories of his marriage that his wife had little regard for either his emotions or needs, so as the years went by, he buried his heart and basically did what she wanted.

I asked Ming if he would show me photos of his paintings as we worked on building his emotional vocabulary. I wanted a direct lens and pathway into the non-rational part of him so that I could use it as a springboard for discussions on how he felt, what he wanted, and more about his needs. In the room together, I could feel his warmth and depth, even more so when he showed me photos of his paintings. His paintings reflected curiosity in others, a spectrum of human experiences, and yes, pain.

For the rage, I encouraged Ming to increase his physical exercise and focus on sports such as boxing, Thai kickboxing, or running. We also used some of his anger to connect with the feelings underneath and to understand what he wanted in his relationships and how to cultivate healthier internal boundaries. Ming was used to letting things roll off his shoulders as he preferred to avoid conflict. I told him that all relationships have conflicts, that how we respond to them is crucial for the long-term health of the relationship and that doing so can lead to growth.

He also decided he needed to move out of the apartment with Yan at the earliest and move to another law firm. We worked on a plan that he would hand in his resignation to the head of human resources instead of going to his boss directly. He told them he would agree to work his notice period yet did not want any further contact with his boss. The head of human resources dared not ask why, as his boss was the managing partner of the firm. Ming accepted he would silently rage against the machine.

He came to see me a few months after the divorce was finalized and told me he had secured a partnership at an American law firm and was in a relationship with a lovely, kind woman named Thang.

I asked what Thang thought of his paintings.

Burning down the house

Over the years, I've worked with several clients who have taken revenge on an unfaithful spouse and/or affair partner. I've also heard many fantasize about taking revenge on social media—wanting to tear down the partner, have the world cancel them, and see their pain validated in the court of public opinion.

This thinking is seductive in moments of anger—believing that revenge will translate into pain for others and peace for ourselves, falsely believing that 'justice' has been served. However, acting on impulse often leads to more distress. To slow down impulse, I have suggested to more clients than I can count to put a note on their devices that reads, 'Urgency is the enemy.'

During the pandemic, I saw an uptick in this sort of behaviour as people were home, on social media a lot, trigger happy. They were also navigating complex layers of stress. Add that to the news of an affair, phone in hand, and the impulse to hurt the other person seemed all too easy.

Before the pandemic, I would hear more about physical forms of revenge, like clients who confronted their rivals face-to-face, or threw their partner's clothing out of the window or burned their belongings—all desperate displays of pain.

I have been very clear not to condone such acts, pointing out to my clients that they can learn ways to avoid indulging their anger. The first step is to name the emotion, not deny its existence—rage is real, like any other emotion. The next is to pause long enough to see there are different ways to process it.

Part of my work is getting people to play out the choices in their lives—to have frequent conversations with their future self.

- If this, then that. If I do this, if I call my husband's affair partner and rip her to shreds, then what? Then, I may feel great and grandiose for about a day—max—and then once the adrenaline leaves my system, I am left no better.
- A year from now, what will I wish I had done? If I tear my partner apart on social media, and my child's teacher sees the post, how will that make me feel?

I also teach clients about how to spot the tell-tale signs their rage is about to show up. For some, the tip-off is physical. During the pandemic, for example, I had a record number of referrals from gastroenterologists and neurologists with patients experiencing psychosomatic stomach aches and headaches. In Asia, emotions are often somatic—people here will sometimes describe their feelings in terms of physical experiences such as a stomach ache when they're anxious or feeling 'tired' when they are depressed. There are even culturally bound somatization disorders such as *Hwa-Byung* in Korea, which is also represented in traditional Chinese medicine, meaning 'neurotic fire'. It mostly manifests as physical symptoms after someone experiences a perceived injustice and suppresses emotions. But for some, the tip-off is cognitive—their thoughts start to spiral, for example. And for others, it's spiritual—they sense that the ground has shifted beneath them.

Things rarely turn out well for the person who exacts the revenge and wants to ruin the cheater, even if they get a fleeting feeling of having accomplished something. After their adrenaline has died down, all that is left is collateral damage.

Of course, it is more productive to focus on how the hurt partner is feeling, and what this all means for their relationship. Rage can be seductive, as it was for Ming when we first met. It tells us so many lies. And the most seductive lie of all is that if we translate our rage into revenge, our pain will disappear.

Chapter 11

The Truth is a Kaleidoscope

Was Hong Kong a graveyard for their marriage?

Tricia and Ben were Americans in their late thirties who had moved to Hong Kong eight years ago. They were college sweethearts from University of Missouri, athletic brunettes reminiscent of Ken and Barbie dolls, and dressed as if they had never left that college campus. They wore khakis and Birkenstocks, and Ben often sported a University of Missouri baseball cap.

Ben, thirty-nine, worked for a global insurance company and had seen his career take off in Hong Kong. He held a senior executive role, travelling extensively in the region. Before they moved to Hong Kong, Tricia, thirty-seven, had worked in Missouri briefly in communications, and, for most of their time abroad, she had been a trailing spouse.

Ben was given the opportunity to come to Hong Kong with his work, and they had two weeks to make the decision. It seemed like an adventure, they thought. Neither had been to Asia before. They figured, why not.

Their first year abroad was full of travel and food porn. Sending photos of street food from places like Cambodia and Laos to their friends and families in Missouri became a habit. Tricia started a blog, full of photos of Ben and her smiling in 'exotic' places, eating 'exotic' food, and meeting 'exotic' people.

When Tricia spoke of their travels, she would punctuate her sentences with 'exotic' whenever possible. Yet, for all her professions of loving the exotic, Tricia also wanted to be in the 'comforts of an American bubble within Hong Kong'. That meant joining an American club, socializing with other Americans, and living in an area largely populated by Americans.

This suited Ben as well. He was travelling the region at his company's expense, climbing the corporate ladder, and loving Hong Kong. Tricia loved the idea of tagging along. When Ben was at work, she would walk the streets of Phnom Penh, Ho Chi Minh City, anywhere his company took him. She would take food photos, write her blog, and marvel at where their travels would take them next. Life seemed so exciting.

By the second year, though, Tricia had started to feel lonely and depressed and wondered how long the thrill of all things 'exotic' would last. She grew disillusioned with the idea of not working. Tricia's closest buddies, a group of American women, told her she should focus first on having a baby while in Hong Kong before thinking of her career. These women all had babies at home and every single one employed a least one full-time 'domestic worker' or 'helper'.

'Helpers' are usually young women from lower income countries—many of whom live in abject poverty—who take on the majority of a family's domestic chores, including baby duties, for startlingly low pay—the average monthly wage is about US$600. By law, in Hong Kong, they must live with their employer, meaning 'help' is on hand round the clock. They are seen as vital to the functioning of Hong Kong society, both local and expat, and with more than 350,000 of them in the city, they make up around ten per cent of the workforce.

Having helpers meant these friends of Tricia were free to spend hours each week on boozy lunches, at which they would often spend their time waxing on endlessly about how great it was to have 'help' and pitying their fellow mothers back in the United States, where very few can afford full-time help. The more Tricia listened to these women, the more she thought it was time to have a baby.

'I told Ben it was time for me to finally go off birth control. I was ready to have a baby. I knew we would eventually leave Hong Kong, and I didn't want to be back in the United States with a baby and not much help. I thought if we wanted a baby anyway, it would be better for the marriage just to have one here. I figured I would look for a job while also trying to get pregnant. I was shocked I got a laid-back kind of communications job a month after applying and was pregnant three months after trying.'

Ben looked at Tricia like there was more to this session than a story about a baby, as much as they both loved their daughter. He shook his head and put one hand on his forehead, covering up both eyes. He took a deep breath as he stared at Tricia who had her eyes glued to mine. They both had their arms folded.

He looked at me and said, 'I have to say, right up front, I'm here to discuss Tricia's cheating, not our daughter. Yes, great, we have domestic help in Hong Kong. What a luxury compared with our friends in the United States. But I don't want to waste time here.' He looked down at his watch and then looked at Tricia with disgust. Like come on, cut the crap, get to it.

Tricia continued to talk about struggling to have an identity abroad and how that shifted into her struggles now with a baby, stuck indoors mostly because of the pandemic. 'Ben doesn't understand how difficult it's been for me here. I loved our first year when we got to travel. The second year, though, I was sure I wanted a baby and thought maybe I'd start applying for a job. Then boom, I got a job within a month of applying, got pregnant three months later, and then the pandemic struck. I don't think he gets how difficult this has all been.'

Ben was not biting. He looked at her and took a deep breath. 'I'm not here, Tricia, to talk about your *tai tai* friends, our daughter, or some sob story,' he said sternly, using a colloquial Chinese term for the wife of an elected leader—or in this case, a wealthy married woman who does not work. 'I'm here to talk about our marriage and your cheating. *Your* cheating, Tricia. So, I'm sorry, but we either get to it, or I'm walking out this door, and I'm also ending this marriage.'

I looked at Tricia and told her I had heard everything she said. It's important that people feel they've been heard, and although Tricia was going off track, I needed to assure her first before redirecting the conversation. I told her I had metaphorically put her story on my bookshelf in a locked box. She could take it off the shelf at a different hour. But not now. Now was about the bleeding wound, a potentially fatal one.

Tricia started to cry, going through tissues at such a furious rate that I had to refill the box within five minutes. 'Allison, I had no identity. I was *that* trailing spouse. I thought having a baby or a job would give me a sense of identity, but . . .'

Ben interrupted her. 'Tricia, this is your final chance. Cut the bullshit.' He kept crossing and uncrossing his legs, arms folded, and I sensed Ben meant what he said. I had no doubt he would end the session and the marriage if Tricia continued building a story that smelt of justification. The years have taught me when someone is bluffing. This wasn't a game of poker for Ben.

'Fine, fine. I will get to it. But I do want space to eventually share more about my feelings and how Ben didn't care about any of the expectations and needs I had,' Tricia said.

I sensed a deep chasm between these two, growing by the second. I had to make a clear choice. Should I listen to more of what Tricia had to say and keep letting her know I had heard her and then attempt to pivot to the real conversation? Or do I refocus right now and assume the leadership needed in this moment? I chose the latter, holding their daughter in my heart. Ben had already made clear he would be out the therapy room door and marriage if this real conversation didn't happen now. It was Triciaville indefinitely, or we're getting to the betrayal.

'Tricia, I don't believe the marriage is strong enough right now to withstand this conversation about your feelings and experiences only. We will get to all of that in time. Right now, we have a potential crisis if we don't focus on the cheating. Ben is clear he will walk out this door and the marriage if we don't discuss what happened,' I said sternly.

She took a few breaths, Ben's seething anger growing with each one. As I watched them, I reminded myself to do my best to remain unattached to the outcome of the session and also their marriage. This is one of the hardest tasks as a therapist—especially working with couples—and one of the reasons I meditate before each session, to anchor myself in helping whoever is in front of me while also reminding myself to stay unattached to the outcome.

'Fine. So, I ended up having an affair. I said it,' Tricia said.

I had to pull out my imaginary dental kit and pull the teeth to get more details. Tricia claimed the affair began as an innocent friendship, with a younger, Spanish co-worker, Joao, full of texts about work projects; then the friendship caught on fire and became erotic. They met at his place mostly, even during the pandemic social distancing restrictions. He was living alone. They ended up falling in love and eventually Ben read email exchanges about their future plans, which included a move to Spain, lots of travels, lots of adventures, lots of references to Joao as 'an amazing Latin lover', and no mention of how their daughter or Ben fitted into this.

It was as if her current reality had been *erased*—something that happens all too often when one is in the intoxicating emotional and sexual throes of an affair. Devalue the spouse, erase reality.

Ben found out about Tricia's affair while in quarantine. One of their mutual friends, who had a common friend with Joao, sent Ben a text saying, 'Let's talk, man. I got some bad news. Text back when you're up, and let's Zoom.'

Bad news indeed.

Initially, Ben had wanted to end the marriage right after getting out of quarantine, but he used the remaining seven days instead to gather his thoughts and process his emotions. He admitted to 'hating' Tricia those seven days, feeling utterly emasculated and traumatized. He vowed to himself to seek revenge right away and decide whether to divorce after.

Instead of confronting Tricia when he got home, he pretended to play happy family and offered to watch their daughter the whole weekend so Tricia could get some time for herself. While Tricia was out of the house, Ben went through all her emails and photos, vitriol churning through his system.

On the Monday morning after, Ben emailed Tricia's boss all the incriminating emails and photos. Within days, Tricia was fired; the company was afraid of lawsuits from her younger male colleague and a potential PR mess. In a further fit of anger, Ben threw out all of Tricia's designer clothes and literally set them on fire. Many of these clothes had been bought by Tricia as a form of 'retail therapy' to relieve her emptiness and loneliness. Tricia was addicted to shopping, and her habit got worse during the lockdown. Self-medication came in the form of designer clothes and Joao.

With all of this on the table, Ben said very directly to Tricia, 'Look, if you love him, then let's end this marriage, and let's just cut to the chase.'

Tricia responded while trembling, 'It will never happen again. It was a mistake. I was so lonely. I want to rebuild. We have a good foundation together.'

'Are you evading yet another question?' he responded angrily. 'I'm asking you whether you love him. What's the answer?'

I turned to Tricia and asked, 'What is the answer?'

Nothing. Not a yes. Not a no. Just an empty silence.

Ben got up and stormed out of the room. I got up and went to talk to him. 'Ben, I fully get why you would want to storm out, and it's ultimately your choice whether you finish the session. I know this must be frustrating as Tricia is moving at a snail's pace. This is all too normal after an affair, yet I imagine the pain for you is quite intense. To be clear, I am not attached to whether you stay married or not. I am instead focused on supporting what Tricia and you want and doing my very best to reduce the vitriol between you two because I know that whatever is done in the therapy room is likely five times more intense at home. I'm holding your daughter in my heart this whole time. She is the victim of this vitriol.'

He filled a glass of cold water and drank it quickly before returning to the therapy room. Tricia was crying as he walked back in, and Ben started to cry as well. He turned to her with a heavy heart and said, 'I never imagined this would happen after moving to Hong Kong. We never should have moved here. It all seemed so exciting, but maybe that was the problem. Maybe we should have stayed in the United States. I want to stay here in Hong Kong, but if it means the end of the marriage, then I don't know, maybe we should go back to our roots.'

Tricia remained silent and ashamed.

'I was loving it here in Hong Kong, and I expected you would just figure it out like I did,' Ben told Tricia. Then he looked at me with a vulnerable look on his face and asked, 'Is that fair?'

I responded, 'That brings us to some important questions to explore next session. In the meantime, your homework is to be kind to each other for the sake of your daughter's wellbeing.

That's all. We will figure the rest all out together.' Being kind to each other is often the most challenging homework for a couple in crisis.

Trailing spouses

We continued for a handful of sessions and worked through some important issues. We spent time processing the affair, tried to heal some marital injuries from the past, and looked at what they wanted in the future. Throughout it all, however, Tricia's lack of heartfelt remorse and a consistent need for her to justify her affair impeded any real progress. It was clear her attachment to Joao was still very much alive. Ben ended up defeated and frustrated. We would inch forward only to take a massive step back. So, I suggested it might be good to meet individually to allow each party to process their feelings and be heard before coming back together for a focused session.

I met Tricia first, and she didn't want to speak about the marriage. She wanted to speak about Joao.

'Allison, I held back so much that first session. You probably thought my tears were about Ben, his pain, and the potential end to the marriage. The truth is that the tears were really about Joao. I think I'm still in love with him,' she shared.

I encouraged her to say more. There was clearly much more.

'Joao is the first man who really wanted to hear how I am feeling. I have tried to share with Ben time and time again my struggle of living abroad. I've told him that after our first year here that I just so wanted to go back to the USA. I wanted the comfort of our family. Ben was so focused on his career, and he just loved the idea of being in Asia. The more he would talk about staying in Asia one more year—for five years straight—the more I wanted to leave. When I met Joao, he made me feel heard, that

I shouldn't compromise. He was also struggling to be in Hong Kong, and we could so relate to each other. We were friends, lovers, all of it.'

I could sense this was just the tip of the emotional and sexual iceberg. I decided to reroute this to Ben to see first if she had once felt like this with him and to see if she wanted to discuss her marriage or was more focused on discussing the affair. 'Did you ever have this connection with Ben?' I asked.

'I did. When we were in college, we had a blast. We were absolutely buddies. We would laugh, share so many dreams about the future, and when we graduated, we moved in with each other and had a great connection. Our conflict in the early years was only centred on our extended family as I struggled to get along with Ben's mom. But we both agreed that we wanted to be together, and that this didn't matter all that much.'

I let Tricia know it would be impossible for her to work on the marriage and remain in a relationship with Joao. At this point, most clients will push back and say something like, 'Maybe some of your other clients can't do it, Allison, but I do believe I can.'

This thought pattern is, in part, what allows people to cross the line. The specialness.

I told Tricia, as I have told many clients, that the two things were psychologically mutually exclusive.

Tricia then wanted to switch gears and talk more about her experiences as a trailing spouse as she said she felt truly unseen by Ben in this respect. I indulged her. 'Sure, let's walk through a different door. What's your experience here been like?'

I talked with Tricia about her identity challenges as an expat and trailing spouse and how that could have affected her decision to have an intimate relationship with her colleague. It is not uncommon for trailing spouses to leave their identity in their home country as they follow their other half around the world.

Many sacrifice careers, connections, and relationships to move abroad and play second fiddle to their partner.

Tricia said that after the first year of being in Hong Kong, a heavy sense of loneliness and depression set in. The constellation of her marriage began changing—Ben was travelling more, they were spending less time together, and Ben started to assert more power over the financial decisions because he was earning more. As the years passed, the higher Ben climbed on the corporate ladder, the more power he would exert over their decision to stay in Asia. He would tell her, 'Our future depends on us staying here. I could never get these kinds of experiences back in the US.'

Tricia coped with those boozy lunches by putting herself in the American bubble, finding a laid-back job, having a baby, and shopping for designer clothes—getting a hit of dopamine from seeing the package arrive, and another hit when she would don the clothing and get a compliment from Joao; Ben barely noticed except when the credit card bill showed up.

There are many who thrive in the role of a trailing spouse and find the novelty and the chance for reinvention thrilling. There are those, though, who feel lost, disconnected, and that their identities have been stolen by another or circumstance. And then there are many who feel a mingling of contrasts—lost and found, lonely and connected, bewilderment and certitude. For Tricia, it depended which man she was with.

I asked Tricia to think about whether she wanted to work on ending the relationship with Joao and work on her marriage. I reminded her she could not be present and work on these two relationships at once. Specialness—grandiosity, in essence—lies to us when we are in emotional, sexual, or substance-induced states. An affair is just like that.

She responded, 'Let me first get my mind around not being able to do both. I'll email you.'

Packing up

Ben's individual session had an entirely different shape. He went straight for the practical before anything emotional.

'Look, I'm aware this marriage may not work out. I've consulted a lawyer already to figure out my options. My buddies have warned me that divorces abroad can be fucking messy, especially when there are kids involved. Luckily, Tricia and I have the same passports. One of my buddies who is American just got divorced from an Australian woman who wants to move back there—talk about a fucking headache. In any case, the lawyer gave me some sobering advice. He told me that I could try and stay in Hong Kong, yet there's a strong chance, especially given how unhappy Tricia is in Hong Kong, that she will ask that she and our daughter be relocated. So basically, he said it's better we stay married, and I keep a tight eye on Tricia's travels and don't allow her to travel to the US without me. Or I just bite the bullet and go back to the USA. He also said with the pandemic, the courts here have been closed for so long that if I do put in an application for divorce, it could be a long time before anything is settled,' Ben said, bluntly.

Because I work with so many couples with two different passports, I am used to these kinds of conversations with lawyers—relocation requests, alimony, custody, care, and control. In Hong Kong and Singapore, I see clients who will retain a particular lawyer just to make sure the spouse cannot. It's strategic, as in, get the Pitbull before my spouse can. And, when there are children in the mix, there is a lot to figure out. While I wondered what Ben was feeling as he said all of this, I couldn't help but feel he had made a smart decision to understand his options.

'Ben, let me ask you, how do you feel sharing all this with me? Because you knew all of it walking in here, but now that you've said it aloud, what's going on inside?' I asked.

'You know what, Allison, I feel I've been on a rollercoaster these past couple of months. I tried to understand whether the move to Hong Kong caused this, and I still think it largely did. Or was Tricia just narcissistic or out of her mind? I don't know anymore. Right when my buddy said to see a lawyer, though, I thought that was the only way to make sense of a path ahead. So, I've decided it's best we all go back to the US together,' Ben said.

After our last session, he asked Tricia to return to Missouri with him to think about their next steps, and she agreed. They boarded the airplane with suitcases full of disillusionment, resentment, and pain—but perhaps also with an ounce of hope and a pinch of that same sense of adventure that once swept them to Asia with just two weeks' notice.

A year later, they emailed to say they had divorced and would share custody of their daughter and 'try' to be kind to one another.

They maintained the narrative that Hong Kong was a graveyard for their marriage. Maybe it was.

Part IV

Healing, Truth, and Pain

Chapter 12

Desperately Seeking Stuart

Mei-Ling slinked into my office in Singapore with a stooped neck, weighed down by a cloak of shame.

She was ten minutes early and eager to talk. Mei-Ling had a pale powdered face made up with coral shadow and blush with a red lip, framed with a wavy shoulder-length cut. A stylish young mainland Chinese woman in her mid-thirties, she was an accountant at an investment bank; wrapped in Gucci from head to toe. Her controlled mannerisms and enunciation all pointed to a determined, focused person used to getting what she wants at work.

She was so intense, I had to lean back.

Mei-Ling had explained her situation in an email requesting an emergency meeting. 'I fell in love with this man. Things went terribly wrong, and I want to have an all-day session with you ASAP. I don't want ongoing therapy, just an all-day intensive.'

I thought, who is this person? No one books an all-day session without at least asking a few questions. I thought it was a scam at first. Five minutes after she sent the email, though, she paid in full. I emailed her to ask for a quick phone call to try and ensure the day for her would be valuable, and later that day we spoke for less than five minutes. She wanted to get started right away. 'I have something to solve. I'm finally ready,' she said.

And, sure enough, without skipping a beat, she launched right in within two minutes of meeting.

'I'm really ashamed to tell you this. I'm a victim of a love scam. I can't tell anyone about it. The only person who knows is my mother, who warned me. I just have this crippling sense of loneliness in my life,' she said, her voice dripping with regret and tinged with sorrow. 'I saw your website and knew this is exactly what I need.'

I leaned slightly towards her to signal compassion and responded, 'Thank you for sharing so honestly and directly about what you've experienced, and I'm sorry to hear that you are a victim of a love scam. Tell me, Mei-Ling, when you saw my website and thought "This is exactly what I need," what did this mean? What would be most valuable for our day together?'

'I want to get to the root of why I allowed myself to be scammed. That's first. Then, I want to figure out how I can let the love I still have for this man go. I realize it's crazy. I know. I just need to move on, but I still feel like I love him. I just don't believe I will find love again. I even still re-read the texts we exchanged during the time I was under his spell. But I must still be under his spell if I'm still reading these?' Mei-Ling spoke in a rushed tone, tripping over her words.

I could sense her urgency to get to the root of why, and I could feel an intense loneliness pulsating in her body. That she did not believe she would find love again was the real reason she was here, I suspected. I held onto this hypothesis lightly, as I have learned never to get too attached to a hypothesis. I owe it to the client to stay present and curious, and constantly mulling a hypothesis can get in the way of this. Ultimately, clients don't care about clever narratives unless those help solve the problem at hand.

'That sounds like a very clear plan. We will do our best as a team to get to the root, understand more about what you mean by moving on and making that happen, and then get to that last line about not believing you'll find love again. Since we will be spending the day together, I want first to ask more about your background. Feel free to start anywhere, and then we can start on our archaeological dig to understand the root cause,' I said.

For most clients, I address the present wound, challenge, or goal early on, yet because Mei-Ling had been clear this was an all-day intensive and that she didn't want ongoing therapy, I needed some background first. We had no time to waste—I sensed an openness in Mei-Ling that I needed to leverage right away.

'I'm an only child because of China's one-child policy. My parents put a lot of pressure on me to succeed. They invested part of their life savings into my education. I went to college in the US. I didn't date much at all. I was too focused on getting an accounting job, and I had a few good friends to hang out with on the weekends. I'm now thirty-six, and everyone calls me a *sheng nu*, a leftover woman. Any woman thirty and older is considered a leftover. My parents are worried our family name will die. They're pressuring me to find any man and get married,' she said, her eyes looking down. 'I'm very senior in my investment bank, I own my own flat in Singapore, and I send my parents a hefty allowance each month. I'm proud of reaching my goals in my career. And, at the same time, I come home to an empty, dark apartment and eat a bowl of noodles in front of the TV most nights. It's kind of depressing.'

I inquired about her past relationships. She said she had never had a 'serious' boyfriend and had been 'awkward' with men in the past. Then she launched right into the online scam and the shame attached to it.

'I stare at numbers all day, yet I couldn't see properly that things didn't add up before my very eyes with my online boyfriend!' Mei-Ling said.

Sometimes we are so hungry, we cannot taste the poison we're eating.

Leftover women

Before falling victim to the scam, Mei-Ling had never discussed with anyone how lonely she felt. She had never connected with a man or felt desired. Whenever she had thought of marriage or was approached by potential suitors years ago, it was simply transactional, calculating, as if she were not even human—*you're in finance, you're twenty-five years old; you're almost a 'leftover woman'*.

Mei-Ling had spent nearly half of her lifetime outside of mainland China and had impressive college degrees and a powerful role in her professional life. Yet she felt immense shame over her status as a single woman at thirty-six. A single woman in China over the age of twenty-five has few prospects of marrying and is considered way past her fertility due date.

Over my years in Asia, I've met many women like Mei-Ling, with Ivy League degrees and influential jobs but racked with self-doubt because of their single status. I believe this stems from something generational—for thousands of years, single women across Asia were considered property and not given names until they were married. These ancient cultural pressures still haunt the region's women like a ghost.

Glimpses of these spirits can be seen in the language used to describe single older women. In Vietnamese, they are called *gái già*, which means 'old girl'. In Thai, they are referred to as *kheun khan* or 'spinster'. In Korea, they are *bihon* or 'willingly unmarried'—a step up from the traditional *noncheonyo hysterie* or 'late maid hysteria'. Meanwhile, in Japan, they are dubbed *kurisumasu keeki*, which roughly translates as 'Christmas cakes', because after their twenty-fifth, they lose their value; on the other hand, working young single women making good money are called *parasaito shinguru* or 'parasite single' for leeching off society instead of fulfilling their duty to bear children.

And it is not just in colloquial language that such attitudes are passed down; it also influences the education system. In

Cambodia, a powerful force still shaping women is a nineteenth-century book of poetry called *Chbab Srey*, which offers a code of conduct on how to behave submissively to one's husband. It says that education is more important for men than women and that 'women cannot dive deep or go far'. The *Cambodia Daily* newspaper stated in a 2015 article that while the entire text is not taught in class, teachers refer students to the entire books of the *Chbab Srey* in the school libraries, and they are taught to follow and memorize the rules and not to critique them.[6]

Even today, compared to the West, societies in Asia remain very marriage-oriented and still largely fail to recognize the influence of women in the workplace.

But there are signs that attitudes towards spinsterhood are changing, and not least because media companies and big-name brands are cottoning on to the spending power of this growing cohort. Marketers now actively target groups such as the 'little sisters' of China, who choose to stay single and are exemplified by one woman who in 2022 went viral for her mantra of 'high-quality singlehood over low-quality marriage'.

Meanwhile, in Korea, some of the latest trends in travel, fashion, and beauty are being driven by 'gold miss' women—those who are consciously single, highly educated, and professional. The 'gold miss' moniker is a twist on 'old miss', which would denote a spinster or old maid.

These changing attitudes are not simply about a marketing epiphany, but demographics. Falling marriage and fertility rates are having profound social and economic consequences across the region.

By 2040, it's projected that one in five women in Japan will never marry and more than half of the country will live

---

[6] Joshua Wilwohl, 'There Is No Place for "Chbab Srey" in Cambodian Schools, *The Cambodia Daily* (9 June, 2015) https://english.cambodiadaily.com/news/%C2%ADthere-is-no-place-for-chbab-srey-in-cambodian-schools-85230/(accessed 15 Feb, 2023).

in single-person households. Similar trends abound in Hong Kong, Singapore and South Korea. In other words, Asia's ageing spinsters may be grappling with loneliness, but they are far from alone and they have more independence than women in previous generations.

Dark empty flats

Like countless singles I have worked with, Mei-Ling felt a deep loneliness when she put the key in her door each evening. She would come home after a long day at work and fantasize about one day opening the door to someone who was happy to see her. In reality, she would dread this moment, knowing that on the other side of that door was an evening of instant noodles, television, and finishing off work emails. She would dread that same night-time routine when she woke up and even as she walked to work. During the day, she had enough work to outrun the loneliness; at night, there was no escape.

Her best friend had recently met someone online and was engaged to marry. So, one night, Mei-Ling thought to herself, why not try? What do I have to lose? I'm already terribly lonely. That night, she signed onto the same dating app her friend used. She didn't post a picture or share much information the first two weeks, and after attracting little interest, she decided to add a photo and some information. She wanted to be 'bold and vulnerable' for the first time in her dating life and posted a casual photo, writing clearly that she was looking for a 'committed' relationship. She was aware that these dating apps are often used by people just wanting sex, and she wasn't seeking that kind of experience.

The next day, she was at home in her dark apartment, illuminated only by the light of her phone, swiping through profiles, before one gave her pause. The photo was of a British man in the UK with a chiselled jawline and piercing green eyes that lit her up. He had a sad story: his parents had died when he was eight and he was raised in an orphanage. Little did she know this was a sob story typical of scammers and con artists.

'I remember the first time I chatted with him, alone in my apartment, and I was instantly attracted to him. I remember his eyes. And then I read his story, and my heart just broke. I also saw he wanted to be in a committed relationship and thought that maybe we could start chatting. I even started imagining meeting him and what that would be like.'

A single photo and a sob story, when combined with years of loneliness, are easily enough to launch the heart into a fantasy of what might be. Mei-Ling sent 'Stuart' a message, which she showed me on her phone. Mei-Ling wrote, 'Hello. I live in Singapore. I think you live in the UK. You have a nice profile photo. Want to chat?' She described this message to me as 'courageous'. And for her, it was.

The first couple of weeks of texting was lovey-dovey. She would even cancel plans with her friends to rush home and text him through the night. One day he said, 'I'm in London. My lawyer said I need to pay a fine. Can you help me?'

She didn't think twice and sent him money. 'Allison, my heart was beating for the first time in so many years . . . in forever. I am so ashamed to say all of this. I was so taken by his charm, and just thinking about being together in the future kept me going each day. I even told my best friend I had met the love of my life. I knew my parents would not be happy that he wasn't Chinese, yet I was even willing as their only child to 'choose love' as my American friends say. We basically just texted the whole time. I wanted to speak on video, and he only would agree to once, and it was so dark wherever he was, I couldn't even see him.'

He said he wanted to visit her in Singapore and asked if she could pay for his ticket. He needed money to pay off his debt in London first, though.

'I need this to make our love possible,' he wrote. She didn't perceive his manipulation. She was swooped away by fantasies. Would they marry? How would she tell her parents? Would their children get his gorgeous green eyes? Would they one day have enough money to travel the world? Stuart was manna to her, medicine for her loneliness.

He continued to ask for more and more money, though. She thought nothing of it even after totalling US$15,000. She said, 'I cannot believe it. I thought this bonded us even more. I saw it as an investment. I think that's the way my accountant brain rationalized it. I kept thinking, this feeling of being in love is so wonderful, we have a future, so why not keep investing?'

Once she hit the US$25,000 mark, she had to tell her mother. Mei-Ling wouldn't be able to give her parents much of an allowance each month. She was concerned that her parents would be disappointed, yet she rationalized the situation once again by hoping they would eventually understand that she needed the money for her future husband.

Immediately, her mother smelt a rat. 'This is a total scam. Stop talking with this guy, immediately,' her mother urged her. 'My friend told me about these kinds of scams. These guys are professionals. Stop it now, Mei-Ling.'

Mei-Ling's heart had a different plan.

We are all Mei-Ling

As more Asian women choose to delay marriage, or stay single for life, many are turning to technology in their search for an antidote to loneliness.

Increasingly, social networks and dating apps are seen as a magic route out of the growing sense of loneliness and isolation many feel.

The young are turning their backs on arranged marriages, and parents are no longer the main matchmakers. Investors know this as well as anybody else. In China, they injected more than US\$5.3 billion as recently as 2022 into dating and social networking apps. Dating apps are now embedded in the modern landscape of love and are here to stay.

Along with this new tech has come an alarming increase in scams like the one Mei-Ling experienced. Often the financial losses involved are considerable.

Studies suggest that women, the middle-aged, and those suffering from anxiety, impulsivity, and addictions are at higher risk of falling prey to online scams.

Mei-Ling was more vulnerable than most, but what happened to her is surprisingly common.

One in four consumers fall victim to online scams in the Asia Pacific according to Experian's Global Identity & Fraud Report[7]. The same report found that Chinese and Indian consumers are the most vulnerable, each accounting for 29 per cent of victims.

Love bombing

Mei-Ling continued to obsess over Stuart and fantasize about their future together. With every over-the-top message she received—saying something like, 'Baby, I miss you! I need you!'—the more she became attached to him. Every text was a 'love bomb' full of exploding adoration that sent adrenaline coursing through her veins. She felt desired and loved. It was her anti-depressant, the spring in her step.

Each time Mei-Ling would respond, 'I miss you, too! I really do,' he became more and more aggressive: 'If you really love me,

---

[7] Aaron Raj, 'One in four consumers are online fraud victims in the Asia Pacific', Techwire Asia (24 June, 2022) https://techwireasia.com/2022/06/one-in-four-consumers-online-fraud-victims-asia-pacific/ (accessed 15 Feb, 2023).

if you really miss me, this is not enough money.' She remembered that last statement because it was their ten-month anniversary. And she thought to herself, 'He's probably right. It wasn't enough.' High as a kite, and then plunged into a dungeon of shame.

As the week went on, there was something about his increasingly aggressive tone that filled the pit of her stomach with dread. She ended up sending Stuart some more money, yet one day, her phone began vibrating non-stop with aggressive messages from Stuart, telling her she was a 'piece of shit', and that she didn't love him enough to send more money. She ran to the bathroom and cried, and her tears told her the truth: this was no fairy tale.

A few days and buckets worth of tears later, she plucked up the courage to give up on her dream and reported Stuart to the police.

'I reported him. I knew this was a scam finally. I guess I accepted that enough to report him. But, Allison, I'm still so in love with him. If I am honest, I don't regret the experience. I regret it didn't turn into a loving romance. It was a dashed romance, I guess. I know these feelings are not real. They're not supposed to be real. How can they be real? Please talk some sense into me. I can't continue like this, living in a fantasy and believing this is reality that someone does truly desire and adore me,' she said.

'I'm so sorry you went through this, Mei-Ling. Acceptance is rarely linear. Most of us weave in and out of acceptance, especially when we are still experiencing the pain in the present moment. I do see the possibility to use this experience as a springboard for transformation, as it tells us so much about what you do want in your life. How did you feel about yourself when you were speaking with him?'

'I felt loved. I felt like a woman—not just a finance woman,' she said.

I asked, 'What was the meaning of this experience for you?'

What was spooky was that he texted her at the very moment I was asking this. I could hear her phone vibrating and watched as her face fell. She turned away to respond to Stuart's text. 'I told him I was busy,' she said sheepishly. I could see the spark was still there.

'When I look at our past texts, I still feel love towards him. I think the meaning is that I want love, yet I just don't know if I can find it again,' she said.

Her heart was so shattered that her mind could not stop generating thoughts and questions about who Stuart was 'in reality'. She spent another US$10,000 to hire an investigator in Cambodia to get photos as well as his life story. She learned that he was based in Phnom Penh. 'He was part of a Nigerian syndicate, sent to Cambodia, targeting women in Asia. He was a former boy soldier. Dark-looking, rough-looking, with short hair,' she explained in hushed tones as if he could hear us.

'It illuminated the yearning, the need for love and connection, I guess,' Mei-Ling said, replying to my question about the meaning of this experience. 'What's crazy is, even after finding out his real identity, I still felt this strong pull of love. Was it love?'

'Mei-Ling, if you felt it, then it was real, an arrow, pointing you in a clear direction of what you wanted—to give love and be loved. In all relationships, though, for them to be healthy and thrive, there needs to be boundaries, not too porous and not too rigid,' I said.

Before I could finish the sentence, Mei-Ling lowered her eyebrows and looked at me utterly confused and asked, 'What do you mean by boundaries?' as she pulled out her phone to search for the word in Chinese.

With that one word, she opened the door to a potentially new world.

Boundaries

Mei-Ling wasn't aware that she was violating her own boundaries whenever she transferred money to Stuart.

Randi Buckley, creator of 'Healthy Boundaries for Kind People', defines boundaries as 'The conditions you need to live the life and have the relationships you desire. With these conditions in place, these boundaries, everything else becomes possible.'

Buckley describes boundaries as expectation management when communicating with others and also as 'values in action'.

'When we see them as values, we're more likely to understand their importance,' Buckley says.

There are many reasons, usually rooted in past experiences, why people do not have healthy boundaries. Buckley identifies six of the most common:

- Fear of disappointing others
- Fear of missing out
- Fear of abandonment
- They have not seen healthy boundaries modelled in others
- They don't know how to articulate or communicate boundaries in the moment
- They feel unworthy

Buckley explains, 'I have my students think of a period (in work or their lives) where things were humming along wonderfully, and they were feeling really good about how things were going. What values were you honouring and what was being honoured by others? Those are likely the values that need to be honoured now, too.'

She advises communicating the conditions you need to be at your best. 'The first thing is to always make sure YOU are honouring your boundaries. It's your action that people see, or not, even more than they hear it. If you aren't honouring the boundary, it's hard to expect anyone else to.'

Breaking out of a shame jail

I began to think about how to help break out Mei-Ling from her shame jail. Boundaries would be one ingredient, but I also suspected Mei-Ling wanted to transform in other ways too.

I asked her, 'If I could wave a magic wand and you'd wake up tomorrow living the life you wanted, one that felt most meaningful, what would that look like? Try not to allow your mind to jump in. Open up. Let it all out.'

I was using a variation of what therapists and coaches call 'the miracle question'—essentially asking the client to visualize what they want if there were no limitations, to remove all shackles. This question is an invitation to dream; creativity can be an incredibly powerful tool for breaking down defences and cranking up the soul. Some clients will respond to the question with a blank stare. Mei-Ling, though, was hungry to answer, and asked if she could draw the answer in her notebook.

Twenty minutes later, Mei-Ling showed me an exquisite drawing of a house. And we entered a different world together.

The drawing included a rubbish bin outside of the house that contained her limitations and burdens. There, she put ideas relating to *sheng nu*, of not being worthy of love, all the straitjackets she had worn over the years. The house itself was a few storeys high, with gorgeous lanterns adorning the front door. On each level, the rooms represented something she valued. The higher the floor, the higher the value. On the top floor, she placed family and love.

'If I could wake up tomorrow and really feel my life was meaningful . . . so much. I can say so much. I would be free from this burden of being a *sheng nu*. That is so heavy. I feel it in my heart, that pain. It troubles my parents so much. I want to respect my parents and I'm so grateful for everything they've done, Allison. They literally sacrificed everything so I could go to school in the United States and become an accountant. I would want to marry a man who is either Chinese or not; I don't care much about that, but again I know my parents do. I would want a man who makes more money than me so he could pay my parents a good allowance because I feel indebted to them. I would also tell people more about my feelings. I keep them all in and believe they don't matter. And I also want to start to play some sport or something. I was always told to stay away from the gym or sports, that my body would be like a man's.'

We spoke about preserving this powerful image, in her soul and on paper. She took a photo with her phone to remind her what was on the other side of her shame jail.

'You're the first to give me permission to go for what I want in life. I have lived out my parents' dreams, and I am glad I could do that for them,' she said. 'Now I feel that I have permission to explore what I want. I didn't know what I wanted before. I thought I wanted a man to choose me, that it was my only way to escape my fate.'

We had some other plans for the jailbreak too. Mei-Ling pledged to join a running group two nights a week after work as this would help with her loneliness and physical strength. Emotionally, Mei-Ling wanted first to journal each day about her feelings and then eventually to share some of her feelings with friends, and maybe one day with family. She wanted to speak with her parents about her desire to be in a loving relationship, and she wanted their blessing to go forth. If they agreed, then she would sign up to different apps or even consider meeting with a matchmaker.

We had spent only a few hours together, but by the end of our emergency session, I had witnessed a profound transformation in Mei-Ling's mindset and outlook on her life.

She went from being tortured by shame and the pain of her loneliness to being hopeful about the future and its possibilities.

I never heard from Mei-Ling again and wonder some days how she's feeling. I often wonder how many people worldwide, if given a promise of love, would empty their bank accounts.

Chapter 13

Legacy Anxiety

'The shame is too heavy for our family to bear. I will end the pain today.' When Tai was thirteen, his father left this suicide note. It has haunted him ever since.

He would later find out his father was about to be arrested for commercial bribery of a business supplier and faced not only prison time but also a hefty fine. This would have brought unbearable shame to the family's name, Tai's mother had explained. She used the term in Chinese—*xiu si ba bei zi xian ren*—that roughly translates to, 'So ashamed, the ancestors of eight generations can feel it.' Tai described his mother as 'well-meaning and aloof' and said she would repeat this Chinese term each time he asked why his father felt the need to kill himself.

At thirty-three, Tai was still analysing, obsessing, and pretending that his father's note didn't exist, sometimes all within the same breath.

I first met Tai for an individual session, and he was a warm, self-deprecating young man. He was Hong Kong–Chinese with jet-black hair slicked back, large sad eyes, prominent cheekbones, and a sharp jawline. A singer and a songwriter, Tai was a factory of creativity and had an incredible mind. When I asked him a question, he would answer with metaphors so deep, so layered, and so colourful, they were like works of fine art. His mind was vibrant, yet violent too, subjugated by self-loathing thoughts about himself and his place in this world.

I asked Tai what his hopes for our work together were.

'I am utterly confused about life. I've been to three other therapists who want to tell me that my life is doomed basically because of what happened with my father and all the pain. I'm not ready to give up, though.'

Tai knew his own narrative better than any therapist. He lived inside it and felt lost already. Their embellishments only led him further into the labyrinth. So, I let him take the lead instead.

'What do you do with your pain?' I asked him.

'The pain is often humming in the background, and when that's the case, I'm humming along. The pain is sometimes so intense, though. I can't bear it. It's like I'm on shore some days, my feet warmly pressed to the sand, and then a giant tidal wave washes over me, and *boom*, I am lost, overwhelmed, and disoriented. I have long wondered why my father left us, why he did what he did, and although my mum has said he did it for us, for the family's name, I sometimes feel he did it *to* us. I don't hate him. I just really am overwhelmed with confusion, with no anchor, no compass in this world, wishing for his guidance,' he said, biting the side of his mouth and holding back tears.

'What are you feeling as you share this?' I asked.

His lips quivered. He was breathing erratically and deeply, then shot out a loud exhale. 'Fuck. This is hard.'

Fuck. This *was* hard. He was right. I could almost see that wave of emotion heading his way.

Tai had a way with words that allowed us to share a reality, and that can be a powerful engine in therapy.

'Tell me more about what the days are like walking on the warm sand of the beach and that giant tidal wave,' I said gently.

'The days that I'm walking on the beach, feet on the warm sand . . . those are wonderful. I feel connected with my partner, my work, and I feel a level of acceptance with my dad. The acceptance isn't a warm, fuzzy blanket—it's still painful. I'm still wondering what advice he would give me now as a man. When the *boom* hits, it's like the ground is shaking, I am disconnected with myself, with everything, and I sometimes lock myself in a room. Other times I drink or take some drugs. I do whatever it takes to escape, and then I hate myself for the drinking, the drugs, the needing to escape,' Tai said with little emotion.

Tai had a deep psychic confusion about what he wanted in life and wished that his father could provide some guidance. His father's presence, paradoxically, felt at once totally present and totally absent in his life.

'I still talk with my dad. I don't know if that sounds weird to you. Since his death, my family has sought support from a Taoist priest, and I speak with the priest sometimes about how to connect with my father. But when the tidal wave hits me, I need to disappear. I get to pretend . . .' Tai did not finish the sentence, leaving me lost in his metaphor.

I told him no, that talking with his father did not sound weird. Many of my clients in Asia see life as circular, not linear, and communicate regularly with their ancestors.

We breathed together deeply for about thirty seconds as I held onto his words. 'You get to pretend what . . . are you able to finish the sentence? If not, then please don't. I will always respect if you want to pass on a question,' I said slowly.

'I get to pretend that the shackles are off, and I can feel grounded and make decisions,' he said before exhaling deeply.

'Tell me, Tai, if you're able to carry the pain differently, then what do you want in your life? What are the decisions you're wanting to make?' I asked.

'One of the big questions right now in my life is whether I want to marry my partner or split up with her. She and I have been together for a while, and if we do marry, then we want to have a baby. But what happens if I just pass the pain onto the baby like an emotional hot potato? Or what if, when I'm fifty, which is when my dad died by suicide, I feel that life is too burdensome, just like he did? Then what? My partner also has her own stuff. I just don't know some days whether we can actually have a relationship in which we both have a lot of stuff. And yet, Allison, when I think of losing her, it's like an endangered language dying.'

I could see that Tai might need his own support, yet I also sensed that doing couples therapy would benefit him. It would help to understand him in the context of a relationship, understand more clearly his relationship with substances, and hopefully support him and his partner as a couple in reaching their goals.

He nodded his assent as I watched him breathe deeply into his chest.

Generational impacts

I met Tai and his partner, Jing, also 33, late one evening. She was dressed in a silky turquoise caftan with her black lace bra peeking through and her bare feet in black Birkenstocks. Glittering round diamond earrings graced her ears and a matching tennis bracelet on her slender wrist juxtaposed her hippie-like outfit. She was also Hong Kong–Chinese and a singer-songwriter. They were both experimental and non-conformist creatives who ran in glamourous entertainment circles. They both loved to party and came from privileged upbringings financially yet emotionally carried many burdens.

Jing nervously twisted one of her earrings as she 'anxiously' described that they were looking for clarity in their next steps— this therapy would be a make-or-break process. Make it, they agreed, would mean marriage and a baby. Break it would mean saying goodbye.

'I've never actually said this out loud—we're either all in, or we're done. I am thirty-three, and you may know that in Hong Kong, Allison, thirty-five and older is considered a geriatric pregnancy. I don't feel old, but we've been together ten years already, and I either have a baby now or risk missing the window. I love Tai so much and can see him as a dad, but I'm also super anxious,' Jing said.

'What is it you love about him?' I asked. I sensed it was more important for Tai to hear the answer than me.

'He's a very genuine guy, super sincere, loving, funny and creative. I can just imagine him running around the flat with a baby. I can sense he would be so super loving,' Jing said as I watched Tai smile in a humble way.

'This is all very helpful to know, Jing, and what a beautiful way to describe why you love Tai. It sounds like there's a lot of love between you two, and at the same time you're at a crossroads,' I said.

They both nodded like bobblehead dolls.

With couples looking to make decisions—whether to have a baby, stay together, separate, or divorce—I tend to suggest a deadline. This allows the couple a small exhale, giving them the comfort that a resolution one way or the other is in sight, even if sometimes, the deadline needs to be extended.

I suggested that Tai and Jing commit to three months, meeting every other week for ninety minutes, as I find it's more effective to meet couples less often but for longer sessions. I also suggested things for them to work on together between sessions.

Making big decisions can help sharpen the focus in therapy. Once they could exhale a bit, I asked Jing more about the anxiety she mentioned, and she said, 'Ha, umm, I've been anxious, like, forever! I actually can't recall a time when I wasn't anxious. This long predates our relationship, yet there are some clear reasons why it spikes with Tai.'

I asked how it showed up with Tai. I am always clear with clients that they can pass on any question I ask. This respects their boundaries and lets them avoid saying anything they may regret.

'I don't mind sharing. My father used to come home super drunk and beat my mum up in front of my brother and me. He would kick her, literally kick her in front of us. When my mum would vomit or scream, he would kick her even harder. My brother even called the police on my dad when he was a teenager, and my dad ended up spending just one night in jail,' she said.

Jing started to open and close her eyes rapidly, trying to stop the tears while grabbing for the tissue box. Tai looked like he wanted to connect with her but was lost as to how. Clumsily, he reached out his hand and placed it on hers.

'My father also weaponized money, and he used to tell my brother, mum, and me that if we ever told people what we saw, he would cut us all off financially. Everything was about money and power with him. I never believed in therapy. In fact, I used to mock it because my father would always say, "Therapy is for sick, weak people." That stuck with me. So, I just went to the doctor and asked for medication as I have had periods when I cannot sleep or I'm having these awful nightmares or flashbacks. Even outside of the flashbacks, sometimes the anxiety will show up out of nowhere. I could be walking down the street, and then I will start to have a panic attack,' Jing said, looking slightly panicked just to be sharing this.

Emotional tidal waves hit them both, it seemed. Like with many couples, when one wave hits, a second usually follows.

'In our relationship, I would say that I get most anxious when he won't commit to the future or refuses to respond to my questions or anything with emotion. I then assume that he's done with the relationship, and that makes me anxious. If he wants to end it, then I would rather we just say that. Now, all he does when I ask him a question about us or share how I'm feeling is drink, get high, or just go in another room and literally lock it for a day,' she said, still panicky. 'But I sometimes cannot tell what he's feeling. It's like sometimes when I express something intense, he tries to numb himself with drugs or alcohol. This happens most often when I tell him I'm anxious about something or even excited about our future. But then there are times I don't know the trigger—he just disappears.'

She looked down, avoiding eye contact.

'Why do you stay?' I asked.

'I think I love him so much. I sometimes wonder if I stay because of my childhood, that I wasn't able to escape then, and maybe I can't escape now. But no, I feel deep down, we do have something amazing together. I think that's it.'

I was watching Tai as Jing shared all this. He was breathing heavily and avoiding my stare. He reminded me of a shy child in class who is hoping the teacher doesn't call on him. So, I didn't. Just yet. Instead, I asked Jing about the substance use. She said they sometimes did drugs together and drank 'a bit' each night. When I asked her about Tai's substance abuse when he was on his own, she expressed deep concern because 'sometimes it's out of control'.

I asked Tai if that were true, that his usage was out of control sometimes, and he simply nodded. Addictions, if not treated, are a barrier to therapy. I wondered what it was going to take to get a truthful answer on what they meant by 'out of control'.

Throughout the session, I could sense a lot of love and a lot of pain with this couple; their connection was palpable, yet so too were their ghosts.

Their different methods of coping when anxiety showed up only made things worse. When a wave approached, Tai would shut down and let it wash him away. He would close his eyes, fall silent and be swept to a place where reality and his emotions had been left far behind. When Jing's wave came, though, she wanted a rock to cling to. Tai was supposed to be that rock, but he was distant and unreachable, borne away by currents of his own. Ultimately, they would both wash ashore alone, numb and waiting for the next wave to hit.

When I put this to them, they both agreed that this is how they had danced together for years, and we agreed we needed to stop the pattern from recurring. We also spoke about something I have coined—'legacy anxiety'—anxiety that gets stored in our nervous systems after witnessing others, often family members, who are traumatized. Jing watched her father abuse her mother, and as a child that abuse lodged somewhere. Tai watched his father suffering and also his mother. Both had waves of anxiety that would hit them. By comparison, 'intergenerational trauma' is trauma that gets passed down from someone or a group who has been traumatized to subsequent generations. With legacy anxiety, though, there's an actual witnessing of pain or trauma.

At first, Tai was unsure of what lay on the other side of all this. He asked, 'Do I have to be so emotional? I don't really get the point if I'm honest.' This made sense given his history of abandonment with his father and his description of a mother and extended family who showed little emotion growing up.

I responded, 'Not everyone wants emotional intimacy or deep connection in their relationships. To largely varying degrees, connection is often the heartbeat of a relationship. If you really don't want any kind of emotional intimacy, then my suggestion is not to be in a relationship. You chose a partner who certainly does want to connect. What comes to you when I say that?'

Although I have worked with many people who avoid their emotions and can genuinely not name or express how they're feeling, with him I sensed something else was going on. He had a deep reservoir of emotion. He and Jing talked about songs they had written together, and their themes overflowed with emotion.

Sometimes with couples, one person's trauma or pain appears front and centre, yet often there are two people in front of me whose pain collides. Legacy anxiety, or any kind of generational pain, is often very burdensome. This is because people may understand the origins of their anxiety on an intellectual level, but they remain disoriented by it on a physical, cellular level. They cannot tell which feelings are their own and which they are carrying for someone else.

'I do feel a lot. I am just clueless about how to express anything painful or challenging,' Tai responded.

Before the next session, I asked them both to be aware of the dance they had become stuck in. Awareness in therapy is necessary yet not sufficient to making changes. I taught them to become aware of when the wave was approaching and how to break free from their usual pattern of responses. We worked on some breathing as well. I wanted to give them something yet knew breathing alone wouldn't move the needle.

They agreed to the homework, and Jing said, 'There's also so much goodness in this relationship. That's what we want to grow yet don't know how.'

I asked them what the relationship looked like when the waves weren't crashing down, and I could see how they had stayed together so long. They were incredibly warm with one another, they laughed, they shared a deep value of creativity, and at their core, they both wanted to care for each other—they were just lost on *how*. We would need to work on their trauma, improve their emotional connection, and cut their substance misuse. It was quite a to-do list.

We ended the session with them holding hands, looking into each other's eyes, and reflecting on a song they co-wrote on a diving trip to Fiji—their first together. They were even talking warmly about becoming parents one day.

I asked them how they imagined themselves as parents.

'We love each other so much that we would even make amazing divorced parents,' Jing said, ending the session with a big, warm smile that lit up the whole room.

Bag of vomit

One Saturday, Jing arrived early to a session and told me that Tai may or may not join. 'He went on another one of his benders,' she said in a frustrated tone. 'Gosh. We've been together for so long, and it seems like every other weekend he parties until he blacks out.'

'What do you mean by blacking out? With alcohol? Drugs? How do you feel about that?' I asked with concern.

'It's mostly drinking. I've gotten used to his ways, but I am feeling more anxious about it these days, especially when we think about having a baby,' she said.

Tai burst in the door without knocking and said hello. Right when I laid eyes on his face and saw his sallow greenish skin and glistening forehead, I knew *this* look. It was a daily look from my upbringing—my father's glazed eyes; there was no way this look was from heavy drinking alone.

Instantly, I flashbacked to the look I saw most days in my father's large brown eyes—windows into a drug addiction. While staring into his vacant eyes and sensing he had drifted off somewhere, I was sometimes so overwhelmed and disoriented, I wondered if I did even have a father. Was he really present in this shell of a body? And there he is, sometimes stumbling down the stairs, other times raging, deliriously high, anywhere but here, his otherwise loving words vacillating between incoherent and cruel.

Immediately, I brought Tai to the room next to ours as there was a nurse at the clinic who offered to keep an eye on him while I continued the session with Jing. I made clear we could not do therapy while he was intoxicated.

Jing launched into more stories of their dangerous dance of avoidance and anxiety and told me what I was seeing in real time was *the* dance. Last night, she had shared with Tai that she was feeling close to him and could imagine them married with a baby. She said he was 'fine' until she started sharing details, like imagining they would wed in Thailand, the dress she was thinking to order, the guests she wanted to invite, and wanting to honeymoon in New Zealand.

With every detail she told him, Tai began to float a little further away. Sensing this, her anxiety increased, and she would try to self-soothe by sharing even more details. It was not long before Tai had walked out the door and turned off his phone.

Later, she received a drunken text. It said, 'What are we doing? I don't think I want this.'

'Jing, how did you respond to this?' I asked.

'My anxiety just skyrocketed. It's like he had shut down, and I turned up the volume. I literally tried to chase him down the hall, but he was not even running. He just shut off, like the walking dead. In any case, I was a wreck last night. I called my best friend to chat, and that helped, but I still felt on edge and had trouble sleeping.'

I could see the anxiety in her chest.

Jing and I spoke about ways she could work through her anxiety. We spoke about seeing a trauma therapist who did a kind of therapy called eye movement desensitization and reprocessing (EMDR). EMDR is a structured form of therapy in which the client briefly focuses on a traumatic memory while at the same time focusing on an external stimulus such as bilateral eye movements, hand-tapping, or audio-stimulation. The idea is that accessing traumatic memories in a safe way, under the guidance of a trained EMDR therapist, will allow the client to form new associations with the memory that are less emotionally distressful. With Jing, the idea was to reduce the emotional distress she had from watching her father assault her mother when she was a child and to see if this helped reduce some of the anxiety she was experiencing.

Jing was also very connected with traditional Chinese medicine, and I recommended she also speak with her practitioner about the possibility of integrating acupuncture.

One of the beautiful aspects of working in Asia is the connection people have to traditional systems of healing. This connection goes beyond simple tradition; many of these systems are being studied in clinical trials, and I anticipate some will satisfy the Western appetite for all things evidence based.

It was clear that if the two of them were going to be healthy, they needed to be healthy together, and that meant doing something about the substance abuse too.

I make no friends when I tell people that mental health is improved by reducing or eliminating substances. The irony is that people often abuse substances to escape their pain, legacy anxiety, and pretty much anything that makes them feel uncomfortable emotionally, yet doing so increases the chances of pain in their relationships and mental health.

Towards the end of the hour, Tai knocked on our door with a bag in his hand full of vomit, likely compiled of copious amounts of alcohol and drugs. 'Hi,' he said sheepishly.

'Are you OK?' asked Jing, standing up to steady him.

His shame and embarrassment permeated every inch of his demeanour. It was an unforgettable entrance, and he was terrified that I would fire him as a client seeing him this way. 'Please don't hate me. Are you going to get rid of me?' he asked earnestly.

The reality was that none of this affected my affection for and belief in him as a client. At the same time, I needed to be clear about the boundaries and what I ultimately felt would be best for his health.

'I care about you and want the best outcome. I also care about Jing and your relationship. At the same time, we cannot do therapy while you're intoxicated or have a possible active addiction that's not being treated. For today, I am asking the secretary to book you in with a doctor downstairs in this same clinic. I want Jing and you to come back for a session next week so we can have a clear plan going forward, one that will finally give you both relief and clarity, I hope. I will also check in with you tomorrow to see how you're feeling. How does all of this sound?' I said lovingly and firmly.

Tai's eyes were still glazed over, his skin sallow green. The outer creases of his mouth were trying to muster enough energy to smile but could not.

'Thank you for not giving up on me,' he said with Jing on one arm, the nurse on the other.

Radical change

As the cosmos would have it, the Tuesday after I saw Tai and Jing, I was hosting a virtual talk for Dr Anna Lembke, psychiatrist, professor, and chief of addiction and dual diagnosis at Stanford University, to discuss her remarkable book that explores the reasons behind addictive behaviours, *Dopamine Nation*. I emailed Tai and Jing to follow up with how they were feeling and also sent them a flyer in the hope they would attend. In *Dopamine Nation*, Dr Lembke discussed some themes I thought would resonate, mainly:

- Pursuing pleasure often leads to pain.
- Explaining dopamine and dopamine-seeking behaviours. Dopamine is a neurotransmitter connected with pleasure, reward, and motivation. For example, eating chocolate will increase dopamine levels about 50 per cent above baseline, sex 100 per cent, and amphetamines 1,000 per cent.

- Chasing these behaviours often has a negative impact, which can result in people leading double lives that are risky.

Dr Lembke explains that the pleasure and pain centre are found in the same part of the brain, and these need to be in balance. Therefore, chasing pleasure (dopamine, the neurotransmitter connected with pleasure, reward, motivation) can often lead to more pain as the brain tries to balance out like a seesaw. If there's been a big tip towards pleasure or a big dopamine hit, then the brain needs to find balance, and that often causes pain and leaves the person feeling worse than before in a kind of 'dopamine deficit'. She also shares that although many people look at a change in functioning as a sign of addiction, what we should really have an eye on is a double life. Many people with addictions function well, and in fact some even fare better for a short duration with the addiction. Tai was definitely avoiding his pain by shutting down his emotions and then seeking pleasure and escape with the substances. He also had a double life as he was totally gone and was like another person while taking drugs.

Jing and Tai returned for a session on Friday, both sober and clear-eyed.

'We've had some difficult conversations since Saturday, and I think we're both ready to just do something about this pain and destruction regardless of whether we stay together or not. Oh, and we went for the talk by Dr Lembke. I think it changed Tai's outlook big time,' Jing said.

'I'm glad to hear you're both ready to do something regardless of the outcome of this relationship and thank you for coming to the talk. Tai, how has your outlook changed after the talk?' I asked curiously.

'Something crystallized in that talk, like when she was talking about how people can still function and be addicted to something.

I told myself a story that so long as I could do my work and be somewhat functional, I was not an addict. Yet, as she pointed out, it's more about the double life, and yes, I had one—one when I was with Jing, and another when I was high or drinking. Something resonated when she said that pursuing pleasure is what often leads to pain. All this escaping, even if pleasurable for five seconds, leads to big, fucking pain. It clearly leads to a lot of fucking pain in our relationship,' Tai said, nodding his head as if he had just heard himself tell the truth out loud and felt released for the first time.

'Wow, that's amazing that those points really connected with you. It sounds like you're ready to do something with all this. What's the truth with which substances you're using, and how often? I ask, Tai, because this will help me be clear with a plan,' I said, looking him in the eyes compassionately yet directly.

'The truth is what walked in your door this past Saturday. That's basically a window into my weekends. Drugs and alcohol? I can't even tell you how much because at some point I just lose track. During the week . . . hmm . . . let's say a bottle of wine each night, sometimes pot, sometimes MDMA if I'm at a party. Cigarettes most days. Blackouts, probably twice a month. Maybe this has been the rhythm since I've been a teenager, and I know it messes with stuff such as work and relationships, but before the talk I just rationalized I was still functioning and fine,' he said with his eyes looking down, while Jing nodded away furiously, as if he had finally told the truth.

'Thank you, Tai, for being so honest. To really treat this, I strongly suggest you go to a proper rehab centre that will help with what sounds like an addiction, or, at the very least, addictive behaviours, and also support you emotionally. Once the addiction is being treated, and Jing also does her own work, then we will be ready to resume the couples therapy and answer with clear eyes whether you two want to be together,' I said.

'I am open to that, Allison, probably open because of the talk by Dr Lembke. Something awakened in me. I've even started reading the book, and I can never usually focus enough to read any book. I hate to admit I am seeing myself in the stories she shares more than I care to admit,' he said.

I was impressed with how perceptive Tai was with Dr Lembke's messages and scheduled a session for him to see a psychiatrist for one session to choose a rehab centre in Australia and come up with a plan for his return, to make sure he had support in Hong Kong. Tai had an uncle he was close with in Australia with whom he was planning to stay before and after the rehab.

After Tai returned from two months of rehab in Australia, and Jing completed the EMDR therapy and bodywork to help regulate her nervous system, they came back for three more months of couples therapy. Tai was regularly attending Alcoholics Anonymous and speaking with his sponsor each week. He was also regularly in contact with his Taoist priest as he had become more interested in regular meditation. Although Jing had never shown interest in Taoism before, she and Tai were now walking to the temple nearby to burn incense for his father before meditating together once a week.

Without numbing his emotions, Tai was able to learn how to express himself and even deal with the pain when it arose. He learned that the waves of pain never stop and began to see them as a way to connect with his father. Now, when the wave heads his way, he no longer escapes into the distance.

After the EMDR, Jing noticed that her nightmares and flashbacks decreased significantly. She began to feel 'enough peace' and that her waves were 'manageable'.

I coached them on ways to take conscious breaks when they saw a wave approaching. They agreed to say 'wave' as a warning signal and to tell each other when they needed a break and for how long. They promised to return to each other when the break was over. Tai found that reading helped when he needed a break; Jing would go for a short walk or take a shower instead.

We also worked on lifestyle changes like choosing healthy foods, exercising regularly together with walks each evening after dinner, saying no to alcohol or drugs, and keeping a regular sleep schedule. They've worked as a team to make these changes and recognize this supported the health of their relationship.

They were fully committed to marrying and having a baby, and we spent many hours talking about how they would transform their pain and become the parents they wished they had had. Tai was right in the first session to wonder if we passed our pain along like an emotional hot potato to our children.

The biggest change they made in therapy was recognizing that all of us, to varying degrees, can choose how much pain we pass on to our children. Most of us sleepwalk through parenthood, carrying loads of generational baggage, myself included, for far too long. Children are often walking, talking triggers, which makes parenting ripe with opportunities to transform this pain.

Eleven months later, a photograph of a graceful, peaceful girl arrived in my inbox, with the subject line, 'We named her 無為, Wu Wei.' I opened Google Translate and pasted the Chinese characters into the search.

I was greeted by a Taoist concept. Wu Wei is an invitation to act peacefully, even when there's internal or external chaos. After working with Tai and Jing, when I am feeling the inner or external chaos present with my own children, I whisper to myself, 'Wu Wei.'

Sometimes we need to become the parents we wish we had.

Shame and suicide in Asia

Suicide is one of the leading causes of death worldwide. It accounts for more deaths than war, homicide, HIV/AIDS, or breast cancer. The World Health Organization reports that more than 700,000 people kill themselves globally every year. In Asia, the suicide rate is at least 30 per cent higher than the rest of the world. Currently, South Korea has the highest annual number of suicides. In Japan, ranked third globally, youth suicide rates are at an all-time high in 30 years. In Southeast Asia, Thailand has the highest rate; in 'The Land of Smiles', someone attempts suicide every ten minutes.

Even though it is an enormous public health issue, the Asia region lacks community-based resources and intervention programmes. At the heart of the challenge is the great cultural stigma and shame surrounding suicide and, indeed, anything to do with death.

Suicide is not openly discussed, which means many people who are thinking of taking their lives are not getting the help they so desperately need.

The cultural factors behind this are complex and include the concepts of 'honour', 'honourable death', and 'saving face'. Each of these in turn is rooted in collectivist ideals that prize conformity and emphasize society over the individual, as opposed to the individualistic Western values of independence, autonomy, and equality.

A 2004 study, 'The organisation of Chinese shame concepts', found there were 113 terms for shame among native Chinese speakers.[8] Among these were terms for the fear of losing face, the feeling after losing face, and guilt. In China and most other Asian cultures, shame is used as a prominent technique of social control and child rearing. When people succeed, their entire family or community basks in the reflective honour, and when they

---

[8] Jin Li, Lianqin Wang, Kurt W. Fischer, 'The organisation of Chinese shame concepts', *Cognition and Emotion*, 18 (6), (2004), pp. 767–797, https://www.gse.harvard.edu/~ddl/articlesCopy/LiWangFischerOrganiztnShame.CogEmotn2004.pdf (accessed 15 Feb, 2023).

fail, they bring shame, dishonour, and ridicule to everyone they know—especially their parents who are blamed for their weaknesses.

So consequential is losing face and experiencing shame that the transgressor's children may be unable to marry well, and their relatives will be barred from succeeding unless they do something to compensate.

Shame in Asia is largely a group concern, rather than an individual one, and occurs when there is a loss of 'face' or honour, which refers to personal integrity, good character, and the ability to conform to society's expectations.

The shame-based roots of Asian culture can be traced to Confucianism, which valued and fostered the power of shame and taught that life's highest purpose is to seek self-perfection. Shame could direct a person in self-examination to move towards social and moral changes but also has had damaging consequences by leading people to hide or escape and even in painful states to want to disappear and die.

Japan has a history of viewing ritual suicide, known as *hara-kiri* or *seppuku*, as an honourable or morally responsible decision—to atone for a deep sense of shame to preserve your family's sense of honour. *Seppuku* was performed mostly by samurai, who in the shame of defeat would stab themselves in the stomach to bleed out. In recent years, the Japanese have begun to view suicide more as a mental health issue; some suicides are even categorized as *karoshi* or death by overwork. But the sense of needing to preserve the honour of one's family remains strong in Japan, as it does in the rest of Asia and among Asian Americans.

According to the American Psychological Association, suicide is the second leading cause of death for Asian Americans aged fifteen to thirty-four. Their immigrant parents have passed on the cultural values of shame and honour, along with the stigma surrounding mental health issues, to the next generation.

As a consequence, many in the younger generation feel terrified of being labelled as 'crazy' if they divulge their struggles. They fear tarnishing their family if they admit to depression or fail academically.

When someone dies from suicide, at least six to ten people are affected. These bereaved are at risk of complicated grief, of developing major depression or post-traumatic stress disorder and suicidal thoughts. They are often in need of more specialized support and care, which is missing in Asia and arguably around the world. Many of my clients in Asia, including Tai, who have experienced a family member or friend dying by suicide suffer in silence and even feel superstitious about talking about the death or the person.

Chapter 14

Fighting the Past

Unjoo and Tim both came in wearing boxing gloves. The fight was on, guns blazing. They were American expats based in Singapore. Both were wearing black tailored suits with crisp white collared shirts and exuded elegance. Unjoo, thirty-eight, had a refined energy and was highly articulate and sometimes a bit rough. Tim, thirty-nine, was likeable with a scruffy aura like he had just gotten out of bed. He had a broken nose and looked like he would be comfortable in a dark alleyway somewhere fending off a mugger. He was steely when he wanted to make a point.

In the first session, they described years of intensity, starting from their very first date five years ago. Tim said that on the first date, they debated US politics so fiercely, they were asked to leave the restaurant in New York City. They shared stories about being on a rollercoaster ride of passion and destruction—replete with plenty of passionate sex, emotional intimacy, and fierce teamwork, but equally with savage fights that dragged on for days, threats of divorce, and cruelty of a grand order.

When they 'spoke' to each other, the room would physically shake. During sessions with Unjoo and Tim, the receptionist called me on more than one occasion to ask if I needed security. This intensity grabbed onto all sorts of conversations—from the most loving and passionate to the most destructive and gnarly. When they were loving, I watched two people getting along like a house on fire; when destructive, I watched them set fire to their house. Over the years, I have learned deep breathing techniques after working with countless raging, cursing couples, and I've become adept at it. Breathe in, breathe out.

They came to see me to learn how to engage with conflict differently, both recognizing on some level that their intense conflict was destructive. The usual pattern of their fights went something like this: Unjoo would descend into a tirade of verbal abuse against Tim, who would then fight back with equal or more intensity; or Tim would rage at Unjoo for a perceived injustice, and Unjoo would fight back with equal or more intensity. Unsurprisingly, they often weaponized each other's words, and so all the emotional intimacy they shared during the intense, good times got used against the other.

I had to be careful not to gasp at some of the words exchanged in my office. I bit the bottom of my lip or side of my mouth regularly and found it both disconcerting and charming that they were so upfront with each other. Many couples will show me texts, emails, or even videos of the conflict, and there's often a large gap with what I see in session and the exchange they have outside the room. With Unjoo and Tim, though, they were who they were on text, email, video, and in the room with me. In some ways, it made our sessions more efficient as I didn't need to wonder how they acted at home.

When they described their first date, they both delighted in being kicked out of the restaurant. Tim remarked, 'How many people on the first date are so blunt about their political beliefs? We were debating one hot topic in politics at the time, and although we were on opposite ends of the spectrum, I knew Unjoo was one hot, passionate woman. We left that restaurant and walked to a bar down the street, holding hands on and off between debating.'

When I asked them to give an example of a day or period in their relationship when they were riding somewhere in the middle lane, they looked at me like I had misread the temperature of their relationship. And they were right.

They stared at each other and laughed (intensely, of course) before Unjoo said, 'Ha-ha, NEVER! Sounds boring! Even when I was given the chance to move from New York City to Singapore, Tim quit his job, and we were on a plane one week later. We make shit happen!'

For this couple, clearly the middle path wouldn't do. That left us with the tall order of trying to preserve the intensity of their relationship—the passionate lovemaking, joyful laughter, fierce teamwork—while channelling the intensity of their conflicts towards something productive.

There was a particular charm to Unjoo and Tim that isn't present with all the intense couples I encounter. Some intense couples are intensely cold, others intensely hot. Undoubtedly, Unjoo and Tim were in the latter camp, but they were not necessarily typical of it and did not have the sadistic qualities I have seen in some such couples. With Unjoo and Tim, I sensed early on that there was at least something from their childhood or past that was showing up, that they were putting on the boxing gloves because of some fight that had been necessary and in them from a young age; the intensity of their tones, harsh word choices, and aggressive body language were suggestive of both fighting from the past and fighting the past itself. I was under no delusion that this would be easy breezy to turn around. Lots of hope, yet lots of work ahead.

The real question was how to motivate them to have conflict with a different vibration, one that was healthier and led to growth, not destruction. Somewhere in their cells, conflict was so familiar, so seductive. Many couples fight this way, à la Unjoo and Tim, to the grave, competing for the final, knockout punch.

'I do not want to take the intensity away from you two. It's remarkable to witness when you're laughing, describing the intensity of the teamwork you're capable of, the fiercely connected lovemaking, the intense joy you have when you join hands. That's all gold. What concerns me is how the intensity grabs onto the conflict and, one day, this destructive conflict will likely eclipse the gold. Tell me, though, why do you want to change how you're experiencing conflict? You two could continue fighting this way indefinitely. Many couples do,' I said.

It was important to know what was motivating them to change, and it was also important to signal to them that it was their life, and if they continued to choose to have conflict this way, then they could. I also wanted to poke them slightly to see the emotional reaction, if any, to hearing they could keep the boxing gloves on indefinitely.

'Although I've never seen it done differently, there must be another way. I just know that my parents used to fight like cats and dogs,' Unjoo responded.

'Yup, same. No clue what it looks like, but there must be another way,' Tim agreed.

'There is absolutely another way so long as you two are willing to put in the work. Unjoo, are you willing to share more about what you mean about your parents fighting like cats and dogs? If Tim pledges not to weaponize your response? I will also ask Unjoo to pledge the same if Tim is willing to share more about his background as well.'

They both nodded.

The next session we all agreed to dig down deep into the roots and see if there was anything of value to pull up. I had no doubt we would dig up something, though I did doubt we could have this conversation with civility. I thanked them both

for their openness and courage for sharing more about their
backgrounds, and I then told them clearly, I don't tolerate abuse
in my therapy room.

'Abuse?! Us?' they said, holding hands, laughing.

Root issues

'One night when I was around nine years old, my mother was
serving dinner, and my father threw a bowl of rice across the
room and looked at my mother and said, "Useless," and stormed
off. My mother took the frying pan and banged on the bedroom
door, screaming back that my father was useless. They then spent
the whole night in a screaming match. I remember my brother
and me under the blanket in our bedroom feeling so scared and
helpless.'

Unjoo had endless memories like this—screaming matches
that lasted into the night, horribly insulting comments given out
like candy by both parents to each other and the kids. She recalled
from a very young age a strong sense that she and her brother
better 'figure out how to survive' and eventually 'get the hell out'.

Unjoo grew up in Queens, New York. Her parents were
Korean immigrants and worked long hours at a dry-cleaning
company they owned and ran together. She was a latch-key kid
and looked after her younger brother from the age of seven.
Her mother would constantly make comments about Unjoo's
appearance and try to make her wear pink dresses and put her hair
up to look more 'feminine'. Unjoo had a natural athletic build and
broad shoulders, and, as a child, she was a tomboy who played
rough with the boys in her neighbourhood. This was much to
the horror of her mother, who embodied beautiful elegance and
prized her 'glass skin'. Unjoo's mother would often make clear she
felt repulsed by Unjoo's 'flat large nose and small eyes', and her
father largely ignored her growing up.

Unjoo grew up feeling 'totally unseen and never heard' as a child, and, to overcompensate, she became a brilliant student and read voraciously at the local library. At eighteen, she was admitted to Yale University on a full scholarship, and during her first semester, she cut her parents off, which she described as 'unthinkable' for a Korean immigrant child where filial piety was supreme. She went on to be a rock star in the banking world and was addicted to her career success.

In her early thirties, she met Tim, a midwestern American architect, and they would get into long protracted all-out wars whenever she wasn't feeling seen or heard by him, even early on. After Unjoo shared all of this, Tim looked at me and said, 'Do you see? That's why she fights like she does.'

Unjoo started yelling at him, 'This is exactly the shit he does. All the fucking time.'

Tim responded, 'How dare you throw that back at me! Did you even hear what I was saying?'

I looked each of them in the eye. 'We're not going to do this. If I allow this, you'll not only walk out of here knowing this was a waste of your time and money but, worse, it'll damage your relationship further.'

With some couples, it is possible to pause and all breathe together. With Unjoo and Tim, I had to get in the ring and separate them.

'Oh, Allison, this is just Tim doing his thing to distract from the truth. I get that I watched some crazy stuff growing up, and OK, I'm sure there's been some influence. Ask him about his sister,' Unjoo responded.

'Look, I was the product of an affair. Never met my dad. No clue where he is, if I look or sound like him. Nothing. Anyway, my mom raised my older sister and me and had to work all the time. My sister, when she was around twelve and I was only eight, started to beat me up after school if I didn't do something.

Sometimes it would be something ridiculous like not sharing my snack. I was basically scared of my sister growing up,' Tim shared with an intensely angry voice, teetering on screaming.

'Tim, was your mom aware of this? What did she do?' I asked.

'My mom. Look, my mom had to work a lot. She did her best. I told her many times, and she even saw some of the bruises. She told me to fight back and to toughen up, that life was hard. I remember being a little boy in physical pain from my sister, which just felt awful and embarrassing, and then seeing my mom in her own pain, struggling,' Tim shared with a touch more emotion.

'What about your pain, Tim? Where did it go?' I asked.

'For years, I just ate too much. I dabbled a bit with drinking, but really food was my drug of choice, and I also got into one more bar fight than I should have,' he said while pointing to his broken nose.

It became clearer how and why both needed to adapt to their environments growing up. After Unjoo and Tim shared their stories, I felt as though I could see a version of them as kids, their so-called inner child, focused on survival, not connection. Part of the therapist's job is to help the couple learn skills to reconnect when one or both is acting out of their inner child.

When Unjoo got the sense Tim wasn't hearing or seeing her, the boxing gloves would come on, and Tim would fight back, only to imagine his sister still attacking him. When Tim got the sense that Unjoo was attacking him, he would finally get his revenge on his sister and fight back.

Rinse and repeat, punctuate with passion, and back to the boxing ring.

As I described the way their inner children interact, they were both holding back tears, softened finally to each other's protective armour. We did some experiential work to connect with these battling children, not for the sake of catharsis but rather to recognize when they were speaking to each other as two children or two adults.

All of us, when we meet a partner, assume we are engaging with an adult only to find that they are a composite of various ages. We all eventually meet our partner's inner child, and sometimes we like what we see, and it softens us. Other times, we are horrified. It's likely in those moments the inner child senses danger and does what it needs to protect itself.

He's watching

The next session, Unjoo and Tim shared that the intensity of their conflict had lessened.

'It's about five per cent less intense! We'll take it,' Unjoo said, half-jokingly. 'We'll take it as a good sign, Allison, because we have some news to share,' she said as she tightened her dress to show me a baby bump.

Years working at a midwives' clinic has me trained to look at a bump and gauge the pregnancy's age. I looked at Unjoo's belly, and in my guesstimate, we had about four months to really turn this around.

I wonder to this day whether this is really what brought them to my therapy room, that perhaps they sensed on some level that their destructive fights could damage their child.

'How are you both feeling about this?' I asked. I've learned long ago not to respond with a reflexive 'Congratulations!' as there is often a mingling of emotions and sometimes ones that don't match a perky 'Congratulations!' one bit.

Unjoo responded, 'Yeah, we're happy! I just worry that Tim isn't really prepared for what's ahead and is going to expect me to step down from my career to take care of our son.'

Tim turned red and responded, 'What! Where do you get this crap from? I never said that, and, in fact, I think you're the one who is going to demand I stop working as hard or give up my running.'

And, just like that, we had gone from happy to attack.

I looked at them both, holding their son in my heart, and said, 'PAUSE!'

They looked at me like deer in headlights.

'Do you have an ultrasound photo of your son?' I asked.

'No,' they said in unison, looking perplexed by my question.

'Here's what we're going to do. After this session, I want you two to go get an ultrasound photo of your son printed off. Every time one of you kicks up, I want the other to point to this photo and say, "He's watching." In fact, every time the two of you start to kick up, I will do the same and point to Unjoo's belly to say, "He's watching." If you'd like, then you can bring the ultrasound photo to session, and we can even put it on a chair next to you both as a visceral reminder that that little boy is forever watching. Whatever you two say and do, he takes that in, and that becomes his blueprint for his future relationships. We have about four months to turn this around, and I totally believe you two can. We have no time to waste, though,' I said and then paused to see if any of this was sinking in.

It was. Their eyes were welling up. Tim looked like he was trying to swallow a golf ball.

'He's watching' became a mantra and a compass. They did the homework and printed out the ultrasound photo. In sessions thereafter, I would say 'He's watching' at the first sniff of an attack, and we worked on ways for them to take healthy breaks before resuming a conversation.

We worked deeper on the inner child and moved the needle from intellectual to visceral. They finally absorbed the damage to their own son that could be done if they didn't start interacting as two adults. During the experiential work, they also could appreciate that, while growing up, these inner children had helped them survive. That was a very important part of the work—to understand that at one point, these inner children were doing an important job, yet in adult interpersonal relationships they could often wreak havoc and make it nearly impossible to experience conflict in a healthy way.

Once they could do all of that, we spoke about the environment they wanted to cultivate for their son. 'He's watching' deepened and became a source of inspiration. If they could channel their exquisite energy towards cultivating a home environment filled with laughter, joy, and healthy relationships, then their son would bathe in the best of their intensity.

We continued sessions until Unjoo was thirty-eight weeks pregnant, and, in the last session, Tim rolled up the sleeve of his work shirt to show me a tattoo on his arm.

It said, 'He's watching.'

Chapter 15

Extraordinary Minds

'I'm at the end of my rope with Phillip's insensitivity and the way he communicates! He's always interrupting me like a child. In fact, he's harder to manage than our five-year-old twins. He blows hot and cold all the time. It's an emotional rollercoaster!'

Tears rolled down Lauren's face as she clenched her fists and grabbed the tissue box in front of her. She was petite and wore a flattering pink shift dress and nude ballerina flats. Her attractive face was framed by a short pixie cut. 'Being married to him . . . it's like a torture chamber,' she said, her face red with frustration and anger. 'I want to pull my hair out every single day. He's got to change, or I'm ending the marriage.'

'Oh, shut up! Come on. I'm not a child. Could a child afford to pay for all your spa trips and designer handbags? First-world problems, baby!' Phillip shot back, his words drenched in disrespect. He had a statuesque figure with chiselled facial features and gleaming black hair like a helmet, gelled in place. His imposing height and presence caused the floor to shake a little as he paced my therapy room back and forth. He was fidgeting the moment he walked in and couldn't sit still.

When I greeted Phillip and his wife in the waiting room, he was charismatic and outgoing, giving me a firm handshake and a wide smile. 'Hey! Great to meet you, Allison. I'm Phillip.' Yet, once he got a whiff of his wife's criticism, he switched gears into a defensive, frustrated version of himself.

'You think I like seeing you spend money like water—on clubs, designer clothes, bags, spas, personal trainers—you waste my hard-earned money! You have everything you want! And you still want more? I don't get it. What about caring for my needs? Why don't we try that for once? What does Phillip need?'

The veins in Phillip's neck throbbed as he spoke, and his words shuttled past like a high-speed train. I would try to slow him down by putting my hands in a 'T' shape, like a conductor. Stop!

'What's it like to hear your wife say she's going to end the marriage if you don't change, Phillip?' I asked.

Turning to me with intense focus he said, 'I don't know why I'm here if she's already made up her mind. Why doesn't Lauren go see a divorce lawyer instead of coming here? Her spa trips and designer clothes will be out the window once the lawyer wakes her up to the fact she'll need to go back to work if we divorce. Flipping burgers, imagine that! Maybe then she'll understand the real pressures at work. She complains about her workouts and how her personal trainer overworks her hamstrings. I'd like her to spend one day in my shoes, and she can experience *real* overwork. I don't need this bullshit! We've already seen two awful therapists.'

'Why are you here then, Phillip? Why even show up to this session if you believe Lauren should be seeing a lawyer to wake her up?' I genuinely wondered.

'Why am I here? I'm here because Lauren says all this crap regularly about me. That I am like her child, that I don't do certain things with the kids. All of what you're hearing now I hear daily. I work a lot and provide the life she wants, and I don't get why she wants more and never asks me about my needs,' Phillip said.

'Why don't you ask him about his work? He loves that more than me,' Lauren said, half choked up.

I went with it.

'May I ask, what is your work? And is it true what Lauren said that you love it more than her?' I asked.

'That's ridiculous. You would have to be a robot to love work more than your wife. I do enjoy my work though. I founded a Singapore-based investment manager catering to the ultra-high net worth,' he said with an ounce of enthusiasm.

'What do you like about your work?' I asked. I needed to push a bit more on the enthusiasm to keep Phillip engaged before building a bridge back to his marriage.

'I'm the boss and get to innovate all the time. Also, all the big movers and shakers come to me, and I can usually get one of them on the tennis court by my office at first light. It's awesome.'

When Phillip spoke about his job, that big, bright smile would return to his lips. He was all high energy, bright lights, high definition, and I'd have taken one of everything he was selling. He was the polar opposite when we spoke about his emotions in the marriage. Then he would float off to an entirely different planet and be bored, frustrated and defensive, or simply zoned out completely.

'This guy is truly a happy guy at work,' said Lauren. 'I don't know how his staff follow the million ideas flowing through his mouth, but yeah, he's super enthusiastic about work and tennis and has endless reservoirs of energy. It sometimes exhausts me listening to his schedule. In fact, if he misses tennis one day before work, I can tell the minute he walks through the front door. He's a puppy dog who hasn't been walked.'

Hmm. Like a child at times. Energy like the Energizer Bunny. Not motivated when bored. Ideas and jokes flowing from his mouth. Charming one minute, deflated from a sense of criticism and rejection the next. Bored when we speak about emotions in the marriage, yet hyper-focused when we speak about his work or playing tennis.

I wondered if Phillip had ADHD (attention deficit hyperactivity disorder). I had a strong hunch he did and knew that unless I was adding a sugar cube to these conversations, some kind of shiny object, Phillip would leave the session by disconnecting in his head. So, I kept a pot of sugar cubes close and did what I could to keep him in the room.

I turned first to Phillip and remarked how genuine his excitement felt for work and tennis—the subconscious subtext being, do you have enthusiasm for your marriage?

Then I turned to Lauren. 'It's clear Phillip is an enthusiastic guy when it comes to his work and tennis,' I said. 'What lights you up about him?'

'Oh, Phillip. He's incredibly spirited when he's passionate about something. You just got to see that. When we first met, he certainly made me feel like the prettiest girl in town, like he had tunnel vision just on me. He used to light up when we were together. He loves to travel and meet people. So when he's talking about his work, it's like a level of enthusiasm I've never seen before. Also, he's super funny and lights up with a good dose of humour . . . although, there are some things that fly out of his mouth that shouldn't. And with our twins, he's super engaged when our son or daughter wants to do an activity he enjoys. The problem is, Phillip can't quite stay focused or engaged with some of the "yuck" stuff with kids like when our son refuses to do something, has meltdowns, or wants to stay somewhere "boring". Phillip can't tolerate it. Yet, when it's something he enjoys, wow, he's a star dad.'

'Wow, so there's a lot that lights this guy up, more than tennis and work. Not everyone I meet, Phillip, has this kind of zest for life. I would bottle your zest if I could. I wonder how the marriage would feel if we applied some of this remarkable enthusiasm and passion to it?' I said, lifting my shoulders slightly to signal *Wow, what if.*

That's not only part of my job description as a therapist but also one of my greatest joys. *Wow, what if?*

'Yeah, well, that would be amazing if we both could be more enthusiastic about the marriage and not always criticize. But yeah, I agree, I could be more enthusiastic and sometimes I don't know why I'm not when she's not criticizing me,' Phillip responded.

'Well, that's a big statement that you could be more enthusiastic. We can work with that,' I said, as if Phillip had just won an Academy Award.

With a client like Phillip, I sometimes need to ham it up a bit, to express that he's made some kind of shift, even if glacial. In general, I don't wait for clients to give ideal or 'perfect' answers. Good enough is good enough. If there's any intent to shift gears and reroute the high-speed train towards relational health, I go with it.

Phillip's enthusiasm was a potential salve if applied to the marriage, and by celebrating it, I also wanted to inject a bit of hope into Lauren, who had turned to me hunched over with her arms in her lap.

'I wanted to ask you something, Allison,' Lauren said. 'I have been Googling things like "Why doesn't my spouse pay attention?" and "Why can't my spouse focus when he's uninterested in something?" And other things related to what I've shared. My description of him as being like a child cropped up repeatedly in group forums where other people were discussing similar issues. Anyway, Google kept coming up with ADHD. I have no idea if he has that or not, but I just wanted to put it on the table. I always think of ADHD as hyperactive six-year-old boys, so who knows, I could be wrong.'

I listened intensely to Lauren while watching Phillip to see whether he was here with us or if I needed to dip into my box of sugar cubes and shiny objects.

'Phillip, is it OK if I respond to that?' I looked at him and received a literal thumbs-up with a boyish smile, as if to say, 'Go forth, dear therapist.'

My guess was he would feel relieved that we had rerouted the focus away from attacking him and towards the unnamed, uninvited guest in this marriage.

'I have been wondering for much of the session about ADHD. I am not a medical doctor or diagnostician so I cannot say with any ounce of certainty, yet I do think it's worth finding out to help the couples work. If you do have ADHD, Phillip, then this will help me understand the support you need, and if you don't, then it will also help. Either way, it'll help me see the bigger picture in the marriage. What's coming to you when I say this?' I asked.

'I always thought there was something different about me, but my dad, who was a medical doctor, would shut down any suggestions that my teachers would make.'

Throughout Phillip's primary and secondary school years, his teachers spoke with his parents about testing for a possible neurodiverse disorder. But Phillip's father, a well-known medical specialist, always shot their suggestions down. The stigma surrounding neurodiversity was too great back then. His father would say, 'The problem is that my son is too smart for some of this schooling. Let him be.'

Teachers, classmates, and family members knew he had difficulty controlling his words and maintaining friendships, but they also loved his enthusiasm, hyperfocus when interested, and his humour. His parents thought that with Lauren, their son had finally found a woman who was patient and understanding of his 'quirks' and that eventually having a family would resolve some of his challenges. They were aware their son's teachers believed Phillip's ability to focus was not at the same level of his peers, even though he was highly intelligent and went on to study at Cambridge University in the UK, obtaining a first-class honours degree in law. He was a successful lawyer until he got 'bored' and decided to open his own business in which he thrived immensely.

Phillip and Lauren came from wealthy Chinese families in Singapore, with ancestral roots in mainland China. While it wasn't exactly an arranged marriage, their parents were close and in the same social circles from the time they were in elementary school. Wistful comments from both mothers when Phillip and Lauren were young encouraged them to date years later when they had grown up. Without critically thinking about whether they really were compatible, they dutifully fulfilled the wishes of their parents and began to date several years after graduating.

It turned out that they had a strong connection as partners. They both loved the outdoors, travel, and tennis, and wanted to stay in Singapore. And they agreed on the importance of family; they wanted children and planned to care for their parents when they were elderly.

When they shared their backstory, I could feel the couple in the room, and I was confident that—whatever the diagnosis—the stalemate had been broken.

Clear as day

When Phillip received his official diagnosis, the psychiatrist called me afterwards and said, 'What a character! He's definitely got ADHD.'

I called Phillip and his wife to discuss briefly so we could come up with a clear plan, and Lauren responded, 'OMG! That's it. I knew when I was reading this stuff online it was basically Phillip. He's been a frustrating enigma for years.'

We then spoke about a plan whereby Phillip would do individual sessions with me for the next three months and then discuss whether to resume couples therapy. In those three months, I also did a session with Lauren to help process the diagnosis and work on ways to support her husband, which in turn would lead to a healthier marriage. Like many, Lauren shared she was both 'relieved and burdened' with this diagnosis. It gave her an injection of hope, but also felt like a lot to carry.

Among her biggest questions were some usual suspects: Why do I have to make these changes? Why am I the one who must accommodate? What if he never makes changes?

Here are some ways I often respond to the non-ADHD partner:

a. I start off by stressing it's normal to have these questions and feelings.

b. I remind them that they don't *have to* change. That's a very important first step so that they don't fall captive to a victim mindset, which will backfire eventually.

c   It may be in their best interest, *if* they want a healthier, stronger marriage, to support their spouse. Their partner will likely be more connected and relational if set up for success.

d. I take the spouse back to the time they wanted to get married. This is to highlight that there was once enough good in the relationship to want to say yes to a life together.

e. I remind the person that I, or someone else, will be working with the spouse to make changes as well.

f.   All marriages involve change. Marriage is not purely about acceptance. Acceptance can be a powerful ingredient in a marriage and a necessary one, yet without some change, it's unlikely the partnership will grow and evolve.

I asked Lauren how it felt hearing all of this, and she responded, 'It's a bitter pill to swallow. I'm not going to lie. But I like what you said about these changes helping the marriage overall, and I do still love the guy quite a bit.'

Once Lauren could reframe her support as not only for her husband but also the growth of the marriage, we got to work.

Here's what I recommended:

a. Take over the administrative work. Too much time in marriages is wasted battling over who does what. With Lauren, I suggested she should either do it or outsource it. Some of the administrative tasks include submitting health insurance bills, paying utilities, rent and credit card bills, filing taxes, and organizing the children's activities. Is it 'fair'? No, of course not. So little in a marriage is.

b. Be more vocal about Phillip's changes but be aware of the tones and words used. It was important Lauren celebrated Phillip's shifts and important not to be too critical as to do otherwise would risk triggering his Rejection Sensitivity Dysphoria (RSD). Almost all people with ADHD also have RSD, which is characterized by intense emotional reactions, to feelings of rejection or criticism, especially by people they love. While no human feels good about rejection or criticism, people with ADHD experience it much more intensely.

c. Set Phillip up for success. Many people in marriages, once they have a theory about the partner—that he won't change, he's a nightmare, whatever it is—they will continually gather evidence to support this 'truth'. I recommend the opposite, which is to ask oneself, 'How can I support my partner so that we both feel better and more connected?' Lauren, for example, started to celebrate Phillip's hyperfocus—such as when he was helping the children with their science projects or coaching them in tennis.

d. Enjoy the exuberance! This suggestion is often overlooked. Often, the non-ADHD spouse will focus on the challenges, and I get it. However, there are also many wonderful qualities that the ADHD spouse brings.

Lauren delighted in much of Phillip's humour—though not the sarcasm he sometimes slipped into—and also his enthusiasm for tasks he enjoyed. She used to love playing tennis with Phillip, so I suggested she should join him once a week before work. She really enjoyed the enthusiasm he had for that time together.

Wild jungle rides

With my ADHD clients, we are often on jungle rides. In our individual sessions, Phillip and I were navigating an exuberant and colourful flow of ideas, with little tolerance for boredom or frustration yet an incredible capacity for creativity and enthusiasm.

These are brains that challenge us in spectacular ways. These are brains that do absolutely need support, yet we should not compel them to aspire to the rigid ideas of success that cater to neurotypicals.

And, as much as therapists, like parents, are supposed not to have favourites, some of my favourite clients are neurodiverse.

I had a strong rapport with Phillip, and we were able to progress at a steady rate. He showed up for every session ready to hit the ground running.

In our first session, I asked Phillip how he felt about the diagnosis. Clients often feel a mingling of emotions. I also wondered what he wanted to get from our sessions.

His eyes widened. 'You know what? I've always wondered if there was something different. I just want to be sure we don't erase different, and yet I get that different can sometimes be challenging for others, and who knows, maybe even myself. I want to work on my relationship with Lauren, yes, yet I also want to work on professional stuff.'

At this point in history, ADHD is thought to be a neurodevelopmental disorder—that is, it's related to how the brain grows and develops. There are three ways it presents itself: predominantly inattentive, predominantly hyperactive, or mixed inattentive and hyperactive.

If you had ADHD as a child, then you will likely still have at least some symptoms as an adult—some people's brains change more than others—and many adults walk around not knowing they have it. Many adults discover they have ADHD when it is diagnosed in their children.

The treatment for ADHD depends on how it presents, but lifestyle and behavioural changes are usually helpful whatever form it takes. Some people also decide to take medication. Phillip was clear he did not want that. After sharing that he did not want to take medication, he turned to me and said, 'You're my human Ritalin! Let's discuss this more next time—I gotta run now!'

He was diagnosed with combined type ADHD, mixed inattentive and hyperactive, and wanted to focus on behavioural changes to help his relational skills at home and at work along with lifestyle changes to help him focus, perform, and simply feel better overall.

With Phillip, I asked him what kind of father and husband he hoped to be and reverse-engineered from there. It required him first to see his identity differently in those domains and then to work on taking action. Phillip was clear he wanted to be a loving and present father, and also felt he could be a 'better' boss. He wanted me to speak with his HR head, Mary, to understand his workstyle and get feedback from his team, and I agreed this would be helpful. Seeing people in different contexts can shine a light on their experiences and how others experience them.

On one level, Phillip reaped the benefits of having ADHD at work as an entrepreneur and to an extent in his business relationships. And he was far from alone in seeing the competitive advantages of his condition.

As Dr Jenifer Chan, a Hong Kong-based psychiatrist and expert on ADHD, explains: 'Successful adults with ADHD have reported that qualities such as cognitive dynamism and energy, and the sub-qualities of divergent thinking, hyper-focus, nonconformism, adventurousness, self-acceptance, and sublimation are positive aspects of their condition.'

Chan adds that entrepreneurs like Phillip excel if they have strategies to manage their workload well and have management skills. 'Entrepreneurs with ADHD have been shown to increase performance due to higher levels of risk-taking, being proactive and innovative. Opportunities to work on novel, exciting, and fast-paced projects and having frequent social interactions will also be helpful to manage feelings of boredom, which are frequently encountered by people with ADHD.'

My supervisor asked me at one point what stage of change Phillip was in when discussing the changes that he wanted to make at work and home. There's a model in psychology known as 'The Stages of Change', which posits that there are five stages a person goes through before making a change. I told my supervisor that ADHD clients mostly do not roll like this. The light switch is either on or off—they either will make a change or they won't. It used to be thought that ADHD included a deficiency of focus. We now know that it's not a lack of focus but a lack of motivation when the person is not interested *enough* in something. But, once my clients with ADHD are motivated *enough* and excited *enough*, they are usually flying.

Here is what Phillip and I worked on together over the course of seven months.
Nutrition:

a. Eat regularly: He shared he often felt 'hanger', and that when it struck, he could not focus.
b. Reduce processed foods and chemicals: I told him if he did not understand something on a food label, then it was likely his body wouldn't benefit from it. I shared the mantra of 'Eat crap, feel like crap.'

c. Reduce sugar: Phillip had a habit of snacking on candy at the office. So, we removed all candy from his office. He coped fine; it was pure habit.

d. Eat more omega-3s: Phillip was vegetarian, so we got him to eat more walnuts, chia seeds, and flax seeds.

e. And more protein: For Phillip, this meant more tofu, beans, and nuts.

Sleep:

a. Prioritize and protect sleep: This meant thinking about sleep early in the day and not waiting until night-time and having a clear bedtime, even on weekends—a maximum of an hour later than on weekdays. It also meant creating a clear bedtime routine. We worked on taking a bath, doing some light stretching, and then reading.

b. No phone or devices one hour before bed: Phillip needed clear boundaries with his phone, otherwise, left to his own devices, he was scrolling all the time.

c. Leave the phone out of the bedroom: Buy an alarm clock instead.

d. Less joe: Eliminate caffeine after lunch. This includes coffee, tea, chocolate, energy bars, and energy drinks that contain caffeine.

e. Mag up: Talk to the doctor about taking magnesium glycinate before bedtime. Many people with a magnesium deficiency suffer from insomnia, and studies have shown that taking magnesium supplements improves sleep quality. There are various forms of magnesium, and only a doctor can properly advise on which form, if any, to take. I have found magnesium glycinate to be the easiest to digest and amino acid glycine improves sleep quality. Some therapists refer to magnesium as 'Mother Nature's Xanax' or 'The Original Chill Pill'.

Exercise:

a.   HIIT the nets: Tennis twice a week before work, and the same for high-intensity interval training (HIIT).
b.   Walk it off: Family rambles on Saturday and Sunday.
c.   Weight it out: Train with weights twice a week.

Marriage and children:

1.   Be aware of RSD triggers: When it comes on, pause, breathe, and take a walk if possible. Try not to respond immediately with an insult—choose words carefully with an intent to heal, not harm. When discussing Phillip's marriage, I would often ask him, 'Do you mean to say *this* and not *that?*' He needed to understand how to frame his thoughts differently. We spoke about how responsive people are to kind tones and word choices.
2.   Empathy with a pause: Ask, 'How might my wife feel when I say this?' Because words shot out of Phillip's mouth like a cannon, he often didn't pause to consider the emotional impact his words could have on his wife. Emotional regulation is often overlooked with ADHD, yet it's one of the most important skills, and this includes being aware of how words and actions impact others. We also leveraged some of the black-and-white thinking that can come with ADHD to draw clear lines of what not to say—these included punching below the belt and anything that felt contemptuous and grandiose.
3.   Be more proactive in spending time with Lauren: Do things that she likes as well. Phillip also started to reach out more during the day to send warm messages like 'I love you' or to ask how she is or how her day was going.
4.   Tolerate more of the 'yuck' stuff with children: Only by investing time now would Phillip have the relationship

he wanted later. We also spoke about there being no guarantees that tomorrow would come and looking at the yuck stuff as time spent with his children.

5. Increase time with the children: This was particularly important for the things he enjoyed doing too, such as teaching them sports. Each Sunday afternoon was a time to take them to the park for a few hours and give Lauren a break.

6. Listen to binaural beats: Even though Lauren was taking over most of the administrative tasks, whenever Phillip did need to do something 'boring', I suggested he listen to what are called binaural beats at the same time he needed to complete tasks. These are sometimes referred to as 'musical Ritalin' as many people report that when they listen to these, they are able to intensely focus.

7. Consult feng shui master: Phillip promised Lauren he would consult their family's feng shui master before making any big life decisions to reduce his impulsivity.

Phillip made many sustainable changes throughout our time together and has made it a priority to still check in from time to time to fine tune his efforts. I also met with Mary, the Head of HR at Phillip's company, and helped improve his workstyle and team dynamics at work.

He and Lauren reported 'massive improvements' in their marriage and return to couples counselling when needed. Lauren shared, at our last couples' session, 'There are fewer moments when Phillip feels like my third child and feels more now like my husband.'

Not a hyperactive six-year-old boy

For the first thirty-three years of my life, I had no idea I had ADHD. I knew something was different, just like Phillip. I couldn't translate my shade of different into words or a diagnosis, nor could I identify the exact shape of it. It sometimes felt like a best friend and other times an enemy. Like many women with ADHD, though, I had gone through life without anyone spotting my condition.

Since being diagnosed, the label has felt like both a warm hug and a straitjacket, often at the same time. When it's a warm hug, it feels like the world makes sense, both my inner world and the world at large. When it's a straitjacket, it feeds limiting beliefs, and I battle with how to get something done or fit in. At times like these, I sometimes revert to 'masking'—essentially trying to hide my ADHD.

As I do with my clients, I take a dual perspective on myself most days. I have my challenges, like every human on this planet, and my superpowers, again, like every human on this planet. Some days feel more 'ADHD-ish' as in the number of windows up in my head at once, overcrowding my mind, all competing for my hyperfocus. Those days often feel both exciting and overwhelming and are some of my most productive yet challenging. My head floods with a million ideas, and I have a strong desire to raise my hand for many things. However, when faced with a new project or task, either a strong flow takes me forward, or I am hit by overwhelm, unaware about where to start, what to do, and how to organize it all.

I've always been hyper-focused on certain topics and can latch on when I'm interested. When I'm bored, I totally switch off, and I have learned tricks to maintain motivation when I am not interested in something or will sometimes outsource tasks.

Years ago in Hong Kong, I had an epiphany while listening to a podcast as I walked along the winding streets of Conduit Road in the area known as Mid-Levels. It was the 'Sounds True' podcast with Tammy Simon, and she was speaking to the well-known Positive Psychology coach and author of *Getting Grit*, Caroline Adams Miller. While I listened, it suddenly hit me: I don't have enough *grit*—this is the missing ingredient in my life. I repeated this obsessively to myself as I fired off an email to Caroline Miller to request a coaching session.

When I met Caroline, she asked me to tell her about my life. I was prepared to be diagnosed grit-less and prescribed a hearty dose of exercises to build up my grit muscle.

She looked at me, shook her head and said, 'No. You basically told me your life story, and it's full of grit. Overflowing with grit. You've told me the grittiest tales. I think you have ADHD.'

In that moment, so much connected. I felt relieved and curious. Like many of my clients, I wondered whether I wanted to get an official diagnosis. With diagnoses, I am aware that most are based on clinical judgement and possibly secondary reporting or filling out questionnaires. There are no blood tests or brain scans like in medicine, and my guess is that in the future, many psychological diagnoses will cease to exist or exist on spectrums. That's why there is often wide variation in diagnosing the condition. Ask ten clinicians, and you may get ten different diagnoses.

I went through the same checklist I offer my clients when they are considering whether to get a diagnosis.

a. Identity: For some people, a diagnosis is a potential or automatic admission into a larger community. With ADHD, for example, some feel connected with others with ADHD and some with a larger neurodiversity community in or outside the workplace.

b. Medication: Some people want to explore if medication is helpful.

c. Lifestyle changes: With many mental health conditions, some symptoms may be improved by eating healthy, getting enough sleep, exercising, and socializing.

d. Accommodations: A diagnosis can be of practical help. For instance, school children may be granted extended time in exams or adults may be able to request quiet rooms at work.

    e.   Behavioural changes: Learning organizational techniques at work and home can help people cope with certain situations more easily.

    f.   Curiosity: Some people simply want to scratch the itch. They want to *know*, but they don't necessarily want to *do* anything with that knowledge afterwards.

I decided to go through with the testing for a few reasons. I did it out of curiosity, to experience what my clients went through, and because I was committed to making lifestyle and behavioural changes that might prove helpful.

Some clients struggle after diagnosis with what their lives could have been had they known earlier. As I awaited my own diagnosis, it struck me that there were upsides and downsides to not knowing.

I met a psychiatrist specializing in ADHD, and she asked me if I often forgot things. I said no, and then interrupted myself five minutes later and said, 'I forgot that I forget things, yes! I forgot to bring my veil to my own wedding.' Well, if that didn't answer her question . . .

When I got home that evening, my husband, Josh, asked how my day had been. I said, 'Oh, today was interesting. I went to see a psychiatrist who diagnosed me with ADHD.'

He replied cheekily, 'There's a name for *THIS*?!'

In one way, having a diagnosis didn't change anything for Josh. We had been married for years, so he was well aware of my ADHD-like behaviour, even if we had not previously labelled it as that.

'Life is never boring. I never know what you're going to text me or what you're working on, or where we're going next,' he pointed out. 'When you're excited about something, you get super excited, and when you're not, you're utterly checked out. Gone.'

Indeed, he'd long come to appreciate many of the aspects of my ADHD, like how I would jump out of bed in the morning, excited about life, and never know if he would be coming home to see the walls painted orange.

But in other ways, there were real advantages to having a confirmed diagnosis. It helped him to understand that when my frustration hit, it would hit like a wave but would soon pass over.

Since my diagnosis, I have referred to Josh as the Make-It-Go-Away Man. This is his official title when performing duties such as picking up my passport at the consulate (too boring), submitting my health insurance forms (no thanks), and dealing with the children when they are melting down (too frustrating) or fighting over who knows what (again, too frustrating) and the acoustics at home reach maddening levels (someone hand me the earplugs!). The one, the only—thank you dear husband—who deals with all things boring and frustrating.

What's important for us is a clear division of labour. For example, Josh does the administrative work, and I do all the cooking. Josh's food is inedible on a good day—he's been kicked out of the kitchen, and he's never coming back. Just like on a good day, my administrative skills are dreadful. We don't waste precious time on arguing with reality.

With my children, too, ADHD has been both a blessing and challenge.

My eldest son described it with wisdom beyond his years. 'Dad is more even with what he feels. You have amazing intensity with your emotions. Dad and you are so different when you're angry. Dad's anger is less intense but lasts longer. You get really angry then you're done with the anger so quickly, like five seconds later, and want to move on to something else.'

It's true. I often feel a range of emotions very intensely. Yet just as often, I move on to something else before I can even name the emotion.

My hyperfocus affects my parenting style in that when my sons are interested in a topic and get excited about something, I'll get excited too and go to the moon and back. My eldest son loves soccer, so we discuss it often. My youngest son loves cars and therefore discuss those often. For the record, neither soccer nor cars are on my list of what truly lights me up, yet I apply enthusiasm and hyperfocus nonetheless. Both my sons love books, as do I, and with these, I display a depth of enthusiasm and high levels of creativity around the stories and characters.

ADHD has in many ways been a gift in my work as a therapist and, like Phillip, my work as an entrepreneur. It gives me a laser focus with my clients and fuels my determination to bring about transformation. With the creativity that comes with ADHD, out-of-the-box ideas come to me during sessions, ones that regularly have me *rethinking the couch*. Still, connecting ideas and thoughts so rapidly can be both a blessing and a burden. Often, I must remind myself to slow down and match the pace of the client in front of me.

With couples, I can juggle many balls and stories at the same time and not get lost. It helps me to see different perspectives and weigh various ideas. I can multitask with ease and keep a dynamic flow to my workday.

The turning point in managing my ADHD came in changes to my sleep, diet, and exercise regimes. I have a strict sleep schedule, and I am fiercely protective of it; having enough sleep moves the needle on my ability to perform. I follow the same nutritional advice I share with my clients and make sure I never let my blood sugar dip—Hanger + ADHD = Volcanic Explosion. Like my clients, the days I eat crap, I feel like crap. I channel my focus through my work and outsource tedious tasks to get things done. It's vital to have a congress of support.

I rarely feel ashamed of my ADHD, even though intellectually I'm well aware there's often a stigma attached to it.

About a year ago, I was having dinner at a café in Singapore with a pregnant female doctor friend when she divulged that she was taking a huge range of vitamins. I asked her how she decided on which vitamins to take, and she responded that the cocktail was a hedge, to 'prevent' her unborn child from having ADHD or autism. She said she would do 'everything in her power' to prevent this. I felt numb, and part of me wanted to respond, 'So, you're hoping your daughter isn't me? The same friend you're having lunch with right now?' I didn't, though, because I was too frazzled to speak.

This experience reminded me that although I do believe there are gifts that come with ADHD, there are also battles—internally and with the outer world.

Neurodiversity in Asia

Neurodiversity (ND) is an umbrella term for ADHD, Autism, Dyspraxia, Dyslexia, dyscalculia, obsessive-compulsive disorder (OCD), and Tourette's syndrome—all are neurodiverse conditions that describe how differently people experience, think, learn, behave, and interact with the world around them. There has been a movement in the West since the 1990s to increase acceptance, recognize ND, and promote inclusion—that there is no one 'right' way of thinking that's better than others, and it's important to not perceive neurological differences as a deficit or as something wrong but as a social category similar to ethnicity, gender, ability, and sexual orientation. Neurodiversity is one of the antidotes to 'ableism'.

There has been little research on the effect of culture on symptoms, diagnosis, and treatment.

In Hong Kong, researchers have found that ADHD symptoms persist into adulthood, at rates of over 80 per cent. A study from South Korea revealed that ADHD occurs more commonly in low-income households, and that the nationwide economic burden associated with a diagnosis of ADHD was estimated to be over US$47.55 million. Overall, figures on co-occurring mental and physical health difficulties and socio-economic factors appear very similar between East Asia and the West, possibly with the exception of substance misuse, which appears less common in East Asia.

Dr Kamani, a psychiatrist in Singapore, explains that the stigma surrounding mental illness in Asia is deeply rooted and often traces back to cultural and religious beliefs. 'In the Asian culture, mental illness is often viewed as a weakness. Sometimes it also has religious beliefs associated with it such as being possessed by evil spirits. There is still significant discrimination towards people with mental illness in society as well as in the schools and workplaces. Very often, mental illness is viewed as a weakness of the mind and character and individuals presenting with these symptoms are often sidelined by the community.'

Kamani says Asian parents often prefer not to get their children diagnosed and treated out of a concern that they will be targeted in school and experience negative bias in the workplace.

She describes the concept of family honour, or 'face', as a barrier that stops people from reaching out for help as it's considered a source of shame to acknowledge mental illness in the family, and it also has consequences on moral standing. 'A study by the Institute of Mental Health's (IMH) research division found that Asian respondents tended to feel more threatened by mental illness as a mark of shame. Similarly, Asians are found to have a lower sense of responsibility towards the mentally ill, as compared to respondents from the other ethnic groups,' she said.

Kamani cites a 2017 study on mental health stigma in Singapore's youth, which found that approximately 44.5 per cent of respondents associated mental illnesses with negative, derogatory terms like 'stupid', 'dangerous', 'crazy', and 'weird', while 46.2 per cent said they would be 'very embarrassed' if they were diagnosed with a mental illness[9].

'The public's general perception of a mentally ill person is one that is violent, unreliable, and unstable,' said Kamani.

Unsung superpowers

Far from unreliable and unstable, some believe that ADHD is a superpower. That is what bestselling author and entrepreneur Peter Shankman calls his ADHD—a superpower. 'ADHD is great because we can come up with an idea and launch it within a few days—while those with "regular brains" are still writing down the idea,' he told me. 'Creativity is a hallmark of the neurodiverse, especially ADHD. Want your company to be creative? Want to have your employees think out of the box? Want to survive and not be eliminated? You'd better be hiring those who think different.'

Shankman is a trailblazer in presenting an alternative image of ADHD, particularly in the workplace. He recommends people with ADHD work in creative fields and not so much with numbers, though there are always exceptions to the rule.

He told me, 'The ability to see things differently—the way no one else in the company ever has before—is a great advantage. Those who are neurodiverse tend to see things with different lenses, much more differently than the norm. This can lead to great advances and incredible ways of shifting your business for the better. What are the possible challenges? To not freak out

---

[9] S. Pang, J. Liu, M. Mahesh, *et al*, 'Stigma among Singaporean youth: a cross-sectional study on adolescent attitudes towards serious mental illness and social tolerance in a multiethnic population', *BMJ Open* 2017;7:e016432, doi: 10.1136/bmjopen-2017-016432.

when they come to you with what may seem like strange ideas. Hear them out before you say no.'

He does admit to a downside, one witnessed with Phillip as well. 'Personal relationships are challenging, no doubt. I'm great in a crisis, but I've been told that I'm not great at the boring "day to day". That's something I've been working on for years,' he said.

Harnessing superpowers in the workplace

Many employers will not be aware of how many of their staff are neurodiverse. People with conditions like ADHD and autism may be reticent to share their diagnosis in all but the most supportive environments. But for those employers willing to actively embrace neurodiversity, there are huge potential gains to be had in harnessing these unsung superpowers.

Asia still lags the West in this regard, yet there are signs that the most visionary companies in the region are coming round to the competitive advantages of hiring neurodiverse staff—a largely untapped pool of talent.

A 2017 study by Nathalie Boot of the University of Amsterdam found that people with ADHD were more creative and out-of-the-box thinkers than those with neurotypical brains.[10]

Globally, there's been a huge shift in the number of leading companies that have refined their human resource hiring process to include neurodiverse talent. These include Microsoft, Ford, SAP, Hewlett Packard Enterprise, Willis Towers Watson, and Ernst & Young. In Asia, companies from HSBC and Ernst & Young to JPMorgan have vouched for neurodivergent staff as

---

[10] N. Boot, B. Nevicka, M. Baas, 'Creativity in ADHD: Goal-Directed Motivation and Domain Specificity', J Atten Disord. 2020 Nov;24(13):1857-1866. doi: 10.1177/1087054717727352. Epub 2017 Aug 28. PMID: 28845720; PMCID: PMC7543022.

being 30–48 per cent more productive than neurotypical staff when they are in roles that are a good fit.

According to the *Harvard Business Review*, a professional with autism is up to 140 per cent more productive than the average neurotypical person when 'properly matched' with the right job.[11] Researchers say that people with autism and those with dyslexia could have higher-than-average skills in mathematics, memory, and pattern recognition, and understanding complex systems. But discrimination against people with neurodiversity is rampant in Asia and around the world because most contemporary workplace systems are geared towards those who are neurotypical.

Dr Kamani has noticed that there are certain professions, such as entrepreneurial ones, that are better suited for people with ADHD. She explains, 'The cardinal symptoms of ADHD, such as inattention and hyperactivity, can impair a person's performance at the workplace as they can get restless or distracted easily. However, looking at their skillset and their passion and finding a career which allows them the flexibility to work at their pace and take frequent breaks often helps. A recent study highlighted how ADHD can be productively harnessed in entrepreneurs. People with ADHD also have the potential to thrive in the creative industries and in self-employed roles, where they have control over the work they do.'

I'm hopeful that corporations in Asia are slowly coming round to the advantages of neurodiverse staff, yet I also see a long road ahead.

With the right support, those with ND brains can excel and bring their unique strengths and superpowers to their work. I have met a number of them: a successful trader with autism who is able to spot number patterns and potential market anomalies, thriving

[11] Ludmila N. Praslova, 'Autism Doesn't Hold People Back at Work. Discrimination Does.' *Harvard Business Review* (13 Dec, 2021) https://hbr.org/2021/12/autism-doesnt-hold-people-back-at-work-discrimination-does.

entrepreneurs making bold decisions, teachers and hairstylists with ADHD, a travel agent with autism who knows every minute detail about flights and hotels in various countries, accountants and energetic TV producers with ADHD, and IT and data analysts with autism. One journalist joked that the newsroom is seemingly full of journalists with ADHD with boundless energy and curiosity, and copywriters with autism who can't let go of a typo and that 'it's like a veritable neurodiversity convention!'

The payback for companies truly willing to embrace ND is clear. If you want extraordinary results, you need extraordinary minds.

Chapter 16

Stressed Out and Burned Out:
Toxic Offices

'At midnight, I'm either watching porn or texting my boss who is a complete prick,' Nigel said, speaking at a million miles per minute.

Nigel was Hong Kong–Chinese with a buzz cut and pimply face. He had been referred to me by a gastroenterologist who was seeing him for irritable bowel syndrome (IBS). But Nigel's problems didn't stop at stomach aches and long trips to the bathroom; he was experiencing chronic stress and anxiety and regularly working around the clock. He was working at a global consulting firm in Hong Kong in a regional role that required him to travel for at least a week every month to another country in Asia. He wore the requisite consultant's casual wear to each session and looked a picture of professionalism. Yet his energy felt frenetic.

'Honestly, I think therapy is a bunch of garbage,' Nigel relayed. 'My father always told me that feelings are for losers, but I am kind of at a breaking point. Plus, the gastro guy basically ordered me to come and see you, and I have insurance coverage, so why not give it a shot.'

'Well, I appreciate your candour and also that you did show up,' I said. 'It must have been a big step for you.'

'I am just stuck and stressed, not only at work but with my girlfriend, Amara,' Nigel sighed. 'Amara is Thai and twelve years younger than me. We met when I was on holiday in Thailand five years ago, and she just kind of followed me to Hong Kong.'

Nigel continued to rattle off his thoughts, lurching from topic to topic without much connection. He needed to purge everything, the stress and anxiety, all at once before we could regroup and gain focus. Boss is a prick. Stressed with an upcoming project. Endless demands. No feelings for his girlfriend. Why is his boss such a prick? Why does his girlfriend want to marry? No, he doesn't want kids. Why is his co-worker now starting to act like his boss?

And so it went.

People walk around feeling stressed a lot. An important first step is to help them articulate what is stressing them out and what they find most stressful. Our minds can be like rubbish bins that never get emptied or washing machines with the same thoughts swirling to no end. Emptying the rubbish and turning off the machine can be a powerful first step in mental housekeeping, my own included.

Once the purge was complete, I encouraged focus. 'Nigel, this all does sound very stressful. Let's focus on one stress at a time, and then we can come up with a plan. What's your biggest stressor right now?' I asked.

'It's all a vicious cycle—my boss and my work, then my girlfriend. My work is probably the most stressful, though,' he said, while folding and unfolding his hands and scratching the back of his head occasionally.

'I'm sorry to hear that. Since your work is most stressful, do you want to focus first on that, or do you prefer to speak about your girlfriend?' I asked.

'Let's just talk about my work,' he said quickly, as if he wanted to solve this yet also wanted to rush past the intensity of what was needed to do so.

'I'm holding onto the conversation about your girlfriend if you want to discuss it at a later point. For now, tell me more about what's happening at work and why this is all so stressful.'

Nigel jumped in before I could finish.

'My boss is a total asshole. He's created a culture whereby he makes an "example" of someone, and that someone is often me. He will often write "250" in Chinese in the subject line of emails. That's a way of calling someone an idiot in Chinese. So, he will send a group email and refer to me as "250". "Oh 250 must have come up with this awful idea." He will sometimes refer to people as *sha bi*. I think the closest in English is something like "stupid cunt". Sorry for that. There are endless examples, and he tears me down in front of the big boss in New York constantly. The guy's a maniac. He will email or text me at midnight, sometimes later, telling me I better get something done or telling me something that another co-worker did wrong. He fucking invades my life,' he said looking stressed just sharing this.

'What about the other people in your office? Is the toxicity solely because of your boss?' I asked.

Usually, toxicity in an office has several roots. There's often a system of cooperation—some reason(s) why the ringleader of the toxicity and their followers are kept in business. There's often a group of people who are terrified to say or do something and are often an incentive to keep the toxicity in place. Toxic workplaces are also sometimes the result of toxic co-workers and team dynamics, not just bosses. Sometimes it's challenging for the naked eye to identify root causes as invisible forces are at play.

Nigel was always 'on'. It was like he was already burned out and miserable and might not be able to see clearly all the factors making his workplace toxic. One thing was for sure: Nigel was being tortured by the boss. He showed me WhatsApp messages and emails from the boss that ranged from abusive to horrifying.

'The other people in my office, hmmm. Let's say that the powers that be know this guy is awful yet don't care. They think he's a golden child. And my other co-workers, you know what, we used to commiserate all the time, and they all pretty much hate him. Yeah, sometimes we still share the pain. But one of my co-workers got promoted and is acting just like the boss now, a total dick.'

Nigel didn't have a say at all as his senior Chinese leaders had an authoritarian leadership style. They turned a blind eye as the boss was a rainmaker with clients and business. They knew about the pressure the boss exerted unfairly on the employees and celebrated it with their wilful blindness. When I asked if any of this had been reported to human resources, he laughed nervously and said, 'They turn a blind eye as well. They know who butters their bread.' It was clear the boss had been given a mandate to push beyond anything humane.

'I can't remove myself from my boss's demands, or he just blows up and makes my life even more unbearable. Last month, I tried to excuse myself from a drinking session with clients in Korea when my IBS was acting up. But he just called me a "pussy" and said, "You better show up, because if you don't, then I am cutting your bonus in half."'

'So, what did you do?' I asked.

'I went. What do you fucking think I did,' Nigel screamed furiously. 'It's always the same with Chinese, Japanese, and Korean clients—it means KTVs [karaoke parlours] and strip clubs. Sleeping with these girls is a requirement too. Our boss doles out hookers to the team as a reward, whether we want it or not. A number of the guys seem to love it, though. I don't and our boss gets reports from the mama-san on how we do. One time I couldn't get it up, and he let the entire team know.'

It seemed the drinking and prostitutes were what I call 'collective misery stabilizers'—very common in Asia. A 'misery stabilizer' is a term Terry Real, author and therapist, came up with for something that's not an addiction but rather a substance or process (gambling, shopping, porn, etc.) that helps people avoid feelings and deal with the pain.

In Asia, where dictatorial bosses are the norm, collective misery stabilizers are meant to help employees cope with the suffering. Drinking, drugs, women, and bonuses—often all in one evening—are usually the collective misery stabilizers of choice.

Nigel said the pressure to take part was immense. 'It didn't matter if you were married or not. You had to be there until the boss left and that was usually all night. It was so different when I worked in the Boston office a few years ago. They never would permit anything like this, especially when it was being expensed. But out here, the firm just thinks it's best to leave the local offices alone if they're hitting the numbers.'

'This sounds awful, Nigel,' I said emphatically. 'Have you tried to disconnect for even just an evening and stop looking at your phone overnight?'

I needed to probe a bit as I was getting the sense that the concept of boundaries was fantasyland to a guy like him.

'I can't. That would make me feel more anxious. I mean, even last night, he sent me a text at 1.37 a.m.—*1.37 fucking a.m.*— and said, "Nigel, you better have that deck done when I see you this morning."'

'You can imagine I didn't sleep much and got the deck done,' Nigel said, looking frustrated. 'Honestly,' he continued while tapping his fingers on his leg, 'I feel like he owns me.'

'Your boss does sound like he owns you. What do you do, Nigel, when you have these feelings?'

This was not the time to offer Nigel some Pollyannish reframe or tell him that he must be learning a lot from this boss. That is cold comfort to someone going through hell. Rather, this was the time to pause and reflect on how aware of his own feelings Nigel was.

I sensed that Nigel was on autopilot—get demand from boss, do demand from boss, rinse, repeat, stressed-out and burned-out robot here to serve. A pause might not change anything his boss did, yet I sensed that without that pause, we weren't going to shift Nigel's responses. I was also aware that with the IBS, his body was already knocking big time, telling him, in no uncertain terms, something needs to change.

'I don't stop to say, "OK this is how I'm feeling." I'm doing it now because you asked. I usually get the shit the guy asks for done. It's automatic at this point. He emails or texts me—he loves to WhatsApp me, and I think he waits online to see if I've read the message—and then I just do the thing he asks. Then I wait for the next thing,' he said, frustration rising.

He was existing, *barely existing,* inside a toxic habit loop.

'When are you sleeping and eating and doing anything that's not work-related?' I asked.

'Sleeping, probably four or five hours a night. Eating, I don't know—I just order in if I am hungry or eat cereal out of the box. At work, I sometimes eat if there's a group lunch. But I always have stomach aches and pains, and even when I'm eating, I'm eating quickly, and I'm still thinking about work and waiting for the next shoe to drop. I also have constant diarrhoea. I don't know, the doctor who sent me here seems to think my work makes this worse. Since he said that, I've started noticing that, yes, my symptoms are definitely worse when I'm stressed.'

'You sound totally stressed out and burned out, Nigel. I feel for you, and I want, *if you want,* to come up with a plan to dislodge you from this awful cycle you're in. It doesn't even sound like you're living. It sounds more like you're a zombie who has been sucked into a vortex. Tell me what comes to you when I say that.'

As I asked this, I looked him straight in the eye to signal that I could sense his suffering.

'You got it, except I don't feel like a zombie. A zombie almost sounds nice compared to what I feel. I have been sucked into a vortex, yes. But it's more like I'm some kind of jacked-up weirdo who is going through the motions and could collapse at any moment.'

'Do you want to work together to get you out of this vortex so you can feel like a human again?' I asked.

'Sure, if there's a way to do it,' he said. 'I'm losing hope.'

2D sex

Nigel returned the next week, looking as stressed out as before, and there had been an 'incident' his girlfriend wanted him to tell me about.

'Just so you know, Amara thinks therapy is for "crazy" people. So, she'll never come here, and yet she wants me to share this. So, here I go,' Nigel said.

It appeared that, just as Nigel always complied with his boss's wishes, so too did he follow his girlfriend's orders.

Comply, comply, comply. Body attacks back—the stress and anxiety triggers IBS.

Nigel told me that he and Amara were already sleeping in different rooms and were more like roommates than lovers. He said that, a week earlier, Amara had popped her head round his door while he was masturbating with a naked woman in Norway via Skype. He was so startled that all he could do was stand up to cover the computer screen. He was speechless as she screamed, 'What are you doing, Nigel?! Turn that off, you cheating prick!' He shut Skype down immediately and reasoned with her that it wasn't cheating because it was all done online. Afterwards, Amara fell speechless and shut down, ignoring him whenever he was around.

How did you respond when Amara said all of that?' I asked.

'I told her that 2D sex is not 3D sex. Sorry, it's just not the same. And she doesn't get that us dudes just like this stuff. Plus, I need a release at night after my hellish days in the office with my prick of a boss. I only watch fifteen minutes of porn a night, and when Amara caught me chatting with that hot Norwegian chick, that was the first time I had even tried that.'

I have had many male clients try to excuse their actions by claiming the sex, for one spurious reason or another, somehow didn't 'count'. One told me it wasn't cheating because the woman spoke Portuguese, and he didn't. Another said it wasn't cheating as he kept the air conditioner on full blast, so they didn't sweat. Another said that the woman looked 'nothing like his wife' and therefore it was acting out a fantasy, not reality.

I added 2D sex to 'The List'.

'How do you know you're watching fifteen minutes of porn each day? Do you set a timer? You don't strike me as a guy who wants to be in therapy for the next hundred years. The quicker you tell me the truth, the quicker we will make progress. So, what's the truth?' I asked.

I wasn't trying to get him. Rather, I was trying to understand more about his escapism and whether the escapism was an addiction. Whenever people are describing hell, there are often attempts at escaping.

To understand someone's escapist tendencies, I need people to invite me into their hell and show me what it is they do to get some relief *despite the cost*. Most are aware this relief is only temporary and that it will cost them more time in hell eventually. It almost always does.

I asked Nigel about the porn, though I could just as easily have asked about the virtual sex; either would be a window into his escapism. It was unlikely he was watching only fifteen minutes a day and equally unlikely the virtual sex was a one-off.

I had a strong suspicion that long trips to the bathroom were not only about IBS but also an escape to watch porn.

Many men with porn addictions, or at least porn escapist tendencies let's say, will come up with clever intervals of consumption—*only* ten minutes! Fifteen minutes from 10.15 p.m. to 10.30 p.m., then the alarm goes off! A lawyer client of mine, utterly addicted to porn, claimed to limit his porn consumption to six-minute intervals.

Nigel laughed and acknowledged that he had no idea how much he was watching.

That was part of the thrill—to get absorbed in a world where nobody was yelling at him, no woman was telling him, 'Ouch, stop, that hurts! You're such a selfish lover!' and no boss was demanding, 'Send the deck now! Your last presentation was awful!'

In this on-screen fantasy world, everything was about gratification. There were no nagging girlfriends, no overbearing bosses.

'How do you feel about your girlfriend, Nigel? One conversation we might have is whether you want to reduce or eliminate your porn usage if it is disturbing your relationship with Amara or causing you more stress. Another conversation is around how you actually are feeling about your girlfriend.' I put both on the table.

When I suggested eliminating porn, he looked like he was about to break out in hives. So, I waited for him to respond.

'Let's just talk about Amara first. Look, I don't know. She wants to get married, I don't. She wants kids, I don't. And she keeps asking if I love her anymore,' he said with little emotion.

'Do you love her?' I asked.

'No. In fact, this relationship feels like a haemorrhoid at this point. It just adds to my stress.'

Again, little emotion.

'Then, why are you with her?' I shrugged, as if I must be missing something.

'Don't know. Because she's there?' he responded.

'Nigel, I'm glad you brought up what happened with Amara, and today has given me good insight into the state of your relationship. My suggestion, if you're not ready to decide about whether to stay in the relationship, is that we focus on your work, and then once your head is a bit clearer, then we re-open what you want to do about your relationship. How does this sound?'

'That's fine. Again, I'm losing hope. Can you hand me the IKEA manual?'

'The IKEA manual?' I asked, puzzled.

'Yes, I need a plan here that's step-by-step, idiot-proof like an IKEA manual,' he said.

Ah, yes, the proverbial IKEA manual.

'Next session I will have an IKEA manual in hand. No problem,' I told him.

Give me the IKEA manual

Nigel returned two weeks later and gave me a blank stare as he sat in the chair. His frenetic energy had turned to focused energy, and I read this as *give me the damn IKEA manual!*

'I've prepared the IKEA manual. Do you want to go through it?'

'Yes, definitely. Please.' He looked at me curiously and seemed shocked when I pulled out an actual roadmap and laid it out, with step-by-step instructions on what to work on.

The manual was an action plan for the next nine months. It went like this:

1. Stuck on repeat: Like so many people when they're stressed, anxious, burned out, or all of the above, Nigel had become stuck in habit loops.

To help him understand what habit loops were, I recommended that Nigel watch a short video online by Dr Jud Brewer, associate professor in behavioural and social sciences at the School of Public Health and Psychiatry at the School of Medicine at Brown University.

The basic idea with the habit loop is that our brains are always looking to make processes more efficient, and there are three main elements of habit formation:

Trigger → Behaviour → Reward

Nigel was stuck in many unhealthy habit loops. When he saw, for example, his boss texting him, his initial reaction was to text back right away. He believed this would relieve him from some anxiety knowing that he had responded. However, all it really did was give him temporary relief until the next text message arrived.

Boss contacts him → Nigel does what boss asks → Nigel gets temporary relief from the anxiety yet endures more anxiety with every message his boss sends; the quicker Nigel gets the stuff done, the quicker the boss adds to his plate.

We also spoke about how the habit loops were exacerbating the IBS.

Feel stress → Reach for processed food → Feel slightly calmer for a short period then return to the stress with a body less prepared to cope with it due to eating non-nutritious foods.

We practised gaining awareness over these loops, and he was clear that he likely wouldn't change the behaviour while he was still employed with his boss. However, he did say the 'minute' he handed in his resignation, he would, and this eventually did happen. He learned that by gaining awareness not only of the trigger but also the behaviour he chose in response, he could work to reduce his overall stress and anxiety. He also read Dr Brewer's book *Unwinding Anxiety* which posits that anxiety is a habit and explains how habit loops are formed and how to create healthier ones.

Finally, we spoke about the concept of 'upregulating' and 'downregulating' emotions. The former is anything we do that increases the intensity of an emotion. For example, Nigel had become aware that when he spoke with his co-workers about difficulties with the boss, this increased (upregulated) his anxiety. He had also noticed that if he shut his phone off an hour before bed, it reduced (downregulated) his anxiety. Becoming aware of these loops helped Nigel regulate their effects.

2. Lifestyle changes: Ultimately, the goal is to create healthy habits and systems with our lifestyle choices involving nutrition, exercise, sleep, some form of community/ social connection, and possibly spiritual practice—if that resonates for the person. Lifestyle changes can have a massive effect on people's mental wellbeing, and it is often a low-hanging fruit.

With Nigel, it was important to shift the feeling that his boss totally owned him. We needed him to start owning some of his decisions, including what he put into his body and how quickly he ate it, because we needed to improve his physical response to stress. When considering lifestyle changes, it's important to realize how detrimental stress can be on *the body*—many people believe stress resides only in the mind.

This is false. When it comes to health, there is no separation between the body and the mind.

Here's how we planned to improve his IBS and calm him down:

- Chewing food slowly to improve digestion
- Swapping coffee for green tea to reduce caffeine
- Eliminating alcohol (his stomach felt 'awful' after drinking)

- Breathing more deeply throughout the day to reduce levels of the stress hormone cortisol
- Once Nigel was able to leave his job with the toxic boss, the lifestyle changes would also include:
- Improving his food intake with healthier choices. He ate fewer preservatives and fewer processed foods, more plant-based meals, and smaller portions. He made it a habit not to eat close to bedtime.
- Taking weekly hikes on the amazing trails in Hong Kong's country parks, sometimes alone, sometimes with friends
- Creating a sleep routine and reconnecting with his love of reading. He started and ended each day by reading for thirty minutes—literally bookending his days with a healthy habit. He also worked on ways to quiet his mind before sleeping and if he got up during the night. Nigel particularly liked the idea of doing a 'brain dump' before bed—dumping out all the thoughts, anxieties, feelings, and to-dos in his brain by writing them down and keeping a pad and paper near his bed if he woke up to dump out more.
- Trying meditation. He ended up at a Buddhist mediation centre in Hong Kong, one evening a week, that had courses for beginners and took a friend along with him each time.

3. The back-up plan: Chances were high that Nigel would leave his current firm. We spent a session weighing the financial, psychological, and emotional costs of staying or leaving. Needless to say, leaving won.
Once Nigel decided to leave, we discussed:

- Getting in touch with headhunters who specialized in his area of consulting.

- Broadening his LinkedIn network and leveraging it. He agreed to make a new connection or set up a coffee date with one he already had, every day.
- Assessing the financial impact of leaving his job and timing it right—he was clear he wanted to wait for his annual bonus before resigning.
- Thinking about what he really wanted to be doing. After he resigned, he became a different person. He had space to think, imagine, dream, and also to look at things logically; previously, the anxiety and burnout were speaking for him.

4. Chase the dream: Nigel really wanted to be an entrepreneur, a feeling that only intensified after going on a couple of interviews at other consulting firms. We spoke about how to make this dream a reality by:

- Creating a business plan and a list of target clients, doing market research, and identifying what would make the brand unique.
- Speaking to a lawyer about his non-compete clause. The lawyer advised him that the non-compete would be unenforceable after a three-month cooling-off period, which gave him more space to breathe and dream.
- Doing the maths: Nigel calculated the annual expenses of running a business based on his savings and whether he needed to go to the bank or his family for a loan.
- Moving back in with mum and dad: This was just a temporary measure. Like many unmarried Chinese people, Nigel had spent most of his adult life living at his parents' home, and they welcomed him back. This allowed him to add another six months of operating costs to the three-year runway he calculated.

5. Becoming the boss he had wanted to have: In his own company, Nigel would cultivate a healthy workplace by setting the tone at the top very clearly that no bullying or toxic behaviour would be tolerated. He would also put together a core values statement that included respect for all team members, and he would monitor his employees' choices and behaviours to ensure they were aligned with the company's values.

6. Impulse control: This was a key in keeping Nigel in place until he received his bonus in three months' time. If Nigel wanted to continue with some of his current clients at his own firm, he needed to be careful about how he left, as the news would get around. Even though Nigel wanted nothing more than to 'torch the place while flipping the bird to that asshole', he realized this wouldn't benefit him in the long term. So, we practised deep breathing and got him in the habit of momentarily pausing before speaking or responding to someone. He needed constantly to ask himself, 'In a year from now, how will I look back and wish I had responded?'

7. Heal the burn: After he collected his bonus, Nigel was drained and wanted to take some time off. Once his parents allowed him to move in, he decided to pay out his notice period and leave immediately. Taking time off was helpful with healing some of the burnout yet also was based on legal advice he received not to work for three months after leaving. It was the first period of extended time off in his adult life. He went back to the beach in Thailand where he met Amara, this time alone. There, he was able to recover from his burnout and decided to end his relationship with Amara. He realized he did not love her or want to be in a relationship and that his avoidance of the issue was holding her captive.

8. Confront the porn: I have seen countless male clients who, like Nigel, have been obsessed with and addicted to porn from their teenage years. Over the years, this has conditioned their brains and dopamine receptors. Porn is one click or swipe away, which makes this addiction all too easy to feed.

Nigel was clear that while still at his workplace he had no 'bandwidth' to talk about reducing his porn consumption and shared that his motivation to reduce porn—rather than eliminate it entirely—was to feel like he was in the 'driver's seat—back in control' of when and how much he consumed.

I usually send clients with severe porn or sex addictions to a specialist or sometimes to an in or outpatient programme. With Nigel, I suggested a thirty-day dopamine fast during which he wasn't to watch porn, have sex or masturbate. This was aimed at resetting his dopamine levels—a neurotransmitter that is connected with pleasure, motivation, and reward. The concept was based on Dr Anne Lembke's book *Dopamine Nation*, which explores the neuroscience behind addiction and offers strategies to reset your brain's dopamine balance including a fast (of a behaviour or substance) for up to thirty days and self-binding strategies. These strategies include placing barriers between our drug of choice and us.

I explained it to Nigel and asked, 'Are you willing to try it?' Nigel nodded, but looked as if he was swallowing a jagged pill. After he resigned, he agreed to try it for fifteen days. He ended up reading Dr Lembke's book and, like countless other clients, found it 'transformative'. It helped him modify not only his porn habit but his gaming addiction too.

We continued working together during his extended time off and for the first six months after he launched his new business. Having left that toxic office, Nigel was a different man entirely—no longer a zombie, but awake and alive.

At our last session, Nigel reached out to give me a firm handshake, and I congratulated him on buying a one-way ticket out of hell. He looked me in the eye and said, 'I've changed my opinion of therapy. It's not complete garbage.'

Toxic offices and burnout in Asia

A toxic office or work culture is one that fosters in its employees' feelings of unsafety, being bullied, and/or of being unheard. I've heard clients describe a toxic office as feeling 'poisonous', 'unpleasant', and 'malicious'. It can also be one that pays poorly, violates trust, and does not recognize great performance. Usually, the tenor and culture of an office is set from the top by the leaders—'the fish rots from the head'—yet there are some instances where the toxicity originates amongst co-workers and even subordinates.

Kathryn Weaver, an international employment law partner based in Hong Kong, says many employees in Asia do not speak out for cultural reasons. 'In Asian culture (as a generalization), employees often find it difficult to speak up against their managers and do not raise grievances or bring claims as commonly as employees do in the West. This can be due to inherent respect for those more senior, a lack of awareness of the law, lack of protection by the law, embarrassment if they were to lose their job as a result of their complaint, and so on.'

In fact, in Hong Kong and in several other jurisdictions in the Asia Pacific, there is no law against bullying, unless that bullying relates to a protected characteristic, such as gender, disability, or race, according to Weaver. Indeed, really toxic bosses can even defend themselves in law on the grounds *they are equally toxic to everyone*. As Weaver explains, 'If a boss or work culture is generally toxic, this can sometimes help a company defend a discrimination claim, i.e., the boss/culture is negative regarding everyone, not one particular protected group of people or person—this is sometimes colloquially known as the "bastard defence". However, if a boss/ culture shows prejudice against a particular protected group, such as women, this can be used as evidence in a discrimination claim. Also, toxic bosses/cultures often feature in claims for breach of the implied term of mutual trust and confidence between an employer and employee.'

Weaver sees glimmers of change in multinationals in Asia that in recent years have introduced mental health policies, training, coaching, and insurance cover. She believes this is inspired partly by the pandemic and partly in recognition of the long working hours culture in much of the region. 'There appears to be an increased awareness that maintaining positive mental health, watching for burnout, and helping rather than penalizing those struggling with their mental health is beneficial to business in terms of talent attraction and retention, increased performance and productivity, and business continuity and profitability. International companies have been increasingly investing in mental health policies, training, and coaching, whereas local SMEs (small and medium-sized enterprises) are still some way behind on this for various reasons, including budget and culture,' she said.

The barriers to changing the workplace culture are due to ingrained mindsets on social and work hierarchies, presenteeism and performance-related pay. Therefore, larger cultural forces— beyond company culture—must be considered for true change to happen.

Behind closed therapy doors, people often tell me the most challenging thing about their workplace is the people who work there. In other words, one of the keys to our wellbeing— whether at home or in the workplace—lies in the health of our relationships.

Toxic workplaces, and workplaces that value profit over humans, are at the root of burnout. Burnout is not a medical condition. Rather, it's classified as an 'occupational phenomenon' by the World Health Organization, though many people who experience burnout will also receive a diagnosis such as anxiety or depression.

And as poisonous as bosses like Nigel's may be, cruel individuals are more usually an unpleasant symptom, rather than the root cause, of a deeper, more systemic problem.

Therefore, giving people time off to heal from burnout or throwing an extra benefit here or there to their employment package is like sticking a plaster on a bullet wound.

When I work closely with companies, we talk about healing burnout, yes, but the real emphasis must be on prevention. Better than any antidote is to avoid the poison in the first place.

I'm hopeful that not only will multinationals in Asia start to shift values and policies, and take preventive measures to ensure wellbeing, but that local companies will as well. This requires a company to understand how to effect change and what this will cost them upfront—it may cost them the status quo, business as usual.

Just as individuals have defences against change—they can't, they don't know how—so too do companies.

I am realistic with companies that there may be some growing pains along the way, yet company culture is something that can change, and ultimately both the employees and those employing them are better off for having healthy workplaces.

For any company that still needs convincing, this alone should be enough to inspire change: *When people feel well, they perform well.*

Chapter 17

The Surprising Cost of Workaholism

'I must have been the only person in history to end up more stressed in the Maldives than I was at work,' Vanessa shared.

Vanessa was a high-powered partner at a private equity firm based in Hong Kong. She was thirty-four, Taiwanese, with shoulder-length black hair and caramel highlights that framed her lovely brown eyes and baby fat in her cheeks. Every step into my therapy room was measured, and her tailored navy tweed blazer and trousers exuded power. She spoke with warmth and trust but also with an edge of aggression and obsessiveness about her career.

The men and women in her office were terrified of her. 'They listen to my every word and do my bidding,' she said, sounding as if she deeply relished the control she wielded over colleagues. 'I've made it clear from the beginning I don't take crap, and I don't celebrate mediocrity. I expect everyone working for me to perform well. I don't expect everyone to love the work as much as I do, but I do expect them to work hard. There's some work-related stuff I want to discuss eventually. However, I also need help to decide whether to freeze my eggs and to address something else.'

Once she had finished, she took two deep breaths.

I could sense work was her comfort zone. We were diving into confronting waters. When this happens with clients, it's often a change of tone, choice of words or body language I notice first. With Vanessa, the deep breaths tipped me off. I imagined her giving immaculate presentations in front of investors, not skipping a beat, just as in the room with me discussing work. It all seemed together, organized and clear.

'It's always been me against all the men who dominate my field, so I've had to be that "strong woman". But when I take a second to think of myself outside of work, I feel so lonely . . . and pathetic for feeling so lonely.' I watched her exhale and could see the relief in her body. 'I can't believe I said that aloud,' she said.

'I imagine you've been holding those feelings in for a long time? What's it like to say it aloud?' I asked.

She took some deep breaths. 'You know what it is with saying it aloud? I have said it so many times to myself. It really hit me the hardest in the Maldives earlier this year. I had been so stressed from work, just utterly at my wit's end with the late nights, late calls, and deadlines so I took a week off to recharge—unheard of for me. Anyway, I was having dinner at the most mind-blowing, gorgeous hotel. I looked around, and I was surrounded by couples gazing into each other's eyes, holding hands, kissing, flowers on the table, the whole thing. I had a terrible feeling in the pit of my stomach. I went back to my room and started reading a book to distract myself. And I just couldn't. I started crying so intensely.'

Tears streamed down her face as she recalled the scene.

I put my hand over my heart and responded, 'I can see why you would have cried so intensely and why the tears are filling your eyes right now. It seems like those tears are messengers—telling you very clearly what you want in your life.'

'Yes and no. There's definitely a part of me that wants a husband,' Vanessa responded.

'Which part of you doesn't want that?' I asked.

People often break their feelings, desires, and dreams into parts—a part of me wants this, a part of me doesn't. It often takes a lot of dialogue and negotiation amongst these parts to get to a decision. Even so, being an adult can sometimes mean playing a card that feels like an emotional gamble.

'It's the feminist in me that's saying I shouldn't want that. That I'm financially independent. That it's wrong to want this. That wanting a husband makes me weak. That a man won't be additive. Oh, and also, I'm aware that I might lose my edge at work if I have a partner as I wouldn't be able to work as much,' she said, quite convincingly.

I held onto that last comment. This moment was about making her feel heard and giving space to all the parts she was describing.

I asked her, 'Have you ever met a man at your firm or another who is a partner and either wants or has a life partner and apologizes for that?'

She half-smiled, laughed and said, 'No. Never.'

I have worked with many men who, behind closed therapy doors, tell me they feel incredibly lonely and empty, irrespective of how much money they make or how much sex they are or aren't having. But I have yet to meet a male client who asks whether he can work the kind of intense hours Vanessa did and still have a life partner. Even so, men, too, must make trade-offs if they are looking to meet someone. Nobody, regardless of gender, has a close partnership with someone without consistent time, energy, and presence.

'Now, which part of you wants a husband?' I asked.

'The part of me that does is the part that wants to be loved and give someone love. It's the part that dreams. It's the part of me that wants to be warm at night,' Vanessa said, the tears once again streaming down her face.

She was melting.

'I will tell you something I've never told anyone,' Vanessa continued, 'When I got back from that trip to the Maldives, for about a month, I spent endless hours watching homoerotic Japanese anime porn. I have no explanation for that other than I couldn't watch any movies about men and women falling in love. I think that watching two men together was distant enough from what I want yet close enough to a love story that I wanted to see it. My work started to suffer as I would go in the next day, after four or five hours of watching, very tired. That stopped me in my tracks. Again, I can't believe I just said this aloud.'

I could see from her face she had shocked herself by sharing this.

'I'm glad you did say it aloud,' I said. 'The tears in the Maldives and the Japanese anime porn all seem consistent with what I think I'm hearing. I'm definitely hearing that work is very important to you, and it seems like you excel massively in that space. It also sounds like you want to finally do something about this yearning you have for a life partner, as in take clearer action.'

I purposely used the word 'action', even if only to send her a message, subconsciously, that she is more than worthy of love. And although connecting with a partner is more than just taking action, there is often a consistent investment that needs to be made in what matters most to us. It's not the worthiness alone that gets us *there* or anywhere.

'Yeah. I think you're right. Yeah, you're right. I do want to do something about this. Because what's the alternative?' she wondered.

'Good question. What is the alternative to this? And what will it cost you if you do start to take action?' I pushed her gently.

'The alternative is more Maldives trips, more Japanese anime, endless nights at the office, deep sadness when I hear my friend's engagement stories, wondering if I should freeze my eggs and risk not having a child ever. And what will it cost me? It'll cost me some time at work for sure,' she said, matter-of-factly.

'How about freezing your eggs? Do you want a child?' I asked.

'I'm not sure I do want a child. I'm sure that my father and mother want me to have a child and become a traditional Taiwanese family girl. I have been trying to escape that all my life. But, to what end? Here I am in Hong Kong, partner at a firm, and I feel such loneliness now.'

Her shoulders dropped as she spoke.

When she talked about wanting a husband, I could feel her connection. But when she talked about having a child, I didn't get a sense one way or the other. I asked whether it mattered that her father and mother wanted her to have a child. Especially in Asia, when a client tells me that a parent wants him or her to do something, then I always ask whether that carries any weight. Often, it does.

Vanessa then shared, 'As much as I'd like to say my parents' opinion doesn't count, it does. I really don't have feelings one way or the other about having a kid. But at thirty-four, I need to start doing something about this, especially because I don't have a husband. And who knows, if I meet the right guy, then maybe I will want a kid. Some of my friends have said that.'

Egg freezing in Asia is its own maze, so I suggested to Vanessa that she do the research outside of session. I told her we could always make space to discuss how she felt about the process and whether she wanted to do it or not. By doing the research outside of session, she could understand the facts and laws. For many clients, ideating or doing something to invest in their dreams or goals in between sessions builds momentum and confidence.

'Sure thing, I'll look up all the information for the egg freezing. I have a question before next session, though. What I'm *really* wondering is, will you be able to help me find a husband?'

With every client I meet, I do my best to highlight what I perceive as their strengths, even if they can't themselves. I look for what they do well and what I imagine to be their strengths and superpowers. However, I've realized that saying this in the abstract often doesn't help people as much as spelling it out. Their reaction also is helpful for me to witness. Some people will eat this up and metabolize it well, others will push back, and some will reject the idea that they have strengths or that many.

Naming Vanessa's strengths was one thing. However, in my experience, people who want to be in a relationship are often really wondering: *Is there something wrong with me?* Some clients ask me this explicitly, others implicitly. I match my response accordingly.

'Even after just an hour of knowing you, I can already sense you have many wonderful qualities. You're kind, engaging, likeable, determined, and focused. And you're honest—you're honest about what you want, and that takes courage. I think this will come down to how much effort you're willing to focus on connecting with someone. Of course, I can't guarantee you'll meet someone, but if I were a gambling therapist, I would say your chances are high.'

Many of us walk around with questions unanswered buzzing in our heads, unable to focus until there is a roadmap. For there to be one, what's often helpful is to close some loops sooner rather than later, to help give the person some headspace to make the big decisions. Connecting with a husband seemed the big-ticket item for Vanessa, yet doing *something* about the egg freezing would ease the pressure to connect with someone soon.

Fertility challenges

In Asia, a seismic shift has been taking place. Even though many Asian cultures place great value on having children, couples are marrying later, and more women than ever are delaying pregnancy due to rising levels of education and longer working hours. According to the International Labour Organization, more than 30 per cent of Hong Kong women work forty-nine hours or more per week.

In some parts of Asia, including Hong Kong and Singapore, many families have the option of hiring a domestic worker. These migrant workers take on the burden of housework and childcare, which in turn allows more women to enter the workforce. However, many bosses are aware of the full-time childcare and will often expect women to work longer hours. Many women in Asia still report taking on the 'mental load' despite having full-time help at home, and therefore question whether having children is 'worth it'. Consequently, many will delay the decision until, for some, giving birth may no longer be possible.

Researchers report that Asia's infamously long working hours are also partially to blame for falling fertility and birth rates. In China, the slang term '996' describes the brutal work culture of clocking in from 9 a.m. to 9 p.m., six days a week, for a total of seventy-two hours, which is common in tech companies. This gruelling work schedule, though, is true in much of Asia where income and education levels have risen dramatically in recent years.

South Korea, Hong Kong, Taiwan, and Japan have some of the lowest birth rates in the world despite government campaigns allowing both parents to take leave after birth and encouraging more men to take an active role in childcare and housework.

To some extent, it is still considered taboo to discuss infertility in Asia, which is perceived as a 'failure' for a married woman in Asian cultures. Compared to the West, there are fewer women having children outside of wedlock because of the heavy stigma in this part of the world and also due to restrictions around adopting and using frozen eggs unless married.

More and more companies in Asia, though, particularly multinationals, are covering the costs of IVF as a health benefit, and several governments are considering expanding parental leave policies to encourage couples to have more children.

Many women in China are struggling to have children or even get married, and the lifestyle of 'double income, no kids' is being embraced as the ideal situation.

The Chinese government legalized IVF in 2001 and has since agreed to cover some of the cost under the national medical insurance scheme in an effort to boost the shrinking population. It plans to have one IVF facility for every 2.3 million to 3 million people by 2025. Currently, about 300,000 babies are conceived by IVF through China's 539 medical institutions. Japan and Korea lead the way in Asia Pacific by offering one year of parental leave for fathers; however, few men take advantage of this out of fear it will have a detrimental impact on their career, and it is still considered the woman's role to care for children.

Purpose-driven workaholic

True to form, I received an email before our next session from Vanessa outlining all the egg-freezing options in Hong Kong and Taiwan with a stellar spreadsheet that compared the two options sent at 9 p.m. on a Friday evening.

I felt impressed with her attention to detail and how she had planned out different scenarios. It was a window into her work ethic and determination, and I noted the irony of reading this at 5 a.m. on a Sunday morning—one purpose-driven workaholic's nod to another's. She also had done research on freezing eggs in other countries in case the cost-benefit analysis outweighed the Hong Kong and Taiwan options.

In our following session, Vanessa told me she had decided to freeze her eggs in Taiwan and planned to do so 'early Q2', as by then her work would be 'less non-stop'.

'Tell me what you mean by "non-stop",' I asked, tilting my head slightly to the side.

This was a bridge to discuss potential workaholism.

Sometimes when people say 'non-stop', it is hyperbole. At other times, I have been shocked to hear the details.

'I put away messages on my email even when I'm in the bathroom. My phone is on twenty-four hours a day, and that used to be the case only when I was working on a specific deal. I realized to really compete with the other firm members, I needed to have it on all the time in case a potential or existing client called. My days average twelve hours of working—as in meetings at the office type of work—and that's six days most weeks. Some of my work is with the USA so I need to be "on" each Saturday in Asia. I couldn't tell you the last weekend when I did something fun outside of work. And the last date I went on? You might laugh, but the guy surely wasn't laughing. Yup, I left the restaurant to speak with a client as my phone rang in the middle of dinner.'

This wasn't hyperbole.

'What happens if you shut your phone off? Or you miss an email from a client?' I asked, my eyebrows slightly furrowed.

Vanessa looked as if my questions were inducing a panic attack—not a good look for a therapist.

Her eyes opened wide, and she responded, 'I don't shut my phone off, and I don't miss emails. Look, obviously I would like more time outside of work to do stuff, but I genuinely like my work. I'm sure some of your clients hate their work in finance, and I guess I'm just different in that way.'

She was right. I have worked with many people in finance and other fields, who found their jobs soul-sucking and were clear they were doing it for the money. They were addicted to the work because they were addicted to the money, the goodies, the ego, all of it. One client told me, 'I leave my soul at the entrance to the bank each morning.'

Yet, I have also worked with many in finance who connected with or cultivated a sense of purpose in their work and felt drawn to it for reasons beyond money. I worked with a trader who was deeply connected with his work and took tremendous interest in researching markets globally. He also took his colossal bonus each year and donated it to charity.

In every industry there are workaholics who may be driven by survival, avoidance, money, and/or ego. However, there are also many who are what I have come to term 'purpose-driven workaholics', and although there are challenges with any kind of addiction, I believe that with work-related addiction, there is a spectrum and, with that, different ways to treat it.

'I believe you. It sounds like you do connect with purpose in your work, and that was even clear in the first session. Tell me, what is it about your work that feels purposeful?' I needed to ask because if she was going to make time to connect with a partner, I needed to know which parts of her work she was most connected to and what was negotiable.

'I feel a sense of purpose in my work as I focus on ESG (environmental, social, and governance) issues that relate to my portfolio companies. Also, I have spearheaded job training programs for impoverished women in various countries. And I really enjoy the complexity of the deals and working with clients.'

'It sounds like you are what I call a purpose-driven workaholic—a person who does have an addiction to the work and therefore suffers some consequences—and/or those around you do—yet feels a tremendous connection to and sense of purpose with their work and are driven mostly by the purpose. That's wonderful in some ways, yet it's still workaholism. What comes to you when I say that?' I asked.

'Oh, I'm totally a workaholic. I like the purpose-driven qualifier. The challenge is I want to continue working hard and do a great job. I want to also make sure I'm leading others towards being great at the work. All that matters to me. Yet, *really*, what matters right now is that we do work on me being in a relationship. I get there will be a trade-off here with how much I'm working.'

There are various practical components to helping workaholics, such as reducing their hours and seeing if they can delegate more. It also helps to make lifestyle changes, as few workaholics, of any kind, will be getting enough sleep, exercise, or nutrition and many will lack any sense of community outside work.

Some workaholics may be avoiding something outside of work—a troubled relationship, feelings that are too painful, or financial woes, for example. But that's not usually the case with purpose-driven workaholics.

'What have you tried so far to meet someone, Vanessa? Are you socializing at all outside of work?' I asked.

'Honestly, I really don't have any friends outside of work in Hong Kong. All my friends are in Taiwan with husbands or families,' Vanessa lamented. 'And, if I'm really being honest, I sometimes ignore them as it feels uncomfortable to see photos of engagements and weddings. On the dating front, I have tried all the dating apps and I just can't stomach another man telling me he loves "strong women" or telling me about how he grew up in a household with a strong mum and sister,' she said, half laughing.

I have lost track of how many women have told me they cringe at men on dating apps who post that they 'love strong women'. There's an undertone of insincerity in that line as if they just want to get into your pants.

'Yes, I can understand why that would make you cringe,' I said as we shared a short laugh together.

I sometimes imagine there's a moustache-twirling executive advising men to say this to attract women. In that moment, Vanessa needed a woman to affirm what she was feeling and say in agreement *yeah, thanks, I'll pass.*

'Let me ask, what do you want in a partner? Of course, we can't perfectly design who he is—that would erase the magical layer of what happens when you meet the person. Tell me, though, what's on your non-negotiable, bottom-line list—as in this guy must be what?' I asked.

'OK, for the non-negotiables. Hmmm. It's important that I meet someone who is connected to some kind of purpose. I don't care if this kind of purpose is work-related for the guy, it could be something else. I also think a non-negotiable would be someone who values environmentalism. It's not just something I value at work. I definitely would need someone who is at least interested in my culture has some interest in visiting my family in Taiwan or is somewhat open to living there. Oh, and kind. I definitely need someone who is kind. I told you that my work sometimes is like a piranha tank, and I want to come home to kindness.'

On the non-negotiables, she sounded confident. 'This all sounds reasonable and clear. Connected with purpose, valuing environmentalism, interested in Taiwanese culture, openness to travel there, and possibly living there, and kindness?' I reflected.

'Yup, and it's helpful to hear that played back. Ahh, and sense of humour—totally non-negotiable,' she said.

'I can see clearly why a sense of humour matters to you. For what it's worth, after working with couples for so long, I think it's one of the most underrated ways to deepen connection, and you have a great sense of humour. Tell me, what's on the nice-to-have list?' I asked.

'I mean, it would be wonderful to meet someone who is handsome and is driven by work. I don't care so much, Allison, about the money he's making, yet I would like to have someone who does connect with work. Again, purpose matters more, yet ideally that purpose could have some connection with work. And, yeah, I think if I could, then I would like to meet someone who is not super attached to having kids. You know I'm not super attached, and so, it would be good to meet someone else like this,' she said.

'Can we speak about what you're willing to change with work and which efforts you're willing to make to date? I will not try to take away the purpose you feel with your work, I promise! Yet, realistically, we will have to talk about making changes at work if you do want to make space for some magic to happen with a life partner.' With workaholics, everything at first seems important to hold onto and do themselves. They're often very attached to being 'on' at all times, feeling that this gives them an edge, an intense focus, an advantage over those who disconnect from work.

'Yes, let's do that. Let's talk about taking action,' Vanessa said enthusiastically.

Here is the action plan we came up with:

1. Amp up the apps: Vanessa needed to up her game on the dating apps. She had not posted a photo of herself and left blank what she was looking for. 'I can't be bothered,' she told me. We upgraded her profile big time, added a recent photo, and made clear in her status that she was looking for a relationship. She switched gears from a passive 'can't be bothered' to an active 'wait, this does matter, and I therefore need to be clear and focused'.
2. Choose your target: Still, Vanessa needed to be discerning with the apps she used. Some of these apps are really tools to connect people for sexual hook-ups. Vanessa needed to choose apps that allowed a real chance at dating as she had no interest in casual relationships. 'I get a lot of my friends do that, and that's fine, but honestly I'd rather work than hunt down sexual partners,' she said. She also needed to be consistent and deliberate in her efforts if she wanted to maximize her chances of success. So, she set a calendar reminder to check her apps daily at 7 a.m. before her workday began. For Vanessa, brushing her teeth became a cue: time to check the apps.

3. Perfect is the enemy of the good: Vanessa had some perfectionistic tendencies, and when she used to send messages, she would check them obsessively to make sure the grammar was correct, and she was painting herself in the 'best light'. We spoke about life being messier than that, and to focus more on shipping stuff—as in actually responding and engaging rather than trying to make everything perfect.

4. Get matched with a matchmaker: Vanessa researched various matchmaker options but decided she didn't want to sign up with any of them. 'If by Q1 of next year I haven't met someone, then I'll reconsider,' she said.

5. Spread the word: She felt 'slightly ashamed' to let all her friends in Taiwan know, and so she told one friend in Hong Kong, a few in Taiwan, and also spoke with some work connections with whom she socialized occasionally outside of work.

6. Join a running club: Vanessa was barely exercising at all when we first met, and with workaholics, I like to appeal to their sense of 'efficiency' by killing two birds with one stone. She had been a runner in secondary school and university, so we reconnected her with this. Doing so helped her health while also offering a way to connect with potential friends and dates.

7. Sleep hygiene: Like most workaholics, Vanessa didn't get enough shut eye. The running helped reset her sleep patterns and she bought one of those 'mobile phone jail cells' in which her phone was locked between the hours of 11 p.m. and 7 a.m. so she couldn't check it. She also started wearing blue-light-blocking glasses during her night calls, reducing night calls where possible, and cutting caffeine after lunchtime.

8. Reduce hours: Vanessa needed to decide what work she could delegate to others, work that she did not connect with. She also learned to discern between 'false urgency' and what's truly urgent, as her workaholism initially coded everything. She was able to reduce unnecessary meetings, which she recognized were 'utter nonsense'. She also built a mental titanium gate around Sundays to disconnect fully from work so she could reconnect on Monday in better form. Usually, workaholics want to see how changes will improve their work quality, and I had no doubt that one day off a week, in addition to the other changes, could help Vanessa. 'I hated Sundays at first yet now look forward to them and do work better once I'm back in the office the next day,' she said.

9. Focus on what matters: We spoke about protecting more time for those activities Vanessa found truly purposeful, such as ESG and helping women in developing countries. Vanessa found she was better able to focus and generate ideas in these areas after a few months of readjusting how she worked.

To her credit, Vanessa tried all of the above over the course of five months and felt life was more 'spacious and enjoyable'. She also applied some of her purpose-driven tendencies to connect with a partner—hyperfocus, determination, and some obsessiveness. As she began dating, there was lots of trial and error, yet she learned that this was part of the process, and instead of getting discouraged, she retained a healthy mindset.

'I guess life projects are sometimes like work projects where you start with an objective and then end up taking different twists and turns. Not linear,' she said.

Around five months into the process, she began dating a warm, lovely Irish man, Conor, who worked for a non-profit organization focused on climate change. They met through a mutual work connection. Vanessa was at a colleague's house for dinner with his family, and her colleague's wife asked if she had a partner. She responded, 'I'm finally looking. Know anyone?' What Vanessa thought was a throwaway comment ended up being the bridge to meeting Conor.

At our last session, she described Conor as, 'Exactly what I need', and added, 'You were correct—dating is not like ordering off a menu. He's got a lot of what I was hoping for, as in he's connected with purpose, kind, has a great sense of humour, yet also an element of mystery. I totally adore the guy.'

I gave her a big smile, and she responded, 'I was really surprised that therapy could be a safe space to share my true feelings yet also a place to inspire action. On TV, it always seems to be about sharing feelings endlessly.' I told her how courageous she had been in therapy, not only with telling the truth but also taking clear steps to make her dream a reality.

'I remember you saying nobody finds a life partner sitting on the couch or staying in the conference room at all hours,' Vanessa said.

Workaholics in Asia

According to Kisi's Global Work-Life Balance Index, the world's top five overworked cities in 2021 were Hong Kong, Singapore, Bangkok, Buenos Aires, and Seoul. Unsurprisingly, four out of the top five were in Asia, while Tokyo and Kuala Lumpur also made the top ten.

Some of the reasons for the deeply rooted work culture in Asia could lie in collectivism and a belief in 'power distance' or a type of social hierarchy where the boss or senior managers are followed without questioning. Workers rarely leave the office before their boss and have a hard time saying no to requests from them. The rise in technology at work like emails and online meetings have made work-life balance all the more elusive, leading to higher levels of burnout and chronic stress, and lower levels of job satisfaction, overall wellbeing, and quality of life. I've learned from clients that many climb the ladder to loneliness only to despair when they discover that what's at the top is an isolating treadmill to nowhere.

People in Asia were less inclined to seek help, due to cultural influences including Confucian values, which uphold collective harmony, and the stigma surrounding mental illness, which is often coded as weakness.

Working with expats throughout the years has taught me much about the origins of their workaholism. Some are workaholics before they show up in Asia and just pack their addictive tendencies in their suitcases, regardless of destination. Others, though, become workaholics because of anxieties related to their immigration status and ability to maintain a working visa. In some places in Asia, such as Hong Kong, a spouse may be able to work on their partner's visa. However, in other places, such as Singapore, each spouse must apply for a separate visa.

This is a very real pressure: lose the visa and an expat may lose both their home and their job.

In addition to the practical reasons expats may overwork and eventually become addicted to the work, there's also the emotional component of not wanting to be perceived as a 'loser' or someone who couldn't make it abroad. This is often an anxiety that expats will have—that they need to prove themselves abroad and then come home a bigger fish. Also, although there is often a perception that expats are wealthy, many are overleveraged financially and need to work non-stop just to keep afloat.

Generational work addiction

The arc of my own work addiction is long. Every morning, I jump out of bed with excitement about my day's work and enjoy copious amounts of green tea while preparing for my therapy sessions with clients and corporate work.

I have deep reverence for the paths my clients are on and feel strongly there is purpose in my work. I feel privileged to hear the stories, secrets, dreams, desires, fears, and wishes of every single person who comes to see me. My high enthusiasm, long hours, hyperfocus, and the trade-offs I make for work mean that, like Vanessa, I am a purpose-driven workaholic. Yet as much as my work is a calling, it's also practical as I need to support my family.

With every addiction, though, there is a downside. I owe more time to my family. There are times when I could be involved in family or interests outside of work and *choose* instead to keep working. This compulsion to keep working regardless of consequences is what makes it an addiction. There's also a high risk of burnout and possible health consequences, and I have suffered with both.

Like my clients, I often ponder the genesis of my work addiction. As with most truths, there are likely various dimensions: genetical, environmental, pathological, and mystical.

Genetical: Addiction has hijacked many people on my father's side of the family. My father struggled with drugs, his father was an alcoholic, one of my cousins died of a heroin overdose, and another cousin spent a lot of time in rehab. I have no idea how much genetic loading for addiction I carry, yet I am aware that if I wasn't addicted to work, then it *could* have been something else. I don't mean that in a fatalistic way—I mean it as something humbling; addiction was the water my family swam in. It's been a painful thread in our lineage that binds many family members, and although I wish the thread was something golden, the reality is much darker.

Environmental: I have watched many people around me become addicted to work, both family members and colleagues—I started working when I was sixteen for the Chinos—and I believe they were purpose-driven workaholics. They showed up at the farm each morning just like I still do with my work—enthusiastic, slightly obsessional, and intensely interested in people and the beautiful complexities around cross-cultural communication and understanding.

As a little girl, I was very close with my maternal aunt, who I adoringly called Mema. She had a very put-together, intense character—a big personality with a big heart. We had a special connection and fits of uncontrollable laughter whenever we hung out and watched ridiculous cheesy movies or took long walks in New York City. She was a fun aunt indeed. In addition to being fun, though, she was also very influential in shaping my work ethic. From around the age of eight, she insisted that I come to 'Take Your Daughter to Work Day' with her and would beat into me the importance of working. 'Never accept an invitation to be a princess and slack off,' she would say.

This will stay with me, always. Some things get tattooed into our psyches.

Pathological: Having ADHD does not mean I am destined to have an addiction, but it does put me at higher risk. My hyperfocus and high levels of motivation and enthusiasm—which are linked to my ADHD—encourage me to keep working when I am interested in something.

Mystical: By definition, it's hard to put this one into words. And I do not want to glorify addiction—it has ruined countless lives, including many of those closest to me. Not even the luckiest addict can escape its grip entirely unscathed. And yet . . . and yet there is something transcendental about my work. About connecting with a higher purpose, answering your calling, doing what you were born to do, using the gifts God gave you, however you want to phrase it. I personally feel blessed to have such an intense sense of purpose. I question many things in life, yet my sense of purpose is not one of them. Indeed, I cannot help but feel my work *deep within my soul*.

So, there it is. Spoken like a true workaholic.

Epilogue: The View from Asia

You've been on a journey. You've witnessed people reckon with universal questions and desires. They could have been from Singapore or Seattle; the issues they struggled with are part of the human condition.

But through their stories, you also saw how culture adds a lens to our experiences. People are far too complex to fit into any formulae, their experiences influenced by too many factors. We are all unique.

Culture is connected with the *how*—how we see things, how we interact with the world, how we respond to our experiences, and how we feel supported. It presents a prism through which to see and experience life.

In the stories I've shared, you've seen support that reflects Asian culture in the form of individuals and couples:

- leaning on ancient systems
- seeking insight and guidance from trusted elders and healers
- preserving value systems and choices that reflect family, harmony, community, and humility
- upholding tradition and rituals while evolving at the same time—think evolution, not revolution

I have a lot of hope for the future of wellbeing in Asia. I see individuals and organizations working to reduce the stigma for *all* mental health conditions and distributing support to *all* in need along with legal, medical, social, and educational changes that support wellbeing. Training more therapists will never be sufficient anywhere in the world.

The biggest shifts took place during the pandemic, which continues to serve as a springboard for change and is likely to do so long into the future. The pandemic was a defining moment worldwide and presented a double-edged psychological sword. It intensified power dynamics: more women suffered domestic violence and abuse, suicide rates skyrocketed, adultery spiked, businesses went under, loneliness spread, and countless people jumped on board the Great Resignation Train and quit their jobs, albeit many couldn't afford to board that train.

I saw many couples forced to confront the truths of their relationships—some for the better, some for the worse. When I arrived in Asia, my therapy room was inhabited mostly by expats and just a handful of locals who would don sunglasses and big hats to be discreet. Over the years, there has been a radical shift. I now see many more locals and many more couples.

As a practising psychotherapist who also works for corporations, I hear what people say behind closed therapy doors and on the trading room floors. This is part of what gives me hope—knowing that outside the therapy room, I've seen more of an openness to supporting employees' mental wellbeing both in local and multinational corporations and a genuine curiosity in understanding how best to support employees. This includes not only increased benefits and training but also tailored support.

I felt honoured to work with AXA on combating the stigma surrounding mental illness and promoting holistic health through their Fit to Flourish campaign that offered a series of ten videos and educational booklets to help people develop ten skills that together can help to optimize their mental wellbeing and improve their quality of life. Gordon Watson, CEO of AXA Asia and Africa, and AXA are at the forefront of mental health advocacy in the Asia Pacific.

Watson says, 'Our annual AXA Study of Mind Health and Wellbeing 2022 showed that in Asia, only 20 per cent of people are classified as flourishing, compared with 35 per cent who are just getting by. The workplace is an important forum for achieving progress in this area. That is why companies need to build a nurturing and supportive workplace environment. This requires a multi-pronged approach. Senior leaders need to set the tone from the top so employees know mind health is a priority and can be discussed, while company policies need to put the right support in place to cultivate a supportive environment.'

The workplace is changing in part due to leaders like Watson who are aware that physical, mental, relational, and workplace health are inextricably linked. AXA is also leading the development of the Mental Health at Work Index, which aims to be the first science-backed framework to establish global standards for workplace mental health. This will be important for companies that want to understand how their efforts are making an impact.

Another admirable multinational I've worked with is Bloomberg—a company with incredible leaders, human resources specialists, and general employees who work tirelessly, compassionately, and genuinely to cultivate an inclusive and caring workplace that prioritizes the wellbeing of its staff. During the global lockdowns, I was honoured to help facilitate a series of global and Asia Pacific-focused sessions on resilience. It was because of Bloomberg's tremendous care and efforts that this could be rolled out effectively. Beyond the efforts made during the pandemic, I have lost count of how many employees have told me they feel cared for and that the company's efforts to promote and support mental wellbeing have helped them and their families.

You've seen throughout the book that people are motivated to grow and transform at work and in their personal lives for a whole host of reasons. Some are motivated by what they might gain, others by what they might lose, and for some, it's a combination of both.

Yet, there is one thing that often has a direct impact on motivation. It is the answer to this commonly asked question: Does this person—my team member, leader, spouse, family member—care about and believe in me?

Most humans are blessed and burdened by knowing whether another human cares about them. There are interactions, moments, and experiences in all workplaces and personal relationships that send strong messages about whether people are cared for, and this has a strong imprint on their trajectories both inside and outside the cubicle. Just as there is no true separation between our physical and mental health, neither is there one between our wellbeing at work and in our relationships.

I am aware, on a cellular level, that my own life could have turned out very differently had it not been for the grace, guidance, and care of many others, including my maternal aunt, Mema. She and I have always had a strong connection; she was there for me during the tumult of my childhood, not only to catch and soothe me but also to believe in me. Armed with a big personality, whenever she wanted to make her point, Mema never backed down and would tell me often, 'You've experienced a lot. Be productive with that pain.'

Whenever we said goodbye from our long walks or lunches in New York City, she gave me a warm, tight hug and said, 'I see you, Allison, and I believe in you.' Her loving words have been a psychological elixir for me, and I still lean on them and the feeling of her warm hug whenever I, like all humans, wobble. Good days, bad days, good days, bad days.

I believe if any of us has just one person who wholeheartedly says, 'I see you, and I believe in you,' it can get into the cracks of our soul for a lifetime, injecting enough confidence and courage that we may feel inspired to leap into the unknown.

Not everyone has a Mema, though. Sometimes we need to become that person for another to experience a Mema of their own. And sometimes we find it's possible to experience that with a therapist.

Acknowledgements

Writing this book has been way more meaningful and challenging than I could have ever imagined. It's hard to put names and words around all that went into this process and equally difficult to describe the immense gratitude I have for others' support. If this book touches anyone, then it's because of the grace and wisdom of the people below and so many others.

Sylvia Yu Friedman, thank you for the incredible support and brilliant edits. This book is what it is because you believed in me and it.

Matt Friedman and the Mekong Club, thank you for working to save the soul of this world. Thank you also for all the support throughout this process and years of thought-provoking, action inspiring conversations.

Andrew Raine, I will forever marvel at your remarkable input and edits. You are an editor extraordinaire and a total star. Thank you from the bottom of my heart for the work you put into this book. You truly transformed it.

Matthew Keeler, thank you for your amazing copyediting. You were so helpful with your ideas and edits, and I could sense your kind spirit even from afar.

Penguin Random House Southeast Asia, Nora Nazerene Abu Bakar, and Amberdawn Manaois, thank you for believing in the book and caring so deeply about mental wellbeing in Southeast Asia.

To my parents, thank you for the gift of life and all the sacrifices you made.

To my family, thank you for all your support.

To my Aunt Mema, thank you for always seeing me and believing in me. You were a role model before I could even walk and talk. You also moved mountains to help me and others, and I love you dearly. How I wish we could still enjoy our *dosa* lunches and uncontrollable laughter in person.

Chino family, thank you for the opportunity to work with your remarkable family. You gave me the gift of a value system and a love for culture. No matter where I am in the world, you are all locked in the vault of my heart. *Okage sama de.*

Stephen and Pervin Clasper at Shakti Healing Circle, thank you for your warm energy and the opportunity to share the sacred space you've created at Shakti.

Annerley Midwives Clinic, thank you to my exceptional Icelandic women and all the incredible midwives and others I worked with at Annerley. We shared endless tears and laughs. That our paths all converged in Hong Kong is still one of the beautiful mysteries of my life.

Géraldine Gauthier and Aurélie Dhellemmes at Go Master Coach, thank you for the opportunity to attend your fantastic coaching programme and the support you provided throughout and after.

Heather Thorkelson, thank you for your unwavering belief in my work and for a friendship that spans so many countries, so many transitions.

Randi Buckley, thank you for years of a solid relationship and creating the space to tell the truth. You are an incredible source of support, inspiration, and just damn good fun.

Evangeline Pedro, thank you for being my co-pilot most days. Thank you for the love you share with our family. We love you lots.

To Terry Real and the Relational Life Therapy (RLT)/ Relational Life Institute (RLI) team including Lisa Sullivan, Anna Sterk, Jerry Sander, and Amy Gordon, you have tremendously influenced how I practice therapy with couples. Thank you for all the wonderful work you're doing.

Dr Sally Breisch, thank you for allowing me to dream and also encouraging me to interpret my dreams in the wonderful Sally way. That big dream is still unfolding.

Dr Susan Mistler, thank you for the support over the years.

Dr Ellen Vora, thank you for tapping into the deeper questions and the deeper meaning of it all.

Dr Anna Lembke, thank you for the groundbreaking work you're doing, which, for so many of my clients and others, has been nothing short of eye opening and life changing.

Cruzanne Macalligan, thank you for your warmth and support.

Kathryn Weaver, Peter Shankman, Dr Jenifer Chan, Dr Kamini Rajaratnam, Ivan Cheong, and Celina Lee, thank you for contributing your expertise to this book and thank you for all the great work you're doing.

Danielle Lim, thank you for your graceful and powerful foreword. You're an incredible writer and are able to access the complex layers of what it means to be a human and one in relationships.

YM, thank you for the deep connection. I will never stop rooting for your family and you.

Bloomberg, thank you for the incredible privilege of partnering with you. The care and support you've demonstrated with your employees is inspirational, and I treasure the relationship we have.

AXA, thank you for the opportunity to work together. I so respect the deep connection you have with mental wellbeing in Asia. A special thank you to Gordon Watson and Sabrina Cheung.

Clients, a big thank you to all my past, present, and future clients. I have such reverence for your paths and feel a tremendous sense of privilege journeying together.

And, finally, thank you dearly to my husband and kids. You're why this all matters. I love you to the moon and back.